The Y2K Personal Survival Guide

Everything You Need to Know to Get from This Side of the Crisis to the Other

Michael S. Hyatt

Since 1947
REGNERY PUBLISHING, INC.
An Eagle Publishing Company • Washington, DC

Library of Congress Cataloging-in-Publication Data

   Hyatt, Michael S.
      The Y2K personal survival guide : everything you need to know to get from this side of the crisis to the other / Michael S. Hyatt
        p. cm.
     ISBN 0-89526-301-7 (alk. paper)
      1. Year 2000 date conversion (Computer systems) I. Title.
   QA76.76.S64H95 1999
   005.1'6--dc21   99-12734

Published in the United States by
Regnery Publishing, Inc.
An Eagle Publishing Company
One Massachusetts Avenue, NW
Washington, DC 20001

Distributed to the trade by
National Book Network
4720-A Boston Way
Lanham, MD 20706

Printed on acid-free paper.
Manufactured in the United States of America

10 9 8 7 6 5 4 3 2 1

Books are available in quantity for promotional or premium use. Write to Director of Special Sales, Regnery Publishing, Inc., One Massachusetts Avenue, NW, Washington, DC 20001, for information on discounts and terms or call (202) 216-0600.

To my wife, Gail, who has been my constant source of strength and joy for nearly twenty-one years.

If you are interested in having Michael Hyatt speak to your group, please contact:

Tim Grable
Ambassador Speakers Bureau
P.O. Box 50358
Nashville, TN 37205

Phone: (615) 377-9100
Fax: (615) 661-4344

E-mail: Tim@AmbassadorAgency.com
Web site: www.AmbassadorAgency.com

Contents

Prep Tips

Tables

Introduction

You Don't Have to Be a Victim

My first book, *The Millennium Bug: How to Survive the Coming Chaos*, almost didn't get published. In the spring of 1998, a couple of weeks before it was set to go to press, Richard Vigilante, vice president of Regnery Publishing at the time, called to tell me they were considering canceling publication. Why? Because they had presold only some 2,500 copies—an absolutely miserable showing. According to Richard, they couldn't *give* the book away. Retailers said they had enough books on this subject and the ones they had simply weren't selling.

I was taken aback, as you might expect. But, being in the publishing business myself, I understood the reality that you can't force booksellers to stock a book they don't want. Clearly, they didn't want this one, and there was probably nothing the publisher could do about it. If Regnery went ahead and published the book, it would likely be DOA, and the publisher would be throwing good money after bad. It simply didn't make sense to move ahead, given the tepid response the book had received from book retailers.

Although I was intellectually resigned to my fate and was already thinking through how I was going to tell my family and friends, my gut was telling me that the book deserved a chance. *Booksellers have been wrong before*, I mused, not quite knowing if I was right or simply engaging in a little self-deceit. *Everywhere I go, people are fascinated by this subject and want to talk about it for hours*. Finally, I persuaded Richard to "throw the dice," as it were, and commit to a small printing just to see if lightning might strike.

And strike it did. Sandy Callender, Regnery's crack publicist, sent out a fax broadcast to several hundred talk radio producers. That was all it took. The phones lit up, and Sandy began booking me for one interview after another. In the first thirty days following the book's publication, I did more than one hundred radio interviews—everything from National Public Radio's *Public Interest* to *G. Gordon Liddy*. Soon after, the book appeared on the *New York Times* "Business Bestsellers" list, where it remained for several months. Since that time, I have been on all three major television networks, CNN, and more than four hundred radio programs.

Beyond Awareness

As gratifying as all of that is, *The Millennium Bug* was really only half the story. It is a book primarily about Y2K awareness. My purpose was to help ordinary citizens understand the Y2K Problem and how it is likely to affect the things they depend on most. As I told Congress on September 24, 1998, when I testified before the House Subcommittee on Government, Management, Information, and Technology:

> Though the experts may disagree about the nature and severity of the disruptions that will occur as a result of the Year 2000 Computer Problem, all are agreed that some level of disruption is now inevitable. We do not know whether this will be a "heartburn" or a "heart attack," but we do know that, in the time remaining, it is impossible to get all of our systems repaired before January 1, 2000. The failure of these systems will undoubtedly affect government agencies, infrastructure providers, and businesses both large and small. But ultimately, it will affect each of us *individually*, including our associates at work, the people in our neighborhoods and churches, and our friends and family. Thus, in a very real sense, *Y2K is a consumer issue*. When these systems fail—as surely some of them will—it is consumers who will feel the impact.[1]

Thus, I wanted to alert our consumer population to the problem and, in the process, motivate people to prepare. (If you are just now getting up to speed on Y2K and would like a brief overview, see Appendix A.) The only problem was that *The Millennium Bug* contained only one chapter on preparedness. From all over the world, I received letters, faxes, and e-mail messages from people who said, "Okay, I'm convinced. Where do I go to get *more information* about preparedness?"

Up until now, I have had to point these people to a dizzying array of books, articles, and websites. For the average person, the process of learning, evaluating, sorting, negotiating, and deciding exactly what to do has been an overwhelming challenge. It's not that the information isn't out there. It is. The problem is that that there is too much of it to absorb and apply in the short time we have remaining.

Moreover, the people I have interacted with are starting from ground zero. They aren't survivalists—at least not in the popular sense of the term—and they generally aren't even campers. Their idea of "roughing it" is staying in a cabin without a TV.

What I wanted—and sensed that people needed—was a one-stop, comprehensive book that would explain, step-by-step, what a person needed to do in order to prepare himself or herself for the world we may experience after January 1, 2000. What you are holding in your hand is, I believe, that book. It is designed to provide everything you need to get you and your family from this side of the crisis to the other.

So How Bad Is It *Really* Going to Be?

I now speak several times a month on Y2K to various trade associations, businesses, and church groups, and I am still a frequent guest on talk radio shows. In addition, I get hundreds of e-mails a day from people visiting my website. All combined, I interact with scores of people on a weekly basis about Y2K. Without a doubt, the number one question I get is this: "So how bad do you really think it's going to be?"

The honest answer is: *I don't know*. I get up each day hoping for good news. I browse the usual Y2K websites along with the major media, reading anywhere from twenty-five to thirty articles a day. On average, the bad news seems to outweigh the good by about twenty to one. While it is true that we are making headway in getting computer systems repaired or replaced, it is also true that the days are slipping by more quickly than progress is being made. Perhaps—just maybe—this will turn around as the year progresses. But right now, based on what we know, I believe that we are still at risk for substantial disruptions after the first of the year.

One of the things that is particularly frustrating is the quality of information available. There are at least three problems related to almost all the reports I'm seeing.

1. The data are almost always self-reported. There is very little independent, third-party verification going on. For the most part, government agencies, infrastructure providers, and businesses are asking us to take their word for it. All of them are carefully managing the information that is released to the public. In some cases, it appears that disinformation is being purposefully distributed. Ronald Reagan's advice at the height of the Cold War seems particularly apropos: "Trust but verify." Until we have someone to do the verification for us, we have to hope for the best but assume the worst.

2. Information about Y2K progress is sometimes overstated. Last year, the General Accounting Office called two federal departments (Defense and Agriculture) on the carpet for reporting as compliant systems that were merely on a list to be made compliant.[2] Programmers are an optimistic lot; they generally promise more than they can deliver. According to the Standish Group International, 73 percent of all corporate software development projects are "late, over-budget or cancelled altogether."[3] In addition, the easier systems are sometimes targeted for repair first, thus distorting the rate of progress. If the more difficult systems are saved for last, things could slow down immeasurably. Far too often, the project seems to be on schedule—until the last month.

3. Conclusions about Y2K progress are often contradictory. Two people can look at the same report and draw opposite conclusions. Everyone has his own agenda (yes, me, too!), and he will necessarily filter the data through his own presuppositions. Some will purposely "spin" the information and willfully distort it for the sake of their own gain or fear of their own loss. It's easy to pick on the people who are selling Y2K books, generators, and food, accusing them of overstating the Y2K Problem for the sake of financial gain. But the truth is that some of those who are downplaying the problem—banks, federal agencies, and utility companies—are doing so for fear of financial *loss*. They have as much at stake as anyone.

The bottom line is that things are only going to get more confusing as we move toward D-Day. The point of absolute certainty will never come. As much as we might like to know what will happen on January 1, 2000, we simply won't know until we get there. *Anyone who tells you differently is claiming to know more than is possible to know.*

How then do we plan? Good question. At some point, you have to make some assumptions about the future and plan accordingly. This isn't easy even under the best of circumstances. You have to accept the possibility that your planning premise is wrong and be willing to live with the consequences if it is. In my view, the issue is not *prophecy*—predicting the future with pinpoint accuracy—but *personal risk management*—understanding what *could* happen and deciding how you can protect yourself from it.

With that in mind, let me tell you what I am *personally* assuming about the impact of Y2K. Understand that I may be right. Or, I may be wrong. Or, more likely, I will be partially right and partially wrong. Nevertheless, I am assuming at least a twelve-month disruption of basic goods and services, including periods of

- No electrical power

- No clean water

- No telecommunications

- Shortages of food, gasoline, clothing, and all retail goods

- Widespread bank failures and inaccessibility of funds

- A stock market crash

- A dramatic drop in real estate values

- An economic depression

- Widespread unemployment

- Civil unrest, including protests, riots, and general lawlessness

- Inability of government agencies to deliver Welfare, Medicare, Social Security, and Veterans benefits

- No meaningful leadership from the Clinton administration

Yes, I know, it's pretty grim. But keep in mind that I am not saying any of this is *going* to happen. I am simply saying that each of these items is a *possibility*, and, therefore, I want to plan accordingly. Think of it this way: What's the risk if I am right and you plan for this scenario versus the risk if I am right and you *don't* plan for this scenario?

From my perspective, there is no downside to preparedness. Sure, I may be out some money and effort if I plan and nothing much happens, but I would much prefer that to facing the scenario I've described above without adequate preparation. Besides, if nothing happens, you can donate what you don't need to charity and keep the rest for some other emergency.

What If I'm Wrong?

Whenever someone tells me he thinks Y2K will be nothing more severe than a winter storm, I always respond with a comment and two questions. First, I say, "I hope you are right." There is nothing I would enjoy more than being wrong in my assessment of Y2K. It would be a small price to pay for continuing our way of life. However, I regard preparing for Y2K like health insurance. I continue to pay the premiums, hoping I never have to make a major claim.

Second, I ask, "If we can't get the vast majority of these systems fixed in the time we have remaining before Y2K, what makes you think we can get them fixed one week after they fail—particularly in a chaotic environment where there may be widespread disruptions?" This just doesn't seem reasonable to me. If we don't get most of the systems repaired or replaced in time—and at this point I personally think it's a long shot—then I think we're in for a much-longer-term problem.

Third, I ask, "What evidence do you have that I'm wrong?" Usually, the person doesn't have anything concrete to offer; he simply responds with some version of "Well, we put a man on the moon, so I'm sure we can fix this problem, too!" or "I'm sure with all the brilliant computer people we have, they can come up with a solution." To which I usually say, somewhat facetiously, "Let me remind you: It was these same 'geniuses' that didn't have the foresight to make sure their programs would work correctly after the turn-of-the-century." I think this kind of confidence is, quite frankly, misplaced.[4]

As I said, I hope they are right. But until I know for sure, I'm going to follow the advice of our colonial forefathers: "Trust God and keep your powder dry."

The Five-Five Plan

When I started talking to people about preparing for the Millennium Bug, I found that they often felt overwhelmed. They simply didn't know where to begin. Contemplating a world without electricity, telecommunications, water, transportation, or modern banking and finance—even for a brief period of time—was more than they could handle. As a result, more often than not, they simply did nothing. Not exactly the result I wanted.

Someone once asked, "How do you eat an elephant?" The answer, of course, is, "One bite at a time." Following that sage advice, I set out to design a system that divides the overall task into manageable chunks, allows people to prepare incrementally, and encourages community action. My plan offers five levels of preparedness in five key areas. Hence, the five-five plan.

The *five levels of preparedness* include the following:

- Level 1: The seventy-two–hour plan
- Level 2: The one-week plan
- Level 3: The thirty-day plan
- Level 4: The three-month plan
- Level 5: The one-year (or longer) plan

The idea is that you start at Level 1 and advance to the next level only when you have completed the previous one. There's no sense buying nonhybrid seeds (the one-year or long-term plan) if you don't have a way to keep your family warm for seventy-two hours! As someone once said, if you don't make it through the short term, *there is no long term*.

At the end of each chapter you will find a "Y2K Preparedness Checklist." The purpose of this list is to give you a "game plan" for getting ready for Y2K. You will notice that the list is sorted by level, so that you can do the first things first and then move up to the next level as you complete the previous one. You may want to circle the level number as you complete the Action Step. You will also find a comprehensive checklist at the end of the book in Appendix B. It is the same material, but it is arranged by level so that you can finish the entire level before moving on to the next one.

The *five areas of preparedness* include the following:

- Area 1: Information
- Area 2: Supplies
- Area 3: Shelter
- Area 4: Money
- Area 5: Protection

The book is organized in terms of these areas, with one section devoted to each area. The chapters are not presented in priority order, and you don't necessarily need to read them in order. I tried to write each chapter so that it is self-contained. Start where you have an interest and go from there.

You will soon notice that I recommend key suppliers for everything from long-term food storage to water barrels. In each case I have tried to find the most reliable, least expensive vendor. (From only one supplier do I receive any personal compensation, and I clearly identify that in the text.) I hired five researchers to work with me on this for approximately six weeks. We tried to make sure that the suppliers could handle the demand we thought we would generate, but I can make no guarantees. These are unusual times, and demand is growing daily. It is difficult for most suppliers to justify ramping up production when they know it will likely come to an abrupt end on January 1, 2000. Also, keep in mind that prices are subject to change.

Don't Wait to Get Started

If you are like most people, you are going to be tempted either to procrastinate or to panic. Neither response is productive. The alternative to both is careful, thoughtful preparation. As you read through this book and begin making preparations, keep these three things in mind:

1. Begin immediately. There is a lot less time to prepare than you may think. Moving from the "thinking about it" stage to real action is the most important aspect of any preparation plan. You can't afford to wait. Time is not on your side. January 1 will be here before you know it. Get busy *now!*

2. Work incrementally. Don't worry about doing everything all at once. It will make the task seem too daunting and may cause you to get discouraged and quit. A little bit each day and each week is much more realistic and effective. Wake up each day and ask yourself, "What's next? What can I do today that will move me closer to my goal?"

3. Prepare in community. Don't go about it alone. Form a preparedness group and let the division of labor work for you. This way you don't have to become an expert in everything. One person can be put in charge of researching food preparation, another water treatment, an alternative source of heat and light, and so forth. Working with others will make the tasks easier and provide you with the opportunity to do more than if you try to prepare alone. For more specific direction, see Appendix D: "Getting Your Local Community Ready."

Finally, remember this: You may not be able to do everything, but you can do something, and something is better than nothing.

Part One

Information

Chapter One

Secure Hard Copies of Important Documents

No tickie, no shirtie.

—Sign posted in a Chinese laundry

It was the day of my best friend's wedding. Thousands of details had been addressed during eleven long months of preparing, and now the big day had finally arrived. Everything was all set—except one minor detail. My friend had completely forgotten to secure a copy of his baptismal certificate, even though the clergyman had made it clear months earlier that he could not perform the ceremony without this document.

Four hours before the wedding, the church office called my friend, reminding him to bring the certificate to the church that afternoon. My friend was frantic. He called his mother, figuring she had it safely stored away. No luck—she vaguely remembered giving it to him when he moved out of state, years earlier. He scoured his apartment—no sign of it anywhere, not to mention that he wasn't even sure what it looked like.

My friend was fortunate. After he pleaded his case to the officiating clergyman, it was agreed that he could get married after all, as long as he promised to find the document and mail it to the church as soon as he got home from his honeymoon. (I think the tear-filled eyes and quivering lower lip of his bride-to-be clinched it.)

Time and again, key documents and paperwork are absolutely crucial. In most cases, nothing—neither a sincere promise nor a beautiful bride on the verge of tears—will substitute for the actual document. So imagine hearing these words: "But we don't have any record that you deposited money here, Mr. Smith. Do you have any receipts or paperwork from 1999… you know, back before the computers went bonkers?"

And you won't hear these or similar words just from a bank teller, but also from insurance companies, your pension plan administrator, Social Security, the Internal Revenue Service (IRS), your lawyer (or someone *else's* lawyer), your doctor, your pharmacist, your dentist, your stockbroker, Medicare, credit card companies, mortgage lenders, and the auto loan company—to which you owe only *one* more payment!

Imagine being unable to prove your age, citizenship, marital status, property owned, debts owed and paid (including taxes), money owed to you, and on and on.

As you know, most of our important personal records are now stored electronically in computer databases rather than on paper documents inside metal filing cabinets. If many of these records get wiped out or scrambled by the Millennium Bug, the post-2000 world will be a very confusing place, to say the least. A lifetime of assets and savings could disappear in an instant—or at least be inaccessible—and there may be no way to prove that you are the rightful owner.

If society is forced to rebuild our modern information infrastructure, reassembling our personal records accurately will be a key task. You can be sure that hard copies—actual physical pieces of paper—will be worth their weight in gold. The person who can walk into a bank, insurance agency, or government office with printed copies of important records, dated before January 1, 2000, will be in a much better position to rebuild his or her life. The person who walks in with nothing will likely walk out with just that.

Once the Y2K Crisis hits, unless you have a hard copy of an important record, you may never have a chance to get another one. The information may disappear into cyberspace forever. Therefore, it is absolutely crucial to plan and take action right away to protect all that you have worked for, and to make sure no one accuses you of owing something you do not.

A Document Shopping List

Before you dive in and begin collecting stacks of paper you may not need, you may find it helpful to develop a specific list of important documents. The issue is not *how many* documents, but *which* documents. Too much paper can be as big a problem as too little—especially if it's not the right paper.

Your list may vary depending on your particular circumstances, but you will probably want to include at least the following:

- Birth certificates for you and each member of your family

- Marriage licenses or certificates
- Baptismal, confirmation, ordination, and other religious records
- Social Security cards and financial information
- Record of military service
- Deeds, titles, and other proofs of ownership
- Mortgages and other loan agreements
- Loan statements showing exactly what you owe
- Credit reports
- Credit card statements
- Insurance policies and proof of premium payment
- Tax returns
- Membership papers
- Contracts and other legal documents
- Diplomas and academic transcripts
- Medical, dental, and pharmaceutical records

Why You Need 'em and Where You Can Get 'em

Wow, what a list. I bet you didn't realize you had been leaving such a large trail of critical paperwork in your wake. If these key papers have been lost, stolen, or destroyed, you need to replace them. Now.

Birth certificates. Although Jack Benny was perpetually thirty-nine years old, and many people would rather give up a kidney (or two) before admitting their true age, it is important at times to be able to prove your date and place of birth. Many government benefits, insurance contracts, and retirement programs are based on age. In the aftermath of Y2K problems, the various methods we use today to prove our age—driver's license, Social Security information, employment data—may be lost or untrustworthy. Being able to produce a valid birth certificate could be vital.

Birth certificates are the type of document that you may not need for decades at a time. Most people I've asked are certain they have birth certificates for their family... somewhere around the house. But when they actually look, the documents are nowhere to be found. So if you can't find them now, take steps to secure copies.

Birth records are held by the municipal government where the birth occurred. If you are missing any birth certificates, you should write to the town or city clerk and request copies. (You might want to call first and find out exactly what the procedure is and how much the charge is. This will save you a step.) Because some government offices are notoriously slow in responding, follow up within a week with a phone call to confirm that they have received your letter. This will also give you the name of the person to ask for during subsequent follow-ups. Every two weeks you should call to see whether the copy has been mailed to you.

If you don't know whom to contact or don't want the hassle of dealing with a government bureaucracy (who does?), another alternative is a company called VitalChek. This company lists every government document provider in the United States by state. Prices for specific documents are listed. You can either write to the agency yourself or fill out an online form and have VitalChek do the work for you. The company's toll-free phone number is (800) 255-2414. Its website address is <http://www.vitalchek.com>. If you want a one-stop shopping place for your most important documents, this is it.

Regardless of who takes responsibility for getting the documents, remember two important points: (1) There is a lot of truth to the expression, "The squeaky wheel gets the grease." A clerk might finally put your request at the top of his "to-do" list just so he doesn't have to take your phone calls anymore. (2) The longer you wait, the more likely it will be that countless other people will be attempting to do the same thing. The year 1999 is certain to be a stress-filled and hectic time for record-keeping employees. Clerks may get so overwhelmed it won't matter how many times you call. You risk not getting the document in time.

Marriage licenses or certificates. Yes, I realize there are some people who would be thrilled if all records of their marriage suddenly disappeared. But for the rest of us, it is important to have a copy of this document.

Marriage licenses are filed in the clerk's office of the town or city where the wedding took place. As with birth certificates, calling or, preferably, submitting your request in writing is the first step. Again, persistent follow-up is important.

Baptismal, confirmation, ordination, and other religious records. I am confident that regardless of how severe Y2K problems might be, religious faith will never become obsolete. In fact, it could be greatly strengthened by sudden and serious social disruptions. At some point, I hope and pray, life will return to something we can call "normal." To be able to participate in certain ceremonies and sacraments, you must have the proper religious documents. These may also prove to be an important secondary form of identification with nonreligious authorities.

The way to acquire copies of these records depends upon your particular denomination, parish, congregation, etc. You may first have to place a few phone calls to determine where these records are kept—the local church or synagogue, the archdiocesan office, or the national headquarters, for example. As with all record acquisitions, politeness, persistence, and follow-up are important to success.

Social Security cards and financial information. For many people, these records are the most valuable assets they own. A lifetime of contributions and crucial retirement income may go down the drain if your Social Security data are lost due to computer crashes.

If you have misplaced your Social Security card, you can apply for a new copy at the local Social Security Administration (SSA) office. But you *must* apply in person. No one else (except your spouse with adequate documentation, such as a certified marriage license, or if you apply for a replacement card for minor children) can apply for you. Furthermore, the SSA will *not* accept a birth certificate as proof of identification for *replacement* of a Social Security card. You must bring a driver's license or passport. On the other hand, the *only* thing the SSA will accept when you apply for an *initial* issue of a card is a certified birth certificate.

Another document you need to secure is a *Personal Earnings and Benefit Estimate Statement* (PEBES) from the SSA. This document lists your earnings and all the taxes you paid to Social Security and Medicare for every year of your working career.

You need to fill out a copy of PEBES form SSA-7004 and mail it to:

> Social Security Administration
> Wilkes Barre Data Operations Center
> P.O. Box 7004
> Wilkes Barre, PA 18767-7004

You can get this form from some insurance agents or your local Social Security office. You can also download a printable copy of the form directly from the Internet at the SSA's website at <http://www.ssa.gov/online/ssa-7004.html>. Complete the form and mail it in. Currently the turn-around time to process your request is about six weeks. But be advised that delays will most likely grow as we move through 1999.

You can also fill out an electronic copy of the form right on the SSA's website. If you use this method, the SSA promises a response in two to three weeks. The form is located at <https://s3abaca.ssa.gov/pro/batch-pebes/bp-7004home.shtml>. But remember that this form is available *only* during certain hours of the day, currently Monday through Friday, 8:00 AM to 9:00 PM (Eastern Time) and Saturday 9:00 AM to 4:00 PM. Again, the longer you wait to take action, well… the longer you will wait to see results.

If you have the time, you may want to repeat this process every few months during 1999 to keep the information as current as possible. But the main thing is to do it at least once. Missing a few months' worth of data is minimal compared to missing a few decades' worth of data.

Records of military service. Many veterans, including those who are disabled or who are retired, depend on military benefits for their livelihood. A disruption in these payments would create a serious hardship. But it may be important for other veterans, even those who don't currently receive benefits, to have these records as well.

If you do not have your Discharge Certificate or, more importantly, your "Report of Separation," which contains the information necessary to determine eligibility for benefits, you can request one from your local Veterans Affairs office. The form you want is SF-800, "Request Pertaining to Military Records." If you want, you can also download this form from the Internet at <http://www.va.gov/forms/data/sf180p1.pdf>. However, you will also need to submit certain forms of identification and mail them, along with the SF-800, to one of fourteen addresses, depending on the branch of service you were in. Be advised that you must have the Adobe Acrobat Reader Version 3 or later to view and print these documents. If you don't have it, you can download it and install it for free at <http://www.adobe.com/prodindex/acrobat/readstep.html>.

Deeds, titles, and other proofs of ownership. Although you may have owned a piece of property (or a car or a boat) for many years, and the idea that someone would ever demand that you prove you own it seems preposterous now, it may not always be that way in the near future. The Millennium Bug threatens to make the preposterous possible.

Without the proper deed or title, the only proof that you own a valuable asset may exist as a microscopic electronic entry on the hard drive of a banking or municipal government computer system. If this information is lost, so is your proof of ownership.

The first thing to do is to determine what valuable assets you own—real estate, vehicles, machinery, and so on. Search for the deeds and titles, and if you cannot find them, immediately take action to get new copies.

Real estate records are kept by the municipal government. Contact your town/city clerk and inquire about the specific forms and procedures you need. Ownership data on vehicles, trailers, boats, and the rest are kept by your state Motor Vehicle Department. Contact your local office to get the appropriate forms.

Mortgages and other loan agreements. The actual contracts of your mortgage and loan agreements are important documents. You may vaguely remember signing a mountain of paperwork the day you closed on your home (or maybe it was so traumatic you've effectively blocked it from your memory). Surely, all those records are safely stored somewhere—at the bank or at the lawyer's office or in Aunt Sally's attic where many years ago she graciously let you store some boxes of miscellaneous stuff.

But a warning: Many document-intensive organizations—banks, insurance companies, legal firms—no longer keep tons of paperwork on file. To save space, many paper records have been digitally scanned and are now stored electronically. Whether your bank or lawyer's office will be able to locate and print out a copy of your contract after the Millennium Bug hits is uncertain. It would be best to secure a hard copy now, before any electronic disruptions occur.

Although these organizations are accustomed to processing requests for summary statements of mortgages and loans, they rarely receive requests for copies of entire contracts. You may run into some resistance or be asked to pay a fee. Remain upbeat, but persistent. And remember that a small fee now may prevent a big financial crisis later.

Loan statements showing exactly what you owe. If all the transactions of your mortgages and other loans evaporate into thin air due to a computer failure, records of your payments, outstanding balances, and the equity of some of your most valuable assets will be gone. Some loans are set up with payment books. A stub for each month lists the payment number, the payment amount, and the remaining balance. This is an excellent hard copy of your loan history, but make sure you can match up each cancelled check for the most recent payments to prove that you have been faithfully repaying the loan.

Other loans or mortgages are more high-tech—a simple bill is mailed each month or the transaction is entirely electronic through automatic withdrawal from a checking account.

You must contact your banks and finance companies and request current statements of the mortgages and loans. Make sure the statements contain all vital information: names, addresses, locations (for real estate), makes and models (for vehicles), date of loan, original amount, detailed payment record, and current balance.

You may choose to request these statements every few months during 1999 to have the most up-to-date information. If you'd rather not do this, make sure to keep proof of payment—cancelled checks, checking account statements, receipts, etc.— for each month after the statement. Keep in mind that you may be called upon to recreate with paper records the history of your loan activity. If you have a summary statement from the lending institution and detailed payment records for the period of time after the summary, you will be in good shape.

Credit reports. In today's economy, lenders, vendors, and others will routinely request a copy of your credit report before doing business with you. These vast data repositories, however, are all computerized and are thus susceptible to Y2K-related disruptions. Therefore, it would be wise to request a copy of your credit report from all three credit-reporting agencies. You can do this by mail, phone, or the Internet. Here are the three agencies and how to contact them:

> Equifax
> Customer Care Group
> P.O. Box 105496
> Atlanta, GA 30348-5496
> Toll-free (800) 997-2493
> Internet: <http://www.equifax.com>

> Experian (formerly TRW)
> National Consumer Assistance Center
> P.O. Box 2104
> Allen, TX 75013-2104
> Toll-free (800) 397-3742
> Internet: <http://www.experian.com>

> Trans Union Corporation
> Consumer Disclosure Center
> P.O. Box 390
> Springfield, PA 19064-0390
> Toll-free (800) 888-4213
> Internet: <https://www.transunion.com>

If ordering by mail, you will need to include your full name, Social Security number, current and previous addresses within the last five years, current employer, date of birth, signature, and home telephone number. All the agencies charge a nominal processing fee, ranging from $3 to $8.

Credit card statements. Luckily there is not much research and request work needed here. The secret is to be organized and to keep accurate records throughout 1999. When you receive your credit card statements each month, as you should always do, first check each charge to make sure you did in fact make those purchases. (If you think credit card statements contain errors today, just wait until *after* December 1999. If the Y2K bug hits the credit card industry hard, the monthly statements may contain some incredible errors.)

Once you make the payment, file the statement. Create a separate file for each credit card account you have. Make sure you can match up the cancelled check as proof that the payment was made.

Insurance policies and proof of premium payment. Insurance policies are simply contracts between you and the insurance company. They agree to provide certain benefits and coverage, and you agree to pay a certain premium. With most insurance companies today, you don't even need a copy of your policy to file a claim. All the details of the contract are stored electronically. Simply give them your name and address and they can access all the information about your policies through their computer systems. This is one of the great benefits of our information age: fast and accurate retrieval of massive amounts of data. But Y2K puts it all at risk.

In the post-Y2K world, if the computer systems crash (thinking the year is 1900), insurance coverage may also revert to 1900 methods: produce the actual policy (contract) or else no coverage. If you don't already have copies of your insurance policies—organized, safely filed, and readily accessible—it is time to do so.

You may have many different insurance policies: homeowner, renter, life (often multiple policies), disability income, auto, boat, motorcycle, business, health, and major medical. And don't forget those specialty policies that may or may not be a rider on your homeowner's coverage for antiques, collectibles, electronic equipment, and so on.

Contact your insurance agent, or the company directly, and request copies of the lost policy forms.

Tax returns. Let's be honest, there are few things more frightening than being audited by the IRS (though I can't think of any at the moment). Some people are predicting that the IRS will be completely paralyzed by the Year 2000 Computer Problem, while others warn that the IRS will drop its "we'll reform and be nice guys from now on" claim and become more ruthless and overbearing than ever. The federal government is worried about a slowdown in cash flow due to Y2K, and may go to extraordinary measures to keep the money pouring in.

Regardless of how the IRS is affected by Y2K, or even if it's not affected at all, it is always wise to have copies of all your past tax returns, including all W-2s, 1099s, receipts, and the rest. If your tax return files contain major gaps, you can call the IRS and request copies.

The IRS's toll-free number is (800) 829-1040. This will put you in touch with an automated phone system, where you can work your way through the options and request Form 4506. This form should arrive by mail in ten to fifteen days. Alternatively, you can download it from the list of forms at <http://www.irs.ustreas.gov/prod/forms_pubs/forms.html> on the Internet. Complete the form, send it back, and photocopies of your tax return will be sent to you in about sixty days. The fee is $23 per tax return. The IRS advises that it may not be possible to get copies of returns more than five years old.

Do not forget your other tax records: state and local income tax returns, property taxes, sewer tax, user fees, and so forth. Request copies of the returns from the tax offices of the appropriate jurisdictions. Acquire hard copies that prove you paid your local taxes: cancelled checks, receipts, or summary statements from your city or town will suffice.

Membership papers. Many people belong to clubs, fraternities, civic organizations, professional societies, trade unions, you name it. It is unlikely that a local club will suddenly forget who you are, even if its data files are lost ("Whataya mean you never heard of me, Nick? I sat next to you at every meeting for the past eight years!"). Whether you owe back dues, of course, is another matter.

But with national clubs or societies, no one will recognize your voice or face. You should secure and store some record of membership. Depending on the group, there might be membership certificates or cards, subscriptions or correspondence, or that old stand-by: proof that you've been paying dues.

Contracts and other legal documents. We have covered mortgage, loan, and insurance contracts in previous sections. There are other legal documents and contracts that may be important. For example: settlements, leases, custody agreements, divorce papers, wills and trusts, and business or employment contracts. Determine which of these apply to your situation and contact the appropriate legal professionals to secure copies.

Diplomas and academic transcripts. You can go decades at a time and never need these documents. But if you apply for a new job, run for office, or simply want to impress someone, you may need to prove that you really did earn that Ph.D. in astrophysics.

From all available reports, it appears that schools and universities will have their hands full just trying to keep the Millennium Bug from paralyzing day-to-day operations. The databases that store the records and grades of students from many years back are surely not on the mission-critical repair list. These computer systems are vulnerable to Y2K glitches and breakdowns.

If you don't acquire a copy of your academic transcripts in 1999, you may never be able to get one. Contact your school's administrative or alumni offices to determine how to get a copy of your grades and graduation record.

Medical, dental, and pharmaceutical records. Generally speaking, doctors and druggists don't give out copies of confidential records. But depending upon your particular situation, you may have a medical condition for which you would want some specific documentation. For example, you or a family member may have diabetes, high blood pressure, or some other illness requiring special health care services.

Contact your health provider to discuss this issue. If Y2K disrupts the health care industry, you may have to see a different doctor under emergency conditions, and it would be wise to have paperwork that explains your special needs.

Stocks, bonds, and other financial investments. Protecting your financial assets is a topic discussed in detail in "Part Four: Money." Regardless of how you protect the value of your investments, you still need to secure hard-copy documentation proving that those investments are actually yours, particularly if you are unable to move your investments into hard assets, as I will recommend later.

Make a list of stocks, bonds, private pension plans, and any other investments you may have. Contact the appropriate broker, dealer, or administrator to determine how to get copies of documents that will demonstrate ownership, regardless of whether the computers work.

Better Safe Than Sorry

Now that you are assembling a library of important documents, you need to organize and store them in a safe and accessible place. You might want to think of a place other than a safety deposit box. If your bank closes because of Y2K problems—God forbid!—you don't want to worry about how you are going to get your documents.

One option is a fire-proof safe or storage box in your home. They come in many different sizes and price ranges. Wal-Mart and other discount retailers sell Sentry Fire-Safe brand products, each designed to protect the contents in the event of a fire.

- The Model 1100 Security Chest has 315 cubic inches of interior space, which will not hold very many documents. It sells for $17.96.

- The Model 1250 Safe has 1.01 cubic feet of space, more than five times the capacity of the Model 1100, and it sells for $79.97.

- The Model 1175 Security File stores standard hanging file folders inside its fire-proof protective walls. The storage area is 13 1/2 inches deep, and it sells for $84.96.

If you choose the small model, there will not be enough room for all of your documents. In this case, use it for irreplaceable items such as cash, savings bonds, and passbooks, as well as birth certificates, deeds, and titles.

You can use a standard filing cabinet for everything else. Organize the cabinet using the same section headings outlined in this chapter. Use plenty of separate file folders within each section to organize your records further.

A simple, inexpensive two-drawer filing cabinet should hold everything this chapter suggests that you collect... but just barely if you have a lot of contracts and such. Why not go the extra mile and buy a four-drawer cabinet? For a little extra money you will have plenty of room to store new documents for many years to come. (What? You think the world is going to end on January 1, 2000? It may change forever, but life will go on. My guess is that no matter what happens, there will always be important paperwork.)

If you store these important documents in a simple file cabinet, you risk their being destroyed by fire. Remember Murphy's Law. If you can't afford or choose not to use fire-proof storage, take the time to make photocopies of all the documents and keep them in a secondary location, possibly a relative's home or your place of business.

Be Wise—Organize

An informal survey I've taken among friends and acquaintances reveals that fewer than one in five would describe their personal record-keeping as "very organized." Let's face facts, keeping meticulous records of the many personal and financial transactions in our busy lives is time-consuming, tedious, and, well, boring. Especially in today's high-tech society, in which verification is only a phone call and a computer print-out away, it is easy to get lazy and assume that large institutions have all the information we'll ever require stored in their massive data banks. Why bother keeping track of it all ourselves?

As most people understand to one degree or another, the unprecedented Millennium Bug problem threatens to disrupt or even destroy all these nice, neat, carefully stored records. The unthinkable must be thought. The impossible is now possible. The details of your life, these records, could simply vanish or be inaccessible when you need them most.

Securing hard copies of important documents is not an easy chore. Uncovering the documents that currently exist in your home could take hours. Requesting copies of the ones you no longer have could take dozens of hours of work over the course of many months. But it must be done. The risk of not securing these documents and trusting that institutional database centers will experience no significant computer failures is too great. The consequences of being unprepared to prove who you are and what you own, in a society attempting to put the pieces back together, could be a personal catastrophe. Many of your rights, privileges, and hard-earned assets may no longer be yours in such a situation. A lifetime of work could go down the drain.

But there is a silver lining to all of this. Once you complete your document inventory and secure these important records, *you will actually have them!*—organized, filed, and stored in one location. These are the records that we all should have in any event, regardless of a pending computer crisis. If the Y2K disruptions prove to be mild, you will have a whole new understanding of what is important and a much more organized system of filing and storage. As my informal survey shows, most of us need to do this anyway.

Y2K PREP TIP #1

Create a Document "Follow-up" Chart

In addition to the Y2K Preparedness Checklist at the end of this chapter, it is a good idea to create a "follow-up" chart. You can either draw it up on graph paper or use a computer spreadsheet program.

Each document you need to acquire can be listed down the left-hand column. In the next column write the date that you called or wrote requesting a copy of the document. Make sure you note the name and phone number of the contact person.

Moving across the columns, write in the date of each follow-up phone call. When you receive the correct document, draw a red line through that item or highlight it in yellow. In the computer spreadsheet, you can change the appearance of the line, or move it to a portion of the page labeled "completed." Whatever you decide, keep it simple. Design your form so that you can see in a glance which documents you are still missing and how long it has been since you last called to inquire about them.

Do not let more than two weeks pass without making a call. Time can slip by quickly, and the more time that passes between your initial request and any action, the more likely it is that your request got buried under a stack of paperwork on somebody's desk.

In virtually every institution, making copies of records to send to customers is not anyone's full-time job. It is one of those low-priority duties that "someone" does whenever he or she has some free time. Which is to say, it is the type of duty that "no one" will do unless you prod and plead and persistently insist that it get done.

That is why it is so critical to have a "follow-up" chart. You can quickly see what documents are still missing from your record library, and how much effort you have expended trying to secure them. This comes in handy if you reach the point at which you must call and speak with someone's supervisor or manager. If you can provide the different dates you called and the exact person to whom you spoke, that supervisor will most likely see that you get what you want.

Admittedly, this can be a tedious and time-consuming chore. Who wants to keep calling and bugging someone to process some paperwork? Unfortunately, in many cases this will be the only way to be sure that you get the important documents you need. A "follow-up" chart will keep you from letting this important task slide.

	Y2K PREPAREDNESS CHECKLIST				
Level	*Action Step*	*Qty*	*Unit Price*	*Total Qty*	*Total Price*
1	Take inventory of important records. Determine which ones you already have.	N/A	N/A		
1	Determine how you will file/store these records for safekeeping.	N/A	N/A		
1	Create a "follow up" chart (see Y2K Prep Tip #1).	N/A	N/A		
1	Assign task of monitoring the "follow up" chart to a family member.	N/A	N/A		
1	Faithfully request, and re-request, the documents until you have them all. Do not let more than 2 weeks pass without working on this chore.	N/A	N/A		
2	Purchase safe, fire-box, and/or file cabinet. Recommended choice: Sentry Fire-Safe Model 1175 Security File.	1	$84.96		

Chapter Two

Build an Emergency Preparedness Library

The man who does not read good books has no advantage over the man who can't read them.

—Mark Twain

A young couple, Nancy and Peter, arrived on the beautiful island of Martha's Vineyard, Massachusetts, for their long-awaited summer vacation. They had rented a house on a secluded part of the island. The weather was spectacular, and the house was gorgeous. They were looking forward to a full week of rest and relaxation, a much-needed opportunity to get away from the stress of their high-pressure corporate careers. They were completely unaware that a tropical storm was slowly working its way up the Atlantic coast.

The first few days of their vacation were spent lounging at the beach, taking bicycle sight-seeing tours, and barbecuing dinner on the grill. One evening, as the wind whipped up a bit, they flipped on the television—their first contact with the outside world in days—and saw a report that Tropical Storm Bob had intensified into Hurricane Bob and was on a path that might hit Cape Cod and the Massachusetts islands.

Within twenty-four hours the quiet and solitude of their idyllic vacation was shattered. The hurricane did not veer out to sea as hoped, but instead rolled directly over Martha's Vineyard with one hundred mile per hour winds.

As the storm began to batter the island, the power went out. Soon after, the water service shut down. Nancy and Peter huddled in the bathroom, clutching a small flashlight and each other, listening to the steady roar of the storm and the periodic sounds of snapping tree limbs and shattering glass.

The next day they emerged from their tub-and-tile bunker to survey the damage. The house was a mess. Rain and tree branches had poured in through the windows, covering the floor with glass, leaves, and water. Outside, things were worse. Power lines, uprooted trees, and sections of porches and roofs were tangled in a silent, surreal landscape of chaos.

Nancy and Peter stared at each other in horror. "Now what?!" they exclaimed in unison. They had no food, no power, no water, no car, no one they knew on the island, and no clue what to do next. All their specialized knowledge of the corporate world was meaningless at that moment.

It is not very often that we find ourselves in an emergency situation. One of the wonderful benefits of living in a modern, prosperous society is that we have greatly reduced the risk of being suddenly thrust into dangerous situations. And when emergencies do occur, an efficient network of police, fire, medical, and relief operations is poised to spring into action and minimize the damage.

But the Millennium Bug threatens not only to thrust us into very dangerous situations, but also to disable those emergency operations we have come to rely on to bail us out. Unlike a hurricane, which hits a specific region, allowing unaffected areas to provide assistance, the Y2K crisis will hit everywhere all at once. Think of it as a hurricane hitting during an earthquake... in a war zone... during a flu epidemic.

If the computers go down, and if they are down for as long as I think, we are going to have to learn to function in a low-tech world. There are many things our forefathers knew and took for granted that we don't. For example, do you know how to:

- Dress a wound, set a broken bone, cure an infection, or treat yourself or others for food poisoning?

- Secure an alternate source of water should your tap water suddenly dry up? Or purify water so you don't make you or your family sick when you drink it?

- Identify edible plants and those that are deadly?

- Deliver a baby or pull a tooth?

- Dress a deer, butcher a cow or pig, clean a fish, or pluck a chicken?

- Dispose of human waste (when the toilets aren't working) in a way that keeps disease from rapidly spreading?

If you answered "no" to any of these questions, you need to educate yourself. The best weapon against uncertainty is knowledge. If the Year 2000 Computer Problem disrupts much of the basic social infrastructure, our usual sources of information—TV, radio, newspapers, telephone, Internet—may not be available to us. It is important to create in advance an emergency preparedness library.

Emergency Situation How-to Books

The following is a list of fourteen emergency preparedness books that I find most useful and informative. There is at least one book for each of the main areas of your life that might be drastically affected by Y2K disruptions and breakdowns.

The books may be purchased at most large book stores, or via the Internet, at <http://www.amazon.com> or <http://www.barnesandnoble.com>.

The American Red Cross First Aid and Safety Handbook by Kathleen A. Handal, M.D. (New York: Little, Brown and Company, 1992), 322 pages, $17.95. This is the official Red Cross classic—the most authoritative and comprehensive guide to giving first aid ever published. The book contains three primary sections: "In an Emergency," "First Aid," and "Personal and Family Safety." It is quite thorough, covering everything from snake bites and bee stings to setting a broken bone and delivering a baby.

This book is written in nonmedical, easy-to-understand language. Section headings are bright blue and easily found, and key words within each paragraph are in bold type. Many informative illustrations accompany the text, greatly increasing understanding and demonstrating proper techniques. The book also contains a First Aid Kit Checklist—the basic items you will want to have on hand before a medical emergency occurs.

The Bible. If our comfortable way of life is disrupted by the Year 2000 Computer Problem and the health and welfare of our loved ones are threatened, we are going to need more than just physical resources upon which to draw. We are going to need emotional and spiritual strength to make it through the tough times.

It has been shown that those who possess an active and strong religious faith are better able to deal with the trials and tribulations of life. In my humble opinion, faith is powerful for one simple reason: It is what our Designer and Creator wants from us.

Just as the designer and creator of an automobile provides an instruction manual so you know how best to operate the vehicle, God has provided the Bible as an instruction manual of how best to operate our lives.

Think of it this way: If the doctor informed you that you have cancer, whom would you call, a clergyman or an economist? If your son's military unit was sent into a war zone, where would you be on Sunday morning, in a church or on a golf course?

When people are suddenly faced with profound and eternal questions, they seek profound and eternal answers. The Y2K Crisis has the potential to jolt millions of citizens away from a relentless quest for pleasure and material goods, and make them face—possibly for the first time in their lives—profound and eternal questions.

The Bible is an indispensable source of comfort and joy, knowledge and wisdom, and should be the foremost volume in every home, not just during tough times, but for all times.

The Complete Book of Survival by Rainer Stahlberg (New York: Barricade Books, 1998), 288 pages, $25.00. The subtitle of this book is: "How to Protect Yourself Against Revolution, Riots, Hurricanes, Famine, and Other Natural and Man-made Disasters." Now, if it weren't for the looming Y2K Crisis, I would probably consider this book a little "far out." Mr. Stahlberg admits in the introduction that he is thinking about the unthinkable (and with a section titled, "Invasion of the Aliens," he's not kidding). But unfortunately, the Millennium Bug does force us to think about the unthinkable.

This book discusses survival considerations of various disasters: economic, climatic, terrorist, war, ecological, political, and bizarre (the alien invasion section). Each scenario is presented in a phase-by-phase format (he calls them "days"). What is likely to occur during each phase of the crisis and what steps you should take to protect yourself and your family are reviewed. The secret, according to Mr. Stahlberg, is the ability to recognize that a crisis situation is unfolding while most other people are still unaware of it. If your self-defense philosophy includes firearms, this book gives an overview of various options and considerations.

If nothing else, this book does a great job of bringing to life the theoretical, abstract ideas of societal disruption. After reading this book you will be convinced that, when the Y2K Problem is factored in, the unthinkable is quite likely.

The Encyclopedia of Country Living by Carla Emery (Seattle: Sasquatch Books, 1994), 858 pages, $27.95. This book is subtitled, "An Old Fashioned Recipe Book," but it is much more than just that. Ms. Emery has compiled in one volume most of the basic food production knowledge rural Americans took for granted a century or two ago—the very knowledge that has all but disappeared from our present generation.

"Today, a general ignorance about food production… makes most people captive consumers," Ms. Emery writes. As a result, citizens are now "almost totally dependent on other people to produce their food, clothing, and shelter."

This is the price we pay for living in a high-tech, prosperous, division-of-labor society. It is also the complex system that might collapse if Y2K disruptions prove to be severe.

This book covers basic farming and harvesting techniques, food preservation and preparation, and livestock and poultry—all from a low-tech, nineteenth-century point of view.

We all hope and pray that the Year 2000 Computer Problem does not thrust us into a situation in which we are required to produce our own food. (With the size of our population and the overall lack of knowledge, equipment, and available farm-land, this would surely result in widespread famine and death.) But this horrific sit-uation is not impossible. If things do get this bad, information about low-tech food production will be unavailable. It's fairly certain that our urban or suburban neigh-bors do not possess this knowledge. If the Y2K Crisis ever reaches this stage, *The Encyclopedia of Country Living* will be an invaluable asset.

Emergency Survival Communications by Dave Ingram (Columbus, Ohio: Univer-sal Electronics, Inc., 1997), 182 pages, $19.95. If the Millennium Bug knocks out power and telephone systems—even for a short time—all of our usual methods of obtaining information and communicating with the outside world will be gone. Television, phones, the Internet, and most radios will be useless. Even if the com-munication blackout proves to be brief, we won't know it at the time. A lack of infor-mation and a sense of isolation will quickly lead to fear and panic.

This book will tell you everything you ever wanted to know (and then some) about emergency communications. After a thorough overview of basic emergency com-munications considerations, numerous specialized chapters speak about the various communication methods. Included are: shortwave radio, scanners, CB radio (citizen's band), and satellite radio. There are also sections on free-playing radios (independent of normal energy sources), weather information, antennas and other accessories, and probably the most important consideration of all: alternate power sources.

Although this book contains many technical discussions and diagrams, the basic information you should know about each device and communication method is clearly spelled out.

Emergency Survival Communications is a good guide to help you make communi-cation equipment purchases. But don't forget: Once Y2K-related problems hit, it will probably be too late to buy the items you need. This book will make an excel-lent addition to your emergency preparedness library—but only if you acquire the right equipment beforehand. Otherwise, this book will do you little good.

The Home Water Supply: How to Find, Filter, Store, and Conserve It by Stu Campbell (Pownal, Vermont: Storey Books, 1983), 236 pages, $18.95. This book is an excellent overview of one of the most precious, if not *the* most precious, commodities in our lives: clean water. Human beings can survive for lengthy periods of time without heat and electricity, food and fuel. But without water, we can survive no more than a few days.

The Home Water Supply is not an emergency how-to book, *per se*. It is designed primarily to educate the reader on the most efficient and effective ways to supply water to a rural or suburban home. The book does a tremendous job of explaining how to construct water supply systems. The various chapters explain how to find, get, move, hold, treat, distribute, control, and conserve water.

The book is based on the assumption that basic plumbing supplies and digging and drilling equipment will be readily available. If you wish to break your reliance on municipal water service before the year 2000 and become self-sufficient, this book will show you how. If you are planning to store an emergency supply of water or secure an alternate source temporarily to deal with the first few weeks or months of Y2K problems, this book will not help.

Regardless, this volume is still a valuable addition to any Y2K library. It contains a wealth of knowledge about a subject most of us have taken for granted our whole lives, and in the event the Millennium Bug causes long-term disruptions and dislocations, it will greatly assist families, neighborhoods, and communities in rebuilding a reliable water infrastructure.

How to Live Without Electricity—and Like It by Anita Evangelista (Port Townsend, Washington: Breakout Productions, 1997), 158 pages, $13.95. Ms. Evangelista and her family of four lived for three years without electricity. All of the knowledge she gleaned during that time—especially the mistakes—are contained in this book. As she writes in Chapter 1: "This book can save you the trouble of learning about power sources from scratch… because I'll tell what worked for me and what didn't work at all."

There are chapters on each of the major aspects of our lives and the possible non-electric solutions. Included are:

- Light—lamps, lanterns, and flashlights

- Water—manual pumps and storage methods

- Cooking—gas, wood, and solar

- Heating—wood, gas, propane, kerosene, and solar

- Food storage—cold rooms, ice boxes, and underground storage

- Communications—battery- and solar-powered radios and CB radios

This book will teach you everything—which kerosene lamps burn clean, which ones fill your home with fumes, the limits of solar power, how to make use of that powerful 12-volt battery sitting in your car. It will be an excellent addition to your preparation library.

Making the Best of Basics: Family Preparedness Handbook by James Talmage Stevens (Seattle: Gold Leaf Press, 1997), 322 pages, $19.95. This is the tenth edition of this classic first published in 1974, and there are now more than 350,000 copies in print around the world. If you can afford to buy only two books, get this one and *The Red Cross First Aid and Safety Handbook.*

Mr. Stevens does a thorough job of covering all the important aspects of family preparedness. Chapter 1, "What is Family Preparedness?", is a wonderful essay that will put you in the right frame of mind and make you aware of the many things we take for granted, and how truly vulnerable we are to any disruptions of our economic and social infrastructure.

There are chapters discussing basic in-home storage problems and solutions, plus chapters on energy and fuel storage and vitamin supplements. The chapter entitled "Water—the Absolute Basic" is not to be missed.

The majority of the book, however, is devoted to food. Ten separate chapters cover everything from basic grains, cooking techniques, and dairy products, to honey usage, kitchen gardening, and dried fruit and vegetables. This is a fabulous book, well-deserving the label "classic."

Portable Wealth: The Complete Guide to Precious Metals Investing by Adam Starchild (Boulder, Colorado: Paladin Press, 1998), 74 pages, $12.00. The best protection against future financial disaster, according to Mr. Starchild, is to invest in tangible commodities—items that have an intrinsic, enduring value. Unlike monetary investments, which are essentially paper or electronic *promises* to pay, tangible commodities won't lose their value during economic, financial, or political chaos.

The three precious metals—gold, silver, and platinum—are discussed in detail, including the history and future prospects of each, and the metals' respective attributes and drawbacks. The options available to investors and various tax strategies are also covered. For those who wish to protect their assets and investments from the Y2K calamity, this book is a must.

The SAS Survival Handbook by John "Lofty" Wiseman (London: HarperCollins Publishers, 1996), 288 pages, $18.50. The subtitle of this book is "How to survive in the wild, in any climate, on land or at sea," and Mr. Wiseman truly covers every possible disaster scenario. A twenty-six–year military career, including years with the elite British Army unit, the Special Air Service, has prepared him well to discuss these "survivalist" topics.

We hope and pray that even the most severe Y2K disruptions will not force us to survive in the wilderness. The chapters on building an emergency shelter in the tropics, constructing an igloo, and navigating by the stars are probably unnecessary. But many sections of this book contain excellent information. For our purposes, the two primary groupings are plants and animals. There are chapters on edible plants and poisonous plants, complete with detailed, color illustrations.

There are also chapters that explain in detail how to hunt, trap, and fish for food—using primitive, hand-made tools. Which animals to stalk and which ones to stay away from is also discussed. There is even a section on—gulp!—edible insects.

If we ever reach the point at which we are down to our last can of beans and it is time to venture out into the woods to "rustle up some grub," this book will show us how.

Spiritual Survival During the Y2K Crisis by Steve Farrar (Nashville: Thomas Nelson Publishers, 1999), 244 pages, $12.99. This nationally known Christian author and speaker explores an often overlooked aspect of Y2K preparations: spirituality. Time and time again history has shown that in a crisis situation, those who are grounded in a strong religious faith are best able to survive and thrive.

Dr. Farrar explains that spiritual truth is also practical truth—that is, it applies to everyday life. The biblical point of view is presented on many Y2K issues: food storage, disagreements between spouses, and self-defense. This book can help you avoid fear, confusion, and panic surrounding Y2K, and discover a biblical and practical plan for your family.

Square Foot Gardening by Mel Bartholomew (Emmaus, Pennsylvania: Rodale Press, 1981), 348 pages, $16.95. This book is *the* book on gardening. My wife swears by it. It sets forth simple techniques for growing more food in less space and with a minimum of effort.

Let's face it, if the Millennium Bug disrupts our society, we may be forced to do something we've never done before (at least not seriously)—grow our own food. The average American has two major problems in this regard: a shortage of knowledge and a shortage of land. This book addresses both issues.

The basics of gardening are covered—what crops are best, soil considerations, watering, weeding, and detailed climate maps of North America.

Mr. Bartholomew also lays out his ingenious "square foot" plan, a system for producing the maximum yield from the minimum amount of ground. A key to this method is vertical growing, whereby crops that usually grow "out"—like cucumbers, melons, and squash—are made to grow "up." (The photo of Mr.

Bartholomew picking cantaloupes at eye-level from a lush "living wall" is fascinating.) The various structures needed for vertical growing and how to construct them are also explained.

Even if Y2K does not force us to grow our own food, this book would make a delightful addition to a home library—for both those who already enjoy gardening and those who may wish to give it a try some day.

The Toilet Papers: Recycling Waste and Conserving Water by Sim Van der Ryn (Sausalito, California: Ecological Design Press, 1995), 128 pages, $10.95. This favorite of the 1970s back-to-nature crowd is once again in print... and just in time for Y2K. A professor at the University of California, Berkeley, since 1961, Van der Ryn takes an informative and sometimes irreverent look at human waste problems and solutions through the centuries. He also discusses in detail safe toilet and privy designs available today that reduce water consumption and avert the need for expensive treatment systems.

Professor Van der Ryn presents detailed designs for dry toilets, compost privies, and greywater systems (greywater is used, dirty water from household activities—except from the toilet). With water and sewer systems threatened by Millennium Bug disruptions, this book can help you deal with one of the most fundamental human dilemmas: how to dispose of human waste safely and cleanly.

Woodstove Cookery: At Home on the Range by Jane Cooper (Pownal, Vermont: Storey Books, 1977), 196 pages, $12.95. This book is divided into two primary sections: the stove itself and the food. The information you need to know about acquiring a wood stove—setting it up, the wood supply, care and cleaning—are explained.

The majority of the book is devoted to recipes. You'd be surprised at the variety of cooking that can be done on a woodstove (I know I was!). Baking and broiling, breads and breakfast, soups and stews—it's all in here. My favorite section is the mouth-watering chapter on desserts: cakes, cookies, pies, and puddings.

Woodstove Cookery is an excellent book to own if you plan to use a wood stove during Y2K. And even after things finally return to "normal," if you want continue using the stove, this book will come in handy.

Magazines

The only Y2K-related magazine I know of is *Y2K News Magazine*, published by Wilson Publications, LLC, in Crossville, Tennessee (24 issues, $44.95). This printed publication is updated every two weeks with current news events and insightful research on all aspects of the Y2K Problem, from business contingency planning to personal preparedness techniques and community action plans, with everything in between.

The magazine's publisher, Tim Wilson, focuses on providing readers with unbiased, objective news stories that give the facts and not the rumors, letting readers decide the truth for themselves. As a result, *Y2K News Magazine* has quickly become one of the most credible sources of reliable Y2K information available. It is well worth subscribing. I personally read every issue from cover to cover.

Internet Sites

The information technology revolution has produced one of the greatest sources for gathering knowledge known to mankind: the Internet. The Internet has been the leading vehicle for sharing information about Y2K on a worldwide basis, although the Internet itself is threatened by Y2K if electrical power and phone service are disrupted.

The Internet contains scores of websites devoted to emergency preparations. The following is a list of the sites I have found to be the most helpful and reliable. I recommend that when you find a valuable article, essay, list, or catalog page, print out a hard copy, and file it with your preparedness books. This way you can access the information even if the Internet goes down for a while. In addition to my own website at <http://michaelhyatt.com>, I recommend the following:

Captain Dave's Survival Center <http://www.survival-center.com>. This site contains a wealth of preparedness resources. Although not totally Y2K-related, you will find Y2K information and preparedness products available. It is written from a survivalist's point of view.

Cheaper Than Dirt! <http://www.cheaperthandirt.com>. Billing itself as "America's Leading Sports Discounter," this site has everything from ammunition to camping gear, from Meals Ready to Eat (MREs) to preparedness books and videos. You can order a hard copy catalog or visit the online store and place orders over the Internet.

FEMA Preparedness <http://www.fema.gov/pte/prep.htm>. This is the official site of the Federal Emergency Management Agency (FEMA). There is a good deal of general preparedness information available here, though not specifically oriented toward Y2K. The FEMA site does have a Year 2000 section, but it is primarily dedicated to explaining why you won't be able to count on the agency if there are Y2K-related disruptions. It can be summarized in one sentence: "You're on your own."

Jade Mountain <http://www.jademountain.com/y2k/y2k.htm>. This company is a leading supplier to homesteaders and others who want to live more self-reliantly. It has Y2K-specific information and suppliers. Products are grouped by category and oriented to those making individual or family contingency plans.

The Money Changer <http://www.the-moneychanger.com>. If you are going to buy silver and gold, you first need to educate yourself. This site has numerous well-written articles on the subject. Franklin Sanders, the proprietor, is a precious metals dealer whom I recommend without hesitation. If you are going to buy precious metals, Franklin's the man to contact. (See Chapter 12 for more information on buying precious metals.)

Montana Marketplace <http://www.mtmarketplace.com>. This is another emergency preparedness company offering a wide range of survival information and supplies. The site is not Y2K-exclusive, but it is actively focusing on Millennium Bug–oriented citizens. The site sells several unique items I have been unable to find elsewhere.

Noah's Ark <http://www.millennium-ark.net/News_Files/Hollys.html>. This is by far my favorite preparedness site. But be forewarned: If you visit you may spend several hours browsing through article after article. If you can't find it on this site, you don't need it. Seriously, it is well worth spending a day reading through this material.

Personal Y2K Supplies <http://www.y2klinks.nct/Y2Ksupplies.htm>. This is a comprehensive list of all the supplies you need for Y2K. It is the most complete list I have found anywhere on the web. This page is part of Ted Derryberry's Y2K website, which is excellent.

Preparing for the Year 2000 Crash <http://www.prepare4y2k.com>. This site is maintained by Dr. Scott Olmsted, a veteran computer programmer who gained national attention when he appeared on ABC's *Nightline* and CBS's *60 Minutes* to discuss the Y2K retreat he has built in the California desert. This site contains preparedness information, essays by Dr. Olmsted, and links to many other useful sites.

Survival & Energy Info <http://www.cairns.net.au/~sharefin/Markets/Alternative.htm>. This is the "mother of all preparedness links." Here you will find a comprehensive listing, by category, of scores of preparedness sites. If you can't find it here, it doesn't exist!

Test2000 <http://www.rightime.com>. Setting the date forward on your personal computer and letting it roll over to the next century is not recommended. A few systems will lock up or cause unexpected results. A much safer method for testing your system is to download a simple program that will check your PC hardware for Year 2000 compliance. This program is free!

Y2K for Women <http://www.y2kwomen.com>. This site is maintained by Karen Anderson and is designed to explain the Millennium Bug to women who have no, or very limited, computer knowledge. It discusses how Y2K will affect women personally and what women can do about it. One of the best features of the site is the "Ask Karen" section. You can even sign up for Karen's free e-zine (e-mail newsletter).

Y2K Supplies <http://www.y2ksupplies.com>. This site is dedicated to Y2K preparedness supplies. Though the site is not extensive, it is worth checking out.

Knowledge Is Power

The difference between triumph and tragedy is whether someone has acquired the proper knowledge and taken steps to prepare for the disaster. An emergency preparedness library is an essential part of your overall program for dealing with the Y2K Crisis. Please do not delay in gathering these critical resources.

Y2K PREP TIP #2
Assign a Research Job to Each Family Member

Assembling an emergency preparedness library is a wise thing to do in light of the potential threat posed by Y2K. It is not too dramatic to say that having this informational resource may prove to be the difference between life and death if the crisis becomes severe.

But realistically, if the lights go out, the tap water stops flowing, and a family member takes ill—all at the same time—emergency how-to books will be little help if no one in your family is familiar with them. Frantically flipping pages and trying to speed-read by candlelight is not a good way to learn. If you wait until an emergency hits before attempting to learn how to respond to it, you may be too late. The stress and panic of an emergency situation make it very difficult to think clearly. And you definitely need to be thinking clearly to absorb new knowledge from a book.

I suggest assigning a research job to each family member. Break down your emergency preparedness library into sections and make one person responsible for each section. Suggested sections might be: health and medicine, food and water, light and heat, money and barter, and safety and waste disposal.

Of course, you want to be sure the family members involved in this plan are old enough and mature enough to handle the task. It won't do much good to assign the health and medicine job to your eight-year-old.

Each person taking part in this program should become familiar with the books and other resources in his or her section. Family members certainly don't have to memorize everything and become instant experts in their fields. They should, however, spend enough time browsing through the books to develop a general knowledge of what information each book offers and how it is organized. Taking notes and writing up an outline could also help.

The point is to have someone in the household who is an "amateur expert" in a particular emergency area. If some sudden crisis hits due to Y2K (or any other reason, for that matter), this person will know which chapter of which book to turn to for help. This plan will save precious moments at a time when every moment counts. It will also increase your family's confidence that you indeed can, by pulling together and working hard, handle any surprise that may come along.

	Y2K PREPAREDNESS CHECKLIST				
Level	*Action Step*	*Qty*	*Unit Price*	*Total Qty*	*Total Price*
1	Visit recommended Internet-sites—print out useful articles, lists, product descriptions, etc. File with preparedness books.	N/A	No cost		
1	Purchase the Bible if you don't already have a copy.	1	$20		
1	Purchase *The American Red Cross First Aid and Safety Handbook.*	1	$18		
1	Purchase *Spiritual Survival During the Y2K Crisis.*	1	$13		
1	Purchase *The Complete Book of Survival.*	1	$25		
1	Assign research jobs to family members.	N/A	N/A		
2	Purchase *The Home Water Supply.*	1	$19		
2	Purchase *The Toilet Papers.*	1	$11		
3	Purchase *Emergency Survival Communications.*	1	$20		
3	Purchase *How to Live Without Electricity.*	1	$14		
3	Purchase *Woodstove Cookery.*	1	$13		
4	Purchase *Making the Best of Basics.*	1	$20		

		Qty Per	Unit	Total	Total
Level	Action Step	Person	Price	Qty	Price
4	Purchase *Portable Wealth.*	1	$12		
5	Purchase *The Encyclopedia of Country Living.*	1	$28		
5	Purchase *Square Foot Gardening.*	1	$17		
5	Purchase *The SAS Survival Handbook.*	1	$19		

Y2K PREPAREDNESS CHECKLIST *(Continued)*

Chapter Three

Develop an Alternative Communications System

What we have here is failure to communicate.
—From the movie *Cool Hand Luke* (1967)

On April 16, 1998, I flew from my hometown of Nashville, Tennessee, to St. Louis. While waiting for my luggage to arrive, I wandered over to a TV monitor to catch up on the latest CNN headlines. The story being presented was about a devastating tornado that had just hit a metropolitan area somewhere in the United States (I arrived after the story started, so I didn't catch the city). Video footage showed buildings that were blown down, children crying, and testimony from residents who were obviously shaken and distressed. I watched with detached concern, having no apparent connection with the citizens but nonetheless feeling sympathy for them. Finally, the reporter happened to mention that the city was Nashville.

I couldn't believe my ears. *Nashville!* I thought. Immediately, my mind was flooded with images of Gail, my dear wife of twenty years, and my five precious daughters. I ran to the pay phone, silently praying to the Lord that my family and friends were safe. I was so nervous I had to dial my phone credit card number three times before I got it right. Finally! It was ringing. But my hopes were immediately dashed: "I'm sorry. All circuits are busy. Please try your call again later." I redialed. Same message.

I went through this sequence again and again for the next hour. I then decided to call my parents in Texas to see if they had been able to get through (my sister and her family also live in Nashville). They were experiencing the same problem and were also concerned. For the next twelve hours, in between business appointments and other commitments, I called twice an hour. Always the same message. It didn't help that CNN kept running the same alarming images over and over again.

Finally, early the next morning, I got through. Gail answered the phone.

"Honey, are you okay?" I said in a voice full of emotion and concern.

"Yes," she said, puzzled by the question. "What's wrong with you?"

"What's wrong with me? I've been trying to get through to you for the past twelve hours and have been scared to death, wondering if you had been hurt by the tornado."

She then explained that the tornado had hit downtown Nashville, twenty miles from our suburban home. Aside from high winds and heavy rain, nothing had happened outside the downtown area. In fact, Gail had no idea there had been a tornado until she saw the same report I had been watching on CNN!

In a crisis, not having accurate information can be psychologically unsettling at best, and life-threatening at worst. Nothing can create a sense of isolation and fear more quickly than being cut off from the flow of information. This is particularly true in our overcommunicated society, where we are almost addicted to twenty-four–hour news updates and immediate Internet access to the latest breaking information. Unfortunately, these same traditional media sources are often disrupted in a crisis.

Whether it's a natural disaster such as a tornado, a hurricane, or a flood, or a technological tempest as a result of Y2K, the communication channels we depend on most are at risk. This includes television and radio broadcasts, Internet access, and even basic phone service. Therefore, it is imperative for your psychological well-being, as well as your physical safety, to have some sort of alternative communications system in place. I want to share several such systems with you in this chapter, including ways to organize the members of your neighborhood or church group so you can stay in touch.

Powering Up, Tuning In

The most common sources of information during a crisis are conventional television and radio broadcasts. Most of us depend on these sources for our daily dosage of news from around the world. But there are at least three problems with being too dependent on the traditional media, particularly the national media:

1. These sources could be disrupted by the Millennium Bug. Even if a given broadcast network makes sure that all of its computers are repaired in time, it is still dependent on an array of third-party suppliers and providers outside of its control to get the word out. These include electrical utilities, telecommunications providers, satellites, and, last but not least, advertising revenue that enables the company to pay its employees and vendors and thus maintain an uninterrupted flow of information. Any—or all—of these could be disrupted by Y2K.

2. These sources are susceptible to government interference and network bias. I do not share many survivalists' antigovernment sentiment, but I have become increasingly disturbed by the persistent "spin" that federal agencies and the major media are putting on Y2K. They continue to assure the American people that "all is well," there is nothing to worry about. I wish this were true. Unfortunately, these assurances are not supported by the data. As a result, you often must go to the original source documents or tune into alternative media to get the real picture.

3. These sources are often drawn to the sensationalistic point of view. Unfortunately, this often becomes "necessary" in the kind of competitive environment in which these media operate, and they seem to be willing to do almost anything to attain higher ratings. The distortion is not so much what the media report as what they *don't* report. Why, for example, didn't CNN make it clear when reporting on the Nashville tornado that it affected only an eight-block area in the center of the city? While the news often masquerades as information, it is, more often than not, just another form of entertainment. Unfortunately, this is not what you need in a crisis.

While the above problems could affect all media to one extent or another, they will undoubtedly have less impact on the local media. Therefore, it is important to have some way to tune into these sources in the absence of reliable electrical power.

Alternative Radios

There are several good AM/FM radios on the market that work with alternative power. Certainly any battery-operated radio is an option. Just make sure you also stockpile a good supply of batteries. However, there are a couple of radios that can run without electricity or batteries. Since they are relatively inexpensive, I would suggest that you acquire one.

The least expensive radio I have found is the Solar Dynamo Radio. Not only is it a radio, but it also has a built-in emergency flashlight. It will run on four different sources of power, including DC (i.e., car battery), solar, hand-crank generator, or two "AA" batteries. The unit features normal AM/FM radio bands, adjustable volume control, LED lights to indicate reception, and an earphone jack. The flashlight comes with two spare bulbs, a clear lens cover for normal use, and a yellow and red lens cover for night or emergency use. A switch flips the flashlight from a steady beam to a flashing warning light. Several survival and preparedness vendors sell the radio. The cheapest source I found was Total Survival. The retail price on the radio is $39.95; Total Survival sells it for $24.95 plus shipping (batteries not included). You can order it from:

Total Survival, Inc.
N. 23 Weber Road, Suite C-4
Deer Park, WA
Voice: (509) 276-1119
Fax: (509) 276-1347
Orders only: (888) 276-2119
Internet: <http://www.totalsurvival.com/communication.htm>

Another possibility is the WorldBand Solar and Dynamo Powered Radio. This radio will pick up AM/FM, four shortwave bands, police and aircraft bands, TV sound, and the National Weather Service. This one runs off four "AA" Nickel-Cadmium (NiCad) batteries (not included). These batteries can be recharged hundreds of times and via solar power, hand-cranking, or DC power. As an example, three hours of sunlight will charge the batteries for four to six hours of playing time. You can order the radio for $89.95 plus shipping from Pioneer Emergency Preparedness Products. If you want more than merely AM/FM radio, this is a good buy.

Pioneer Emergency Preparedness Products
P.O. Box 686
Pioneer, California 95666
Toll-free: (800) 330-4234
Internet: <http://www.prepare-now.com/818.html>

A final option, and seemingly the most popular one, is the BayGen Wind-up Radio. It has AM/FM and shortwave and will play for approximately thirty minutes on a thirty-second wind. This is the one recommended by the Red Cross and the United Nations. It currently sells for around $100 plus shipping. This is the one I bought, and I have been very happy with it. (If I had known about the WorldBand Solar and Dynamo Powered Radio above, I probably would have bought that instead.) The BayGen radio is available from several sources, including retail outlets such as Sports Authority. Pioneer Emergency Preparedness Products also sells it (see above). It is available from that company for $99.95 plus shipping. You can get an optional AC power supply for $10.95.

Shortwave radio provides one of the best alternative sources of news on the planet. You can tune into broadcasts from around the world—everything from BBC radio news to survivalist-oriented programs with some good and some questionable content. It's safe to say there is something for everyone in the world of shortwave radio. How many of these broadcasts will continue to air in a Y2K-related emergency is anyone's guess. Even in a worst-case scenario, it is probably safe to say that at least some broadcasts will continue without interruption. If so, it will give you a means to find out what people are experiencing in other parts of the country or the world.

One of the reasons I like the BayGen radio described above is its ability to receive shortwave radio transmissions. You can, however, find much more sophisticated, dedicated shortwave units at any radio supply house. If you are new to shortwave radio, you may also want to order *Passport to World Band Radio*. This guidebook contains up-to-date program schedules and frequencies for most international broadcasters, peeks behind the scenes, and equipment reviews. It is available from Jade Mountain for about $23. You can order it from:

Jade Mountain, Inc.
717 Poplar Avenue
Boulder, CO 80304
Toll-free: (800) 442-1972
Fax: (303) 449-8266
Internet: <http://www.jademountain.com/y2k/y2kBayGen.htm>

Commercial Broadcast Options

Once you have a radio, the next question becomes, "What are you going to listen to?" Obviously, your local AM/FM stations will be possibilities. Most stations have some sort of emergency back-up, so even with a power outage they won't go off the air immediately. But you may want to round out the perspective you are getting locally with news from around the country. One option is to tune in to "clear channel" AM stations.

During the day, AM and FM radio have about the same approximate range. But "during the night, signals from lower frequency AM stations 'skip' off the earth's ionosphere and are easily received throughout North America. Fancy or expensive receivers are not required for receiving these signals."[1] Many "super stations" broadcast on what are called "clear channels" and operate at the maximum power allowable: 50,000 watts. Table 3.1 contains a list of "Clear Channel AM Radio Stations and Frequencies." This will provide you with several options for tuning in to extra-local news. Be advised, however, that some frequencies are occupied by more than one station. The one you actually receive on any given day is dependent on a number of factors, including geography, weather, and atmospheric conditions.

Noncommercial Broadcast Options

In addition to the various commercial broadcast stations, there are a number of noncommercial broadcast frequencies that you may want to monitor. Most simple radios

Table 3.1:
Clear Channel AM Stations and Frequencies

State/Territory	City	Station	Frequency
British Columbia	Vancouver	CKLG	730
California	Fresno	KFRE	940
California	Los Angeles	KFI	640
California	Los Angeles	KNX	1070
California	San Francisco	KCBS	740
California	Santa Monica	KBLA	1580
Colorado	Denver	KOA	850
Connecticut	Hartford	WTIC	1080
District of Columbia	Washington	WTOP	1500
Florida	Marathon Key	RADIO MARTI	1180
Georgia	Atlanta	WSB	750
Illinois	Chicago	WBBM	780
Illinois	Chicago	WGN	720
Illinois	Chicago	WLS	890
Illinois	Chicago	WLUP	1000
Illinois	Chicago	WMAQ	670
Iowa	Des Moines	WHO	1040
Iowa	Waterloo	KXEL	1540
Kentucky	Louisville	WHAS	840
Louisiana	New Orleans	WWL	870
Maryland	Baltimore	WBAL	1090
Massachusetts	Boston	WBZ	1030
Massachusetts	Boston	WHDH	850
Massachusetts	Boston	WRKO	680
Michigan	Detroit	WJR	760
Minnesota	Minneapolis	WCCO	830
Missouri	St. Louis	KMOX	1120
New York	New York	WABC	770
New York	New York	WBBR	1130
New York	New York	WCBS	880
New York	New York	WEVD	1050
New York	New York	WFAN	660
New York	New York	WINS	1010
New York	New York	WOR	710
New York	New York	WQEW	1560
New York	Schenectady	WGY	810

State/Territory	City	Station	Frequency
Ohio	Cincinnati	WKRC	1530
Ohio	Cincinnati	WLW	700
Ohio	Cleveland	WKNR	1220
Ohio	Cleveland	WWWE	1100
Oklahoma	Oklahoma City	KOMA	1520
Oklahoma	Tulsa	KVOO	1170
Ontario	Windsor	CKLW	800
Oregon	Portland	KEX	1190
Pennsylvania	Philadelphia	KYW	1060
Pennsylvania	Philadelphia	WOGL	1210
Pittsburgh	Pennsylvania	KDKA	1020
Quebec	Laval	CKLM	1570
Quebec	Montreal	CBF	690
Saskatchewan	Regina	CBK	540
Tennessee	Nashville	WLAC	1510
Tennessee	Nashville	WSM	650
Texas	Fort Worth	WBAP	820
Texas	San Antonio	WOAI	1200
Utah	Salt Lake	KSL	1160
Virginia	Richmond	WRVA	1140
Washington	Seattle	KING	1090
Washington	Seattle	KIRO	710
Washington	Seattle	KOMO	1000
West Virginia	Wheeling	WWVA	1170

do not have the capability of accessing these frequencies, and you will need a specialized scanner to do so. Such a device will enable you to tune into everything that is being broadcast locally, including National Oceanic and Atmospheric Administration (NOAA) weather, police, fire, ambulance, and amateur radio. You can generally also monitor more esoteric transmissions such as railroad communications; Alcohol, Tobacco, and Firearms (ATF); border patrol; U.S. Customs; ship-to-shore; aircraft; airport; and a variety of other government and private transmissions. Table 3.2 contains a list of "VHF/UHF Communications That Can Be Monitored on Scanners."

Be warned, however: The Communications Act of 1934 prohibits you as a third-party from revealing the contents of two-way conversations with others or using this information for personal gain. In addition, the Electronic Communications Privacy Act of 1986 makes it illegal for private citizens to monitor cellular telephone frequencies. The Telephone Disclosure and Dispute Resolution Act of 1993 adds addi-

Table 3.2:
VHF/UHF Communications That Can Be Monitored on Scanners[2]

Alcohol, Tobacco, Firearms (ATF)
165–168 MHz
406–420

Amateur Radio
144–148 MHz
222–225 MHz
420–450 MHz
902-928 MHz

Ambulance
155.0–155.5 MHz
462–468 MHz

Aircraft
118–128 (Air Traffic Control)
123.5–123.7 (Arrival and Departure)
Note: above aircraft use AM mode

Border Patrol
408–417 MHz

Business Bands
150–162 MHz
461–465 MHz
502–512 MHz
851–853 MHz

Cellular Phones
870–896 MHz
Note: Commercial aircraft cell
    phones use the 894–896 MHz range

Cordless (Home) Phones
46.6–49.9 MHz (older models)
900–902 MHz (newer models)

FBI
162–167 MHz

**Federal Emergency
Management Agency (FEMA)**
166.2–170.2 MHz
Also 138.225, 141.725, 408.40, 410.48,
413.21, 417.66 and 417.05 MHz

Fire
154.0–154.5 MHz
451–454 MHz

General Mobile Radio Service (GMRS)
462.5–467.7 MHz

Military Aircraft
236.4–236.7 MHz (Air Traffic Control)
243.0 MHz (Emergency)

**National Oceanic and
Atmospheric Administration (NOAA)
Weather Radio**
162–163 MHz

Naval Aircraft
277.5–278 MHz
340.2 MHz (Air Traffic Control)

News Media
450.0–455 MHz

**Nuclear Regulatory
Commission**
167–172 MHz

Police
154–159 MHz (Smaller cities and rural areas)
453–454 MHz and
460.0–460.6 (Larger cities and metropolitan areas)
and 810–816 MHz (new 800-MHz band activity)

Railroads
159–161 MHz

Secret Service
164–167 MHz

Strategic Air Command (SAC)
311.0 MHz

Police and Municipal Trunking
856–867 MHz

U.S. Customs
165-166 MHz

tional restrictions, making it illegal to produce or import a scanner that allows the user to monitor these frequencies. Also, you should be aware that some states (e.g., New York and New Jersey) prohibit private citizens from monitoring police communications.

There are a number of options when it comes to scanners. It all depends on what frequencies you want to monitor, what features you desire, and how much you have to spend. Prices start at about $100 but can escalate to a few thousand for some desktop models.

Reach Out and Touch Someone

Simple radio receivers or scanners are great when all you want to do is listen in on a broadcast or someone else's two-way transmissions. But what if you want to engage in two-way communication yourself? What if you want to talk as well as listen?

Cell Phones

Forget about cell phones if Y2K problems hit the telecommunications infrastructure. They may be working in some areas, but they depend on much of the same systems that traditional phones use. If your telephone doesn't work, there's a good chance your cell phone won't either. As a result, you need to think of a truly *alternative* system.

Citizen's Band

One option is a CB ("citizen's band") radio. As you may recall, these were very popular in the 1970s, before the availability of cellular phones, but are now making a comeback. You can pick them up very inexpensively—usually less than $100, and even cheaper if you are willing to do a little garage sale shopping. They supposedly have a range of ten to twenty miles if the channel is clear and the terrain permits; or about four to five miles if the channel is congested. In actual use the range is usually about a mile and a half. However, if you wire them to an antenna and elevate them on a PVC pipe or other device, you can extend the range by several miles. (You will need to do some experimenting to find out if this will work in your situation.)

I recently had Alvin Foster at ALF Enterprises design a CB system for me. I told him that I wanted a base station for the Y2K Task Force Coordinator in our subdivision and handheld devices for every family that wants to purchase one. The advantage of the base station is that you can hook it up to a mounted antenna and extend the range by several miles. (Remember: As it says on new car stickers, "Your mileage may vary.")

For the base unit, he recommends the Cherokee CBS500 Base Station. It is a forty-channel AM radio with a number of bells and whistles. It operates on AC or DC power and has a low-power switch to conserve battery power when full output is not needed. It is also reasonably priced (see Table 3.3, below).

For handheld units, he recommends the Cherokee AH27F. This also is a forty-channel AM radio. These are the latest and greatest technology, with power circuitry designed to save batteries. They can be powered by alkaline batteries, NiCad rechargeable batteries, or automotive cigarette lighter adapters.

The most expensive part of the equation, particularly for the base unit, is a solar panel and attendant hardware. You can't actually power the base unit directly from your solar panel; you have to charge deep cycle batteries and use them instead. If you already have an alternative source of power, you won't need the solar panels. I had him include them in case you don't have any other way to gener-

Table 3.3:
Handheld CB Unit

Description	Qty	Unit Price	Extended Price
Cherokee AH27F Handheld CB	1	$80.39	$ 80.39
Subtotal for radio only			$ 80.39
Panasonic AA NiCad Batteries Rechargeable 8-pack	2	$12.95	$ 25.90
AA Solar Charger #806	2	$17.95	$ 35.90
Subtotal for solar recharging unit only			$ 61.80
Total for both radio and solar charger (does not include shipping)			$142.19

ate your own electricity. (The prices in Tables 3.3 and 3.4 are Alvin's discounted prices.)

The handheld unit can work with normal alkaline batteries; however, they do have a shelf life, and the rechargeable NiCads are cheaper over the long run.

As you can see, a big part of the expense is the solar recharger. If you already have a generator, a solar energy system, or some other way to generate electricity, you won't need to buy the recharger (more about this in Chapter 8). You can order directly from:

ALF Enterprises
P.O. Box 671
Mukilteo, WA 98275
Voice and Fax: (425) 267-9267
Internet: <http://www.alfenterprises.com>

Family Radio Service

Family Radio Service (FRS) is yet another option. FRS is a radio band that the Federal Communications Commission (FCC) designated for anyone to use for virtually

Table 3.4:
CB Base Station Unit

Description	Qty	Unit Price	Extended Price
Cherokee CBS500 Base Station	1	$125.25	$125.25
Solarcron Antron 99 Base Stion CB Antenna	1	$ 59.99	$ 59.99
100' Coaxial Antenna (to run from your base unit to your antenna)	1	$ 29.99	$ 29.99
Subtotal for radio only			$215.23
Solarex PV/SX VLX-53 (53 watt, 3.08 amp solar panel)	1	$359.00	$359.00
ASC Solid State Charge Regulator PR/SC-ASC-12/8	1	$ 49.00	$ 49.00
Blocking Diode	1	$ 2.00	$ 2.00
Solarex Omni Mount Kit MH/SX-OM-2X	1	$130.50	$130.50
RV or Marine Deep Cycle Battery (purchased at Wal-Mart, etc.)	1	$ 50.00	$ 50.00
Subtotal for solar recharging unit only			$590.50
Total for both radio and solar charger (does not include shipping)			$805.73

any purpose. In comparison to regular handheld CB radios, there is less traffic, the radios are somewhat smaller, and they have better battery life. Power output is the maximum legally allowed at one-half watt. The audio is very crisp and clear from the speaker, and the range is advertised as more than two miles, though most users will not get more than about half a mile, especially in wooded terrain. They are easy to tote around, since they are only a little larger than a pager and weigh just eight ounces or so. Table 3.5 compares CB radios with FRS radios.

The prices for FRS radios are about the same as for CBs. Models start at about $40 at Radio Shack and go up from there. My personal favorite is the Cherokee FR465Plus. This is a fourteen-channel radio with LCD display, "Vital Link" radio range finder system with voice alert and panic button, six user-selectable "Call Tones" to alert other FRS users, improved Incoming Call Tone Ringer operation, and a ten-segment "Fuel Gauge" for more detailed battery level indication. At this writing, ALF Enterprises sells these units for $109.95 plus shipping. (You can see a wide variety of FRS radios, including the FR465Plus at <http://www.alfenterprises.com/FRSRadios.html>.) Since these radios are also powered by two "AA" batteries, I recommend the same rechargeable system described in Table 3.3, above.

Table 3.5:
Citizen's Band (CB) vs. Family Radio Service (FRS)

Feature	Citizen's Band	Family Radio Service
Band	HF	UHF
Modulation	AM	FM
Maximum Out Power	4 watts	0.5 watt
Range under ideal conditions	5–20 miles	2 miles
Average range	1.5 miles	0.5 miles
Comparison	• Handheld or base stations • Can get additional range with right antenna • The AM signal has the ability to follow the terrain • Best suited for outdoor use	• Handheld units only • FCC rules prohibit modifying the antenna • The FM signal transmits better through walls • Better suited for indoor use

Amateur Radio

For more reliable communication over greater distances, you might want to consider obtaining an amateur radio license. With an amateur radio band handheld radio, communication over distances of one hundred miles or more can be accomplished using one of the six thousand–plus amateur radio repeater systems in place across the United States and Canada. Use of the repeaters is free, but be advised that some of them may be down because of Y2K-related disruptions.

A ten-year license for amateur radio is only a few dollars. You must pass a licensing exam, but just about anyone can pass the Technician Class "no code" exam with a little study. Books published by the American Radio Relay League (ARRL) will help you pass the test. You can learn more about this organization and the license requirements at <http://www.arrl.org>.

Amateur radios vary widely in price, from less than a hundred dollars for some entry-level models to several thousand dollars for serious hobbyists. Entire books have been written on just the equipment, and "hams" generally have strong opinions about what kind of equipment you need.

If you are serious about diving into amateur radio, you should probably talk to several vendors. If you simply want to "get your feet wet," you might begin with the Alinco DJ-190-TD handheld radio. With four "AA" batteries in its dry cell battery case, output power is more than two watts FM, which under normal conditions will give you the ability to access a repeater up to fifty miles away. Through the repeater, you will have the coverage of the repeater system, which is usually located as high as possible on a mountain or on tall buildings. This gives handheld radios and mobile units the ability to communicate over distances much greater than otherwise possible. This system is much the same as that for police, fire, rescue, ambulance, and business radios. At this writing ALF Enterprises is selling this unit for $159.95. You can get more information at <http://www.alfenterprises.com/Alinco.html>.

Summary

Regardless of what system you decide to go with, you need some way to stay in touch with the world around you. Whether it's a $25 solar-powered radio or a $1,000-plus amateur radio system, you need a means of receiving information and, if possible, transmitting it. This is important not only for your personal safety, but also for your psychological well-being.

Y2K PREP TIP #3
Before You Buy a Two-way Radio...

Before you rush out and purchase a bunch of fancy communications equipment, you need to determine your communications needs and decide what you want to accomplish. To do so, follow these steps:

1. Make a list of the people you want to stay in touch with in an emergency. This will undoubtedly include family members, business associates, church friends, and neighbors.

2. Determine what it would take to stay in touch with each person. For example, to stay in touch with my parents, who live in another part of the country, will require an amateur radio. To communicate with my fellow church members, who are scattered over a wide geographic area, may require the same. But I can use either CB or FRS radio to talk to the neighbors in my subdivision.

3. Consider your resources. Make sure that you attend to first things first. As important as staying in touch may be, it's not as important as food, water, and shelter. Make sure you take care of those things first, *before* you blow a bunch of money on high-tech communication gadgets. If you have less than $100 to spend, get a simple AM/FM radio that will run on solar power or via a hand-crank mechanism. If you have a couple of hundred dollars, you can add a CB or FRS radio.

4. Get a commitment from the people you want to talk to. It won't do you any good to buy a radio if the people you want to talk to don't have one. Duh! That's why buying a radio is often a group decision. It's best if you are using similar equipment so you can help one another with problems.

5. Develop a communications plan. How often to you want to talk to the people in your network? What are your procedures and protocols? These are things you need to figure out *together*, long before you are in the middle of a crisis.

6. Run periodic test drills. Take a page from the military: practice, practice, practice. You want a system you can depend on in an emergency. The only way to do this is by getting comfortable with it before you need it.

	Y2K PREPAREDNESS CHECKLIST				
Level	Action Step	Qty	Unit Price	Total Qty	Total Price
1	Buy an AM/FM radio, preferably one with shortwave capabilities.	1	$100		
2	Consider two-way communication. Discuss options with your family, friends, and neighbors.	N/A	N/A		
2	Buy one or more two-way radios, either CB or FRS.	Varies	Varies		
3	Consider getting an amateur radio license.	1	$10		
3	Consider buying a ham radio for long-range, two-way communication.	1	Varies		

Part Two

Supplies

Chapter Four

Stockpile Food and Common Household Goods

Give us this day our daily bread.

—The Lord's Prayer

John and Sarah knew that a storm was coming, but they didn't think much of it. The newlyweds had just relocated from California to the tiny town of Goulds, Florida. Days before Hurricane Andrew was to hit, longtime residents warned the newcomers to immediately get to the hardware and grocery stores for supplies.

But John and Sarah Myers, who had never been through a hurricane warning before, believed they had plenty of time to get everything they needed. "Why not enjoy another day at the beach?" they reasoned, while everyone else is "overly concerned" about a swirl of wind and rain hundreds of miles away.

Unfortunately, by the time they decided to prepare, a human hurricane had already swept through the town's retailers, leaving empty shelves and frazzled clerks in its wake. When Sarah finally made it to the local market early on Sunday morning—about twenty-four hours before Andrew's arrival—she almost fainted when she rounded the corner into the bread aisle. Where bread and sandwich buns once filled the racks, only gaping space remained. Not even a loaf of rye or pumpernickel had survived the assault.

The same scene greeted her at nearly every turn: no water, no milk, no juice, no soft drinks, no peanut butter, no soups—nothing she had come to buy was still in stock. All she could do was go back home and join John in a closet, cowering under a mattress, as Andrew approached. It was going to be a very long night.

When the storm finally passed, Sarah and John emerged, thankful to be alive, and yet hardly comprehending the struggles that would be their daily companion for literally months to come. In the immediate aftermath of Andrew's destruction, Sarah discovered one more problem: Even the little food she had in the pantry was inaccessible because there was no power for her electric can opener. The Myers were totally dependent on the planning, and mercy, of others.

                                              ▯ ▯ ▯

Supply-chain problems almost always precede a severe storm by days. Once people are convinced that danger or weather-related interruptions are imminent they rush to the store, en masse, grabbing anything they think they might even remotely need. The same is likely to occur with the Year 2000 Computer Problem—only with much greater and broader impact.

Unlike natural disasters, Y2K will not be restricted to one location, and that means there will likely be a run on food and other common household supplies—from coast-to-coast—as we move into the second half of 1999. When it comes to you, your family, your loved ones, and your neighbors, you certainly don't want to be a day late getting to the store.

Remember as you follow the advice in this chapter that purchasing food and supplies when they are plentiful, and storing them for an emergency, is *not* hoarding (despite what some government workers and media reporters might have you believe). Gathering items during a time of plenty is *stockpiling*. Since grocery and retail stores can turn over their inventory of essential items sometimes two or three times a week, and since they can be emptied in hours during a crisis, you need to plan ahead and store now what you will need later.

The Food Chain

Many of us have absolutely no experience dealing with food shortages. Practically, that means the first thing you need to overcome is the natural paralysis that accompanies an unfamiliar task of unknown size and scope. Time is not your friend right now, so make an initial assessment of your needs based on the following information, and then take action… immediately!

If you're like most people, the first thing you'll be tempted to do is run to the local grocery store and buy up anything and everything you see. This might calm your fears for a time, until you realize that much of that food may have spoiled, or lost its nutritional value, before you really need it. Regular canned foods have a shelf life of approximately two years, but, believe it or not, they're not the least expensive way to stockpile.

Now that I've said that, let me clarify that store-bought foods *are* an important supplement for the short term. The "Grandma Strategy" of emergency preparation was to have a pantry filled with the basic necessities. We would do well to learn from what she used to do as a matter of habit. A well-stocked pantry will get you through most typical emergencies. So let's start with some simple principles about creating a home food-storage program.

James Talmage Stevens, author of *Making the Best of Basics* and *Don't Get Caught with Your Pantry Down!*, advocates the following three rules:

1. Store what you eat.
2. Eat what you store.
3. Rotate, rotate, rotate.

While these principles were developed for food storage under "normal" conditions, they also provide helpful clues for Y2K preparations.

Store what you eat. While most Americans will almost certainly have to make changes in their diet if the food chain is disrupted, it is still wise to consider whether you will eat something before you buy it. Simply put, it won't do much good to purchase three cases of asparagus on sale if no one in your house will eat it (unless you believe it will make an attractive barter item, in which case it may be a good idea after all).

Eat what you store. While you'll want to save most longer-term storable foods until after January 1, 2000 (more on these products below), you should already be eating the canned and other typical grocery store foods you store. Most regular food products have a shelf life of between six and twenty-four months, meaning that some things bought early in 1999 may already be losing their nutritional value by the time the Millennium Bug bites. Which leads to the next point:

Rotate, rotate, rotate. The best strategy with items whose nutritional life is less than two years is to stock up on several months' supply, and then continue to buy more as you use them. The newest purchases should be placed in the back of your pantry (or other storage area), and the older items rotated closer to the front for usage, based on age.

One caution here is that a canned item you buy today could actually turn out to be older than the one you bought last month. Identifying the exact age of canned and prepackaged foods takes a little bit of time on your part but is critical for the health of your food-storage effort (and, therefore, the health of your family, neighbors, and loved ones you hope to sustain with your supplies).

Product Coding

Have you ever picked up a food product in the store and tried to decipher the cryptic code stamped on the package? In many cases, this seemingly nonsensical collection of numbers and letters contains all you need to know about the freshness of the contents. Typical information contained in the code includes: the date—and sometimes even the time—that the package was filled, the specific processing line that handled the item, and the batch or supplier from which the raw product was purchased. All of this information is crucial in determining the exact age of the contents, and for those rare instances when food poisoning is linked to a product and a recall is deemed necessary.

Because some items sit in regional warehouses for a time until ordered by your local store, you'll want to investigate the particular form of coding used on the products you purchase. Most use some variation based on the Julian calendar, using a single digit for the year, and a number between 1 and 365 for the day of the year. Others merely use a month designation using 1 through 12, or even A through L (where "A" would be January, "B" equals February, etc.).

Unfortunately, there is no universal method or standard used throughout the food processing industry, so identifying the exact age of canned and prepackaged foods is up to you. While I would love to provide all the answers here, it would exceed the full length of this book to list all the food producers in the world and the distinctive coding systems they use on each individual product.

But just to give you some examples, the code number on a can of Del Monte sliced peaches may read 8243X-SRR59. Believe it or not, this tells me the peaches went into the can on August 31, 1998 ("8" = 1998 and "243" = the 243rd day of 1998, or August 31). Since canned fruits have a storage life of approximately one year, these peaches should be eaten before September 1, 1999. If the white lettering on a jar of Jif peanut butter says 9021Y206 ("9" = 1999 and "021" = 21st day of 1999, or January 21), I'm able to add the six- to nine-month storage life for unopened peanut butter and make sure it's used by October 21, 1999. A slightly different variation of Julian coding is found on Underwood canned meats. When the code reads A9Z26, the "A" = January and "9" = 1999, and since shelf life is approximately two years, this product will be usable until January 2001. Unfortunately, some systems make absolutely no sense without some clues from the manufacturer. A list of about forty examples can be found on the Internet at <http://www.waltonfeed.com/self/lid.html>.[1]

Learning the shelf life of all of your foods is a critical exercise. The only thing worse than not preparing at all is spending the time and money to prepare, only to discover that your preparations have spoiled or lost their nutritional value before you ever need to use them. Appendix E contains the shelf life of various foods along with various storage tips. You can utilize these guidelines as you put products into your storage program, marking packages or cans with a date by which they should be used.

Storing what you eat, eating what you store, and rotating new items into your pantry as you use them are three foundational elements of any food-storage program. In the event of any typical disruption, these steps will help tide you over until help arrives from outside.

Unfortunately, Y2K is not a "typical disruption." Practically speaking, this means that relying solely on canned foods from your local supermarket or warehouse club may not be sufficient to ensure your family's well-being; they simply don't last long enough. When the Millennium Bug begins gnawing away at our food chain, long-term storable foods will become an absolute necessity.

Long-term Food Storage

Long-term food storage presents you with several options: (1) bulk foods, (2) dehydrated foods, (3) canned or packaged foods, (4) freeze-dried foods, and (5) Meals Ready to Eat (MREs). Each option has its pros and cons. Pick an option—or combination of options—congruent with your resources and goals.

Bulk Foods. When I speak of "bulk foods," I am referring to bulk purchases of wheat, white, or brown rice, dried beans (especially pinto beans), lentils, corn (popcorn makes a good source of corn meal when ground), salt, sugar, honey, oil, and vitamin supplements. The chief advantages are:

- Extremely low cost per meal—about 35 cents

- Low front-end investment—you can buy a year's supply for approximately $300 per adult

- High nutritional value—so long as you stay away from white rice and white flour

- Long shelf life—twenty years or more

- Ability to purchase incrementally—you don't have to buy everything at once

- Short delivery times—if you can find it locally you can take immediate possession; if you order from a source that is not local, it generally takes a month or so before you actually receive your order

The primary disadvantages are:

- Low variety—you may find it difficult to go from your current diet to a bulk food diet

- Difficulty of preparation—you often have to grind grains or soak beans before you can cook them

You can purchase many of these items at a relatively low cost in warehouse stores, such as Sam's Club and Costco. Another source for bulk foods, particularly wheat and brown rice, is Y2K Feed & Supply. This company sells bulk foods prepacked in nitrogen and, as of this writing, offers guaranteed shipping within seventy-two hours. You can order at:

Y2K Feed & Supply
P.O. Box 284
Phippsburg, ME 04562
E-mail: <info@y2kfeedandsupply.com>
Internet: <http://www.y2kfeedsupply.com>

Unfortunately, it accepts orders only via postal mail. Please see its web page for details. You can also find bulk foods at local farm or health food cooperatives in many areas around the country. If you check around locally, you may find a very inexpensive source close to home.

It is possible to survive for a short time on these bulk foods alone, but if the crisis is prolonged, there is a danger of "food aversion." Simply put, you can't go from Twinkies and Coca-Cola to 100 percent whole wheat and water without something "giving" in the form of gastric distress. If you get an infection and need good nutrition to fight it off, this diet may leave you not wanting to eat when you need nutrition to survive. Your ability to overcome food aversion could mean the difference between a winter cold and life-threatening pneumonia. That's why it is best to supplement these kinds of foods with some of the others listed below.

If you have minimal resources, bulk foods are the way to go. You can also supplement with a vegetable garden, which will add to your variety. Regardless, I suggest that everyone store some bulk foods. Even if you opt for dehydrated or freeze-dried food as your "core" package, bulk foods make excellent staples and should be included as part of your overall diet.

Dehydrated Foods. This kind of food storage is far and away the most popular form of long-term food. There are several important advantages:

- Low cost per meal—at 75 cents per meal, this is the second least expensive form of food storage

- Good nutritional value—among the highest of the long-term options

- Moderately long shelf-life—ten years or more, depending on how and where you store it

- Good variety—numerous foods lend themselves to dehydration

- Low storage space requirements—a one-year, four-person supply takes up about the same amount of space as a typical refrigerator

Yet there are some drawbacks:

- Moderately high front-end investment—these usually come in one-year packages that must be purchased all at one time

- Difficulty of preparation—you must make sure you have extra water on hand in order to rehydrate the food, and you must cook dehydrated foods before eating

- Long delivery times—because of Y2K, demands for dehydrated foods have increased significantly

Although there are other good reasons, I recommend the dehydrated food program because of the cost factor alone. Y2K Prep has put together two excellent programs that, as of this writing, provide a year's supply for one for $850, plus shipping, and a year's supply for a family of four at $3,350, plus shipping.* (The contents of these packages are listed on the company's website.) Depending on your needs, I believe you'll find both of these to be excellent choices.[2] You can contact the company at:

Y2K Prep
251 Second Avenue South
Franklin, TN 37064
Toll-free: (888) 925-2844
Fax: (615) 794-8860
Internet: <http://www.y2kprep.com/food.htm>

If you can't afford a prepackaged, long-term food-storage program, you might consider learning how to dehydrate or can your own foods. This information is beyond

---

*You should know that I have a financial interest in this company. The reason I got involved was because I became convinced, as a result of my research, that it had the best value at the best price. It also has one of the shortest delivery times available.

the scope of this book, but many county extension offices provide free instruction on canning, dehydrating, and even "root cellaring." And they often offer free or very-low-cost classes on developing these skills.

If you can afford the front-end investment, dehydrated foods offer the best option at the lowest price for the "core" of your long-term food-storage program. This is the foundation of my family's personal program.

Canned and Packaged Foods. Of all your food options, canned and packaged foods are the ones most familiar to us. You probably use them already, and they are readily available at any supermarket. The primary advantages are:

- Low front-end investment—you can buy them incrementally, purchasing a little bit each week

- High variety—there are a huge number of options available

- Ease of preparation—generally these foods require simple warming; they are already pre-cooked

- Quick delivery times—these foods are readily available at numerous local sources

The disadvantages include:

- Cost per meal—over the long haul, this option is about *twice as expensive* as dehydrated food

- Short shelf life—two years or so is the average, but compared to other options, it is relatively short

- Low nutritional value—this is a generalization, and there are certainly some exceptions, but canned and packaged foods are usually not as healthy as the other options

- Sizable storage requirements—about four times as much space will be required as for the equivalent amount of dehydrated food

Freeze-dried Foods. These products are the "Cadillac" of the long-term, storable food market. If your financial resources are plentiful, and your taste buds very discriminating, freeze-dried foods are an outstanding choice. Benefits of freeze-dried foods include:

- Ease of preparation—food is "ready-to-eat," including seasonings, and the rehydration time is shorter than regular dehydrated foods

- Contain real meat products—you can compare and contrast this with the "textured vegetable protein" (TVP) included in most dehydrated food packages[3]

- Moderately long shelf-life—ten years or more, depending on how and where you store it

- Good variety—there are numerous foods that lend themselves to being freeze-dried

- Low storage space requirements—about the same as dehydrated food

Of course, there are a couple of drawbacks, including:

- Much higher cost-per-meal than dehydrated food—about $2.50 per meal

- Moderately high front-end investment—these also usually come in one-year packages that must be purchased all at one time

There are numerous suppliers for freeze-dried foods; I cannot recommend any one in particular. The important thing to decide is whether you want to go with dehydrated food or freeze-dried. You probably don't need both. If there are some items you want to have that come only in freeze-dried form, I recommend that you buy a dehydrated package as your "core" unit and supplement with specific freeze-dried items. It will be less expensive in the long run.

Meals Ready to Eat (MREs). These self-contained meals were originally designed by the U.S. government for the military. They have several advantages:

- Moderately long shelf life—the taste actually deteriorates before the nutritional value does

- Ease of preparation—this is the best feature; they are ready to eat without any cooking, though you may want to warm them

- Method of purchase—you can purchase them a case or two at a time rather than having to buy a full year's supply

There is one major drawback:

- Cost per meal—at about $4 per meal, this is roughly equivalent to going out to eat at a fast food restaurant

MREs are generally packaged in triple-layer plastic or aluminum–plastic pouches that have better storage qualities than heavy cans, with no need for a can opener. The food in these pouches is precooked and sealed at a high temperature so that bacteria is neutralized. They do not require refrigeration and can be stored at room temperature. Emergency Essentials offers MREs at competitive prices:

Emergency Essentials
165 South Mountain Way Drive
Orem, UT 84058
Toll-free: (800) 999-1863
Internet:<http://www.beprepared.com/Product/mreprod.html>

In my opinion, MREs are best used in the early days of the crisis, when you may not have the time or energy for elaborate food preparation. I have purchased some for just this purpose.

Table 4.1 contains a comparison of each of your options. Remember: The information is approximate.

In addition to the above foods, you will also want to store plenty of spices, including salt and pepper. You will probably also want to store other condiments, such as ketchup, mustard, salsa, honey, baking soda, cooking oil, sugar, yeast, and so forth.

Finally, remember when ordering that you'll want to get more than just what your family alone will need. If you can get almost four times as much food for the same money by purchasing dehydrated foods instead of freeze-dried, why wouldn't you? Sure, there's a convenience factor with the more costly products, but there may very well be a lot of hungry people living around you in 2000 and beyond. How long do you think it will take your neighbors to learn that you're eating "gourmet food" while they're starving? Think about it. Better to eat beans and rice with many friends than filet mignon amidst an angry, starving crowd.

Now that you've determined what kinds of food you'll store, there are a few more issues you need to resolve before turning your attention to other household needs. Even the best long-term food can be severely harmed if you don't have proper storage containers and a location that controls the five greatest enemies of stored food: heat, sunlight, humidity, vermin, and oxidization.

Table 4.1:
Comparison of Food Storage Options

Criteria	Bulk Foods	Dehydrated Food Packages	Canned and Packaged Foods	Freeze-dried Food Packages	Meals Ready to Eat (MREs)
Cost per meal	35¢	75¢	$1.25	$2.50	$4.00
Front-end investment	Low	Moderate	Low	High	Moderate
Shelf life (stored at 70° F)	20+ years	10+ years	2 years	10+ years	8 years
Variety	Low	Medium	High	Medium	Medium
Storage space requirements	Medium	Low	High	Low	Medium
Ease of preparation	Difficult	Moderate	Easy	Moderate	Easy
Nutritional value	High	Moderate	Low	Moderate	Moderate
Method of purchase	Incremental	All at once	Incremental	All at once	Incremental
Delivery times	Immediate to 1 month	8–10 weeks	Immediate	8–10 weeks	Varies
Its place in your total food strategy	Long-term or staples	Long-term	Short-term or supplement	Long-term	Beginning of crisis

Storing What You Stockpile

Imagine that it's March of 2000 and you're extremely thankful for the preparations you've made. Stored food has kept your loved ones and a few of your neighbors alive, but today when you open a new container you're greeted by a collection of creepy, crawly critters who are also giving thanks for your stored rations. If you think that's a depressing picture now, consider how you'll feel when you really need that food to survive. And bugs are just one of five major threats to your supplies.

Help your foods keep their cool. Ideally you should keep your foods in a cool, dry place. A U.S. Department of Agriculture study suggests that foods stored at 70 degrees Fahrenheit will last approximately ten years, whereas those stored at 80 degrees will last half that long. Drop the average temperature to 60 degrees and your shelf life doubles again to around twenty years. Find a cool, dark place—like a basement—and your long-term foods can be with you for a long, long time.

Never let them see the light of day. Ultraviolet light (UV) is another foe you want to avoid. Most food grade buckets are largely opaque, but it's still a good idea to keep them out of the light. A little UV over a long period of time can zap the nutritional value of your foods.

And speaking of buckets, we came across an excellent supplier, Nutraceuticals 2000, based in Newberg, Oregon. It has "Super Seal Buckets" made of food-grade plastic, with a patented lid called the "Life Latch." The top rotates on and off like a Mason jar, and seals with a special O-ring that is recessed into the lid. This design allows for an airtight seal each time it's opened and closed, and enables it to maintain a vacuum. We have seen standard buckets selling for $7.95 or more, but through Nutraceuticals 2000 you can get a five-gallon "Super Seal" for only $5.95 ($5.49 when you order twelve or more). The buckets also come in a 3.5-gallon size for $5.70 each for up to fifteen buckets ($5.25 for sixteen or more), and a 6.5-gallon size for $6.85 ($6.25 for eight or more). You can get more information from its website at <http://www.nutraceuticals2000.com> or by writing:

Nutraceuticals 2000
1102 N. Springbrook Road, Suite 284
Newberg, OR 97132
Toll-free: (800) 929-9972
E-mail inquiries: <nutra2000@geocities.com>

If you're working on a very tight budget, you could buy Nutraceuticals's standard five-gallon buckets at $4.99 each, and use "Super Seals" for each product that is currently in use. In other words, begin by storing all of your foods in the standard buckets, then as you open one, transfer the contents to a "Super Seal Bucket" that will seal and reseal effectively. This allows you to leave the original seal on the standard buckets intact until you really need the product.

Don't let mold bend you out of shape. Preventing your self-stored foods from growing moldy requires that the contents be properly dried before sealing the bucket. Desiccants (moisture absorbers) can be added to the bucket just before sealing and should effectively absorb any residual moisture. For about 25 cents per bucket, you can have extra peace of mind knowing that you've thwarted another of your food's greatest enemies.

Desiccare, Inc., provides high-quality desiccants at an affordable price. The "One Unit Clay, Unit Pak" is just the right size for a six-gallon or less food-storage bucket. Desiccare offers consumers a forty Unit Pak box for just $9.95. Since Desiccare also provides the oxygen absorbers discussed in the next section, I will include its contact information following our look at a pair of final threats.

The air we breathe, and bugs that breed. As we all know, it's an unfortunate fact of life that bugs enjoy our food almost as much as we do. What you may not know is that the air you breathe is also harmful to your food's long-term health. Air oxidizes many of the nutritional compounds in food, drastically reducing its shelf life. Thankfully, bugs and oxidation can be overcome with the same solution: oxygen absorption.

Taking the air out of a bucket is not as difficult as it may sound. Desiccare provides oxygen absorbers in a variety of sizes to fit almost any food-storage application. When sealing five- to six-gallon buckets, the FT-200 is the absorber of choice. You will need four per bucket. The FT-200 comes in bags of seventy-five absorbers for $21.95; that's just under 30 cents each. A product listing is available online at <http://www.desiccare.com/homeprod.htm>. You can also contact the company at:

> Desiccare, Inc.
> 10600 Shoemaker Avenue, Building 'C'
> Santa Fe Springs, CA 90670
> Toll-free: (800) 446-6650

If you've never used oxygen absorbers before, there are a few things you should know before proceeding. First, you will want to keep the absorber in its packaging until you're just about ready to place it in your bucket and seal. As soon as you open the bag, it will begin absorbing oxygen, whether that oxygen is in the bucket with your grain or simply in the room where you're working.

Second, realize that your container will have to withstand some level of vacuum. If oxygen is slowly drawn into a leaky bucket to replace what has been absorbed, the absorber will keep on working until it is full, and finally won't be able to assimilate what's in the bucket.

Another option for dealing with bugs is *diatomaceous earth*, also known as "fossil shell powder." Diatomaceous earth is composed of microscopic fossils of diatoms, a type of green algae, or phytoplankton, that produces a shell made of amorphous silica. When the diatoms die, they fall to the bottom of a freshwater or saltwater lagoon, building up layers of microscopic shells. These shells are razor-sharp at the microscopic level and are lethal to insects. They work by cutting through the insect's waxy outer cuticle and absorb body fluids until the insect dies of dehydration. Thus, the process is physical, not chemical. It is effective against rice weevils, lesser grain borers, flat grain beetles, merchant grain beetles, saw-toothed grain beetles, red flour beetles, confused flour beetles, granary weevils, and the larvae of the Indian meal moth. Best of all, it is completely harmless to humans and pets.

You use diatomaceous earth by simply mixing it with your stored grains, beans, rice, and seeds. Every kernel should have a light coating. As a general rule of thumb, you should use about one ounce of diatomaceous earth for every eighteen pounds of grain. You can order diatomaceous earth from a number of sources. The best source I have found is Perma-Guard:

Perma-Guard, Inc.
115 Rio Bravo, S.E.
Albuquerque, NM 87105
Voice: (505) 873-3061
Internet: <http://www.permaguard.com/Pages/index.html>

At this writing, a fifty-pound bag of diatomaceous earth sells for $24.95 plus shipping.

One final threat to your food, even in many plastic buckets, is larger vermin such as rats. One of my friends who had stored years worth of food in plastic buckets suddenly noticed that his local rat population needed to go on a diet: they had gnawed through his "super pails" (five-gallon plastic buckets lined with Mylar and filled with nitrogen to remove the air and keep it out).

An airtight seal should stop this problem in most cases, but not all. In rural areas, a well-sealed tin storage building with suitable traps may be required. Poison can be distributed strategically but should not be placed where children or pets can get to it. Nor should it be in the food handling area, where it could contaminate the food.

This is one more good reason to consider dehydrated foods; they come in #10, nitrogen-packed, metal cans that completely lock in the aroma that attracts critters.

Seeds of Destruction, Seeds of Life

Modern farming is typically conducted using hybrid seeds. While hybrids are supposedly designed to produce a more robust grain or vegetable, one negative by-product is that the seeds cannot be harvested for a second-generation crop. South America is ranked among the worst regions for Y2K preparation, and that is where many of our hybrid seeds are produced. What this means is that even a small disruption could lead to massive food shortages.

Growing your own vegetables and grains with nonhybrid seeds—also called open-pollinated or heirloom seeds—can provide an excellent, fresh supplement to your stored foods. The Ark Institute is perhaps the best, most knowledgeable source for nonhybrid seeds. Its "Survival Seed Package" was designed to feed a family of four both fresh and preserved vegetables for a year, and contains fifty varieties of garden vegetables, fruits, grains, and herbs. Cost for the package is $159 (shipping included), and includes a free copy of Ark founder Geri Guidetti's book, *Build Your Own Ark! How to Prepare for Self-Reliance in Uncertain Times*. You can visit the institute's website at <http://www.arkinstitute.com> or by writing:

The Ark Institute
P.O. Box 142
Oxford, OH 45056
Toll-free: (800) 255-1912

In case of seed shortages, another good source is a group called Back to Eden. Its seed kits are specially designed for various regions in the United States and can normally be purchased for $129 (though it is also known to run periodic specials for as little as $97). You can see its packages on the web at: <http://www.tlchub.com/seeds/thekits. shtml>. There is a link on this page to a United States Department of Agriculture map so you can determine your growing zone, enabling you to select the correct package. If you have a group, you can order four packages and get a fifth free.

Back to Eden
c/o TLC Greenhouse, Inc.
3976 M-50 Lane
Paonia, CO 81428
Voice: (970) 527-3375
Fax: (970) 527-6221
E-mail: <seeds@tlchub.com>

If you plan to garden, I encourage you to begin this year. You need to practice now, when it's not essential. Like most things, the more you do it, the better you get.

Ideas for Families with Small Children

Before we leave the subject of food, I should add a few words for those who have small children. In many cases the Year 2000 Computer Problem will be toughest on those who can't understand why Mommy and Daddy no longer take them to McDonald's once a week.

For the sake of your children, try to stock up on long shelf-life foods that they especially enjoy. This would include spaghetti, macaroni and cheese, and other pasta products. Stockpiling some favorites will allow you to sprinkle in familiar foods here and there as you explore the new culinary realm of dehydrated foods.

Also, be careful with ground wheat. The digestive systems of small children are often very sensitive to a change from fine flour to flour that is more coarse. Grind as finely as you can.

In addition, don't forget that if you have, or are expecting, an infant during these times, he will have special needs that cannot be met through stored-food programs. You may also want to consider breast-feeding a little longer than you ordinarily would.

Pets

In your food preparations, don't forget your pets. You can stockpile for them, just as you do your family members. The good news is that most of the food is already dehydrated or canned. Simply determine how much food your pet consumes per day and then multiply by the number of days you are trying to prepare for. If stockpiling is not possible, dogs can live off table scraps, as they did before the days of prepackaged pet food. Obviously, providing for pets is not the same priority as for family members, but for many people it is a close second!

Concluding Thoughts on Food

I hope you've decided, no matter what level of problems Y2K brings, that you're not going to be dependent on your neighbors—or the government—to provide your daily bread. If you truly believe there's any significant probability of disruptions to the food chain, it is, in fact, selfish *not* to prepare.

There is certainly no time to waste in taking action. While it is impossible to forecast exactly when food shortages will become apparent to the general population (though I saw early food industry reports about minor shortages in retail channels as early as December 1998), I am sadly confident that the day will come. You don't want to be standing in a line at that time, hoping there will be something left by the time you get to the counter. You also don't want to be dependent on some government-ordered rationing program that may limit the amount of food you're able to get, regardless of the size of your family.

No matter what you've done to this point—and no matter where we are in the progression toward shortages—if you begin doing something today you'll be much better prepared than many others. You'll be in a position to be at least a small part of the solution, instead of part of the problem.

Household Supplies

In good times we take innumerable items for granted, but in an emergency they become conspicuous by their absence. When Y2K hits the supply-chain, many basic items may not be available. Others that are unneeded when power is plentiful, cheap, and reliable may become popular once again. In this section we will list a large number of items you should begin to gather now, in preparation for the year 2000. Consider which ones you will need to acquire for yourself, and those you can afford to get as barter items. While many commentators have decried those who are preparing, the reality is that as we buy these materials, the supply chain will actually increase production to meet the demand. This will mean more of these items for everyone, something that would not happen if everyone were to wait until the last few months of 1999.

In many cases there is no special supplier for these items. You will find them at a typical retail or discount store in your area. In instances in which a particular provider is necessary I will list it for you. Again, the most important thing is to begin getting the items you need immediately.

More Power to You

Although knives, forks, and spoons will perform admirably whether the electricity works or not, you'll want to have a little insurance for everything that requires power. Table 4.2 lists a few of the things you'll need to replace in your food preparation and clean-up arsenal, with a suggested back-up or two.

Table 4.2:
Alternative Kitchen Appliances

Microwave, electric, or gas oven	Solar oven, camp stove, cast iron Dutch gas oven, etc.
Electric can opener	Manual can opener
Blender	Jars with lids
Dishwasher	Liquid dish soap and plenty of cloth towels
Electric skillet	Cast iron skillet
Electric or gas stove	Wood stove
Refrigerator	Food that doesn't require refrigeration
Mixer	Nonelectric hand-mixer
Garbage disposal	Various composting options
Toaster or toaster oven	Cast iron skillet
Electric food processor	Knives
Coffee or espresso maker	Stove-top coffee pot

Some of these alternatives (like the espresso maker and trash compactor) are easier to do without than others (such as the microwave and refrigerator), but you need to think through how you'll live if all of them are out of commission due to lack of a dependable supply of electricity. True, almost all appliances *can* be powered using alternate energy, but in many cases that would be prohibitively expensive (more on that subject in Chapter 9).

It's also possible that your equipment choice in one area will force other changes. For example, you may need to switch your cookware if your alternative for baking and cooking is a wood stove (due to the more extreme heat produced by many wood-burning stoves).

Cookware for the New Millennium

Although I will deal with heat sources for cooking in Chapter 8, I want to mention cookware here. Cast iron cookware is ideal for use with wood-burning stoves.[4] It provides durability, even heat distribution during cooking, and heat retention from stove to table. Some medical authorities even say there are health benefits from the extra iron that finds its way into the food. A simple and functional collection of cast iron cookware would include a skillet or two, a Dutch oven, perhaps a casserole dish, and a pair of bread pans. The sizes needed will depend on how many people you expect to be cooking for—and remember to expect more than just your family.

Though cast iron has been used for cooking since the Middle Ages, finding manufacturers today is not easy. Lodge Manufacturing, operating in South Pittsburg, Tennessee, since 1896, provides a wide variety of products, at very reasonable prices.

> Lodge Manufacturing Company
> 6th Street at Railroad
> P.O. Box 380
> South Pittsburg, TN 37380
> Voice: (423) 837-7181
> Fax: (423) 837-8198
> Internet: <http://www.lodgemfg.com>

You can browse and order on the Internet, or call for its catalog. Even better, if you are planning to travel between Chattanooga and Nashville on Interstate 24, stop by and take advantage of its "Factory 2nds." These pieces with minor cosmetic blemishes can be purchased for 50 percent off regular prices. Unfortunately, they are available only to those who stop by the outlet store in South Pittsburg, right in front of the foundry. Another option is to shop for cast iron cookware at flea markets, garage sales, and Army and Navy surplus stores. One of the things you will see immediately is a wide range of prices.

Grinding Your Daily Bread

If you're going to store and use wheat and other whole grains, one essential item you'll need is a hand-powered grain mill. A mill is among the first things you'll want to order, because this is a niche-market item whose supply is severely limited. I recommend a couple of different mills based on your resources and product availability.

My first choice is the Country Living Grain Mill. Not only is this mill among the fastest and most durable on the market, it comes with a built-in, "V-grooved" flywheel. This allows you to hook it up to a bicycle, using a belt, and do some exercise as you grind (not that you'll necessarily need the exercise if everything else has broken down, but it's a lot easier than doing it all by hand!). One accessory you'll definitely want to get is the "Power Bar," which increases the twelve-inch flywheel to nineteen inches, making grinding even easier (a huge consideration if you're grinding several times per week).

The biggest problem as of this writing is that delivery time on the Country Living Mill is three-and-a-half to four months. This timeframe may improve as production increases, but you'll want to measure carefully how long you're willing to wait for such an important item.

A friend of mine placed his order through Homestead Products and was pleased with the service of Dan Youngquist and his team. If the Country Living Mill is back-ordered beyond your comfort level, Homestead also carries the Family Grain Mill featuring both electric and hand-powered operation. Whereas the Country Living Mill with the "Power Bar" weighs in at $343, the Family Grain Mill with electric and hand base is $295 (the many attachments you can add to this configuration raise the price).

> Homestead Products
> 3925 N. Clarey Street
> Eugene, OR 97402–9708
> Voice: (541) 688-9263
> Fax: (541) 688-9775
> E-mail: dany@teleport.com

My friend actually ordered both of these mills and, during testing with families that have been grinding their own wheat for years, found that the Country Living Grain Mill produced a finer flour and thus was the preferred model. You can see the two mills and read more about the products on Homestead's website at <http://www.teleport.com/~dany/mill/index.htm>.

Let's Get Personal

Some of the most important items you need to stockpile are toiletries. Contrary to many of the things we've discussed to this point, these are resources you're familiar with—very familiar. No special suppliers are needed, but that doesn't make these items any less important. In fact, forgetting to take care of these items could lead to some of the greatest discomforts the Millennium Bug can bring.

There is not space for me to discuss every little personal item you will need. Suffice it to say you would find yourself severely inconvenienced without your daily dose of deodorant, a good supply of lotions and creams, and, for women, feminine hygiene needs. One innovative option for the latter is a product called "The Keeper," an internally worn, soft rubber, reusable menstrual cup. I know many women who swear by it. You can order it from:

> Internet Store Keeper
> 3332 Harwood Blvd., Suite 102
> Bedford, TX 76021
> Toll-free: (888) 882-1818
> Internet: <http://www.thekeeperstore.com>

For other Y2K needs unique to women, you will want to visit Karen Anderson's popular Internet site at <http://www.y2kwomen.com>.

Another item that you don't usually think about it—until you're out—is toilet paper. My children can't imagine life without toilet paper, and, quite frankly, neither can I. I know that human beings got along without it for millennia, but this is one aspect of the "good ol' days" that I can live without. Try to buy an extra package of toilet paper every time you go to the store. At Sam's and other discount clubs, you can often buy it by the box. The great thing about toilet paper is that it will undoubtedly make a great barter item, if things should disintegrate that far, and will be useful whether or not there is a crisis related to Y2K.

Use the Y2K Prep Tip and Preparedness List at the end of this chapter to help you think through basic household necessities. A little thought and preparation today can make you more thankful for what you have now, and more prepared for what you may not have access to later.

⌨ ⌨ ⌨

1992's Hurricane Andrew proved to be the most expensive natural disaster in human history. Seven years later, John and Sarah Myers still recall the feelings of helplessness they experienced in the days and weeks after the storm passed. They remember their dependence on others for the most basic necessities, and are doing everything in their control to ensure they'll never be in that position again.

Before Hurricane Andrew, they believed nothing "that bad" could ever disrupt their lives. They assumed the best, and ended up wishing they could turn back the clock on those last few days before the storm. Older, and a bit wiser, they now realize there is no substitute for thoughtful preparation. The time to get ready for a storm is on the first warning, before the leading winds arrive and the rains begin to fall.

Y2K PREP TIP #4
Make Use of Little-known Storage Spaces

As you begin stockpiling items in preparation for Y2K, one of the first questions you must answer is, "Where do I put all of this stuff?" This is particularly so when it comes to bulky items like food and water.

Let's assume that you have already "dejunked," reclaiming usable space in closets and cupboards. However, sooner or later, these spaces are going to be full. Now what? Let me suggest seven storage spaces that you may not have thought of:

1. Under the bed. If your house is anything like mine, these spaces are already taken. A quick inventory revealed Christmas wrapping paper, missing books, toys, and the usual junk that, for whatever reason, got shoved into these spaces when the kids were "cleaning." Okay, clean 'em out and turn them into extra Y2K storage spaces. These are particularly good for canned goods, dried pasta, etc. If you want to get fancy, you can buy some rectangular plastic containers, fill them up, and slide them under the bed.

2. Under furniture. This doesn't offer a lot of space, but it's something. You can fit smaller, soup-sized cans under a sofa. If there's not enough room to stand them upright, you can lay them on their side. End tables often have a large space under them where you can stack various items, too.

3. On top of shelves. I'm not talking about the shelves themselves—if yours are like mine, they are already full. But often on the top of bookcases or even kitchen cabinets there is a flat surface that provides a good deal of storage space. Even a refrigerator top can be used; however, you have to be careful about the heat generated by the refrigerator. This doesn't have to look tacky. In fact, many restaurants store items on these kinds of spaces as part of the decor. One caution: If you live in an earthquake area, this may not be safe.

4. Crawl spaces and "cubby holes." If you don't have a basement, you may still have several spaces that often go unused. In our home, we don't have a basement, but we do have a crawl space under the house. It's about three feet high and difficult to get to, but it's a good source of extra space. (It's also cool and dark, both of which are helpful when you are storing food or water.) In our upstairs recreation room, we have three large "cubby holes" that are simply the dead space between the exterior and interior walls. These are excellent storage spaces but are also subject to temperature extremes, so be careful what you store there.

5. Return air vents. This may not be a usable space, but it's worth checking into. Obviously, you don't want to block the flow of air. But for small items—especially valuables—this can be a good choice. It's usually one of the last places thieves will look. Studies show that they will check your dresser drawers, deep freeze, and even closets. But they want to be in and out in ten minutes. As a result, they will not take time to check things like air vents.

6. Partition off part of a room. You can buy a folding screen and create a partition in the corner of a room. These are generally inexpensive and will allow you to store a number of items in an organized way that is out of view.

7. Use a bathtub or shower. Okay, I admit this is a bit radical. However, if you have more than one bathroom and are desperate for storage space, you can convert a bathtub or shower to dry storage. It has the advantage of being out of the way and hidden from view. (If you use a bathtub, you can pull a shower curtain closed.) This will likely create an inconvenience, but it's better than nothing.

This list should get you started. With a little ingenuity, you can imagine other spaces as well.

	Y2K PREPAREDNESS CHECKLIST				
Level	Action Step	Qty	Unit Price	Total Qty	Total Price
1	Purchase canned foods.	Varies	Varies		
1	Purchase Styrofoam cups.	Varies	Varies		
1	Purchase paper plates and plastic utensils.	Varies	Varies		
1	Purchase napkins and paper towels.	Varies	Varies		
1	Purchase baby foods (if necessary).	Varies	Varies		
1	Purchase matches (for candles, cooking, etc.).	Varies	Varies		
1	Purchase cooking timer (wind-up).	1 per family	Varies		
1	Purchase crayons, pencils, erasers, pens, paper.	Varies	Varies		
1	Purchase needles, thread, safety pins.	Varies	Varies		
1	Purchase work gloves.	2 pairs/ person	Varies		
2	Purchase dried foods (pasta, macaroni, beans, etc.).	Varies	Varies		
2	Purchase salt, sugar, honey, cooking oil, spices.	Varies	Varies		
2	Purchase thermometers.	2 per family	Varies		

Y2K PREPAREDNESS CHECKLIST *(Continued)*					
Level	*Action Step*	*Qty*	*Unit Price*	*Total Qty*	*Total Price*
2	Purchase special treats (candies, puddings, cookie mix).	Varies	Varies		
2	Purchase dishwashing liquid.	Varies	Varies		
2	Purchase can opener (heavy-duty, hand operated).	2 per family	Varies		
2	Purchase manual kitchen utensils.	Varies	Varies		
2	Purchase aluminum foil, plastic wrap.	Varies	Varies		
2	Purchase knife and utensil sharpeners.	Varies	Varies		
2	Purchase board games and cards.	Varies	Varies		
2	Purchase rubber gloves.	4 pairs	Varies		
2	Purchase clothesline and clothes pins.	Varies	Varies		
2	Purchase laundry detergent.	Varies	Varies		
3	Purchase long-term food-storage program (per person price) or...	1 year	$850		
3	Purchase long-term food-storage program (per four-person price).	1 year	$3,350		
3	Purchase food-grade storage buckets (amount assumes no packaged long-term foods).	12/year	$6		

(Continued)

	Y2K PREPAREDNESS CHECKLIST *(Continued)*				
Level	*Action Step*	*Qty*	*Unit Price*	*Total Qty*	*Total Price*
3	Purchase desiccants—One Unit Clay, Unit Pak.	1	$10		
3	Purchase oxygen absorbers— FT-750.	1	$5		
3	Purchase cast iron skillets.	2 per family	Varies		
3	Purchase cast iron Dutch oven.	1 per family	Varies		
3	Purchase colander.	1 per family	Varies		
3	Purchase food scale.	1 per family	Varies		
3	Purchase shoelaces.	Varies	Varies		
4	Purchase basic grains, beans, corn (popcorn), rice, etc. (amount assumes no long-term foods).	40 lbs per month	Varies		
4	Purchase a grain mill (Whisper Mill, Family Mill, or Country Living Mill).	1	$229 to $366		
5	Purchase nonhybrid seeds.	1 pkg/ family	$129 to $159		

Chapter Five

Develop an Alternative Source of Water

Water, water, everywhere,
Nor any drop to drink.

—Samuel Taylor Coleridge,
"The Rime of the Ancient Mariner"

Years ago I went salt-water fishing with a good friend off the coast of New England. We brought along sandwiches, sun screen, Dramamine, and a one-gallon container of fresh water. After catching a few bluefish (you should've seen the one that got away!) we took a break to have lunch. As I reached to pass the water jug to my friend, it slipped from my hand and fell right into the cooler containing the fish we had caught. Half of the water poured out before I could grab the jug. The half remaining in the container was now mixed with fish slime and scales.

At first we thought, *Oh well, no big deal.* But within minutes our throats became parched, the sun felt much hotter, and we quickly decided to cut our fishing trip short and head back to shore. The thirty-minute boat ride back to the marina seemed like an eternity. Coleridge's words were appropriate. We were surrounded by water, and yet there was not a drop to drink.

If there is one thing that we cannot live without, it's water. The average person can survive for three weeks without food, but only three days without water. And if there is one thing we take for granted in our civilized society, it is clean water. For most people, it's as close as the nearest faucet. Perhaps the only time people consider the importance of clean water is when they venture away from our modern society—camping, hiking, or fishing—or completely out of the country. Those who have had the misfortune of drinking contaminated water know firsthand how incredibly debilitating the experience can be. Few things can incapacitate a person faster than ingesting bad water.

The Millennium Bug threatens the supply and distribution systems that bring most people clean water. Water companies and municipal water utilities have many embedded microdevices and software monitoring systems throughout their operations. Y2K glitches could stop the flow of water—or even worse, send contaminated water into people's homes. These firms are also dependent on reliable electrical service, phone networks, and other third-party vendors.

For people who get their clean water from a well rather than a water utility, electricity is, in most cases, required to run the pumps. There is no doubt that our supply of clean water is at risk because of the Year 2000 Computer Problem.

Our Daily Needs

We use a lot more water than you think. In fact, the average person uses fifty-four gallons every day! The following chart shows the breakdown:[1]

Table 5.1:
Typical Water Use Per Person Per Day

Shower	25 Gallons
Toilet Flush (Four flushes @ 5 gallons each)	20 Gallons
Hand washing (Twice @ 2 gallons each time)	4 Gallons
Brushing Teeth (Twice @ 2 gallons each time)	4 Gallons
Drinking and Cooking	1 Gallon
Total	54 Gallons

In an emergency situation, however, you need to plan on only one gallon per person per day. This is the bare minimum to cover cooking and drinking needs. Even though this amount is a fraction of normal usage, it still adds up quickly if the crisis situation drags on for weeks or months.

The first thing to do is calculate how much clean water your family requires, depending on which of the five levels you are preparing for: seventy-two hours, one week, thirty days, three months, or one year or more. Multiply the number of family members by the number of days to determine the minimum amount of water you will need to survive. (If you want to be able to do a bit of washing and cleaning, figure *two* gallons per person per day.) As you can see, the amount of water required—even for basic survival—is immense.

Storing Clean Water

Water is very heavy—almost eight pounds per gallon—and it takes up a lot of space. Fortunately, water is inexpensive, and if stored properly it will keep for many years. Of course, it is inexpensive *before* a crisis hits; afterward, it will be worth its weight in gold. This is why my advice, regardless of how long you think Y2K disruptions might last, is to *store as much clean water as you possibly can.*

Bottles

Water can be stored effectively in plastic soft-drink or juice bottles. I do not recommend using glass containers, which are heavier and can break. The thin plastic jugs used for milk are usually biodegradable and will disintegrate over time. Do not use these either.

I also do not recommend buying off-the-shelf bottled water. There are several reasons for this. First of all, at approximately $1 per gallon, it is far more expensive than other methods. Second, water quality varies widely. Some is advertised as "spring water" but is nothing more than tap water. Other water is distilled or produced by reverse osmosis. None of these methods will prevent the growth of bacteria over time; therefore, you still need to treat it with chlorine or by some other means if you are going to store it for the long haul.

I prefer the two-liter soft-drink bottles. They are a manageable size, even for young family members; they have screw-on caps that can be secured tightly; and most of all, they are plentiful. Clean them out thoroughly and follow the purification steps listed below before filling with water. Even if your Y2K water plans include large storage containers or a self-sufficient source (wells, springs, etc.), it is wise to store water in these smaller bottles, too. They are convenient to use and can be stored in various places around your home—preferably places that are dark and not subject to extreme temperatures.

Food-grade Drums

One of the best methods for storing a lot of water is to use fifty-five–gallon, food-grade, plastic drums with tight-seal lids. Most suppliers I surveyed on the Internet sell them for $65 or more. The cheapest price I have found is offered by Bay Tech Containers. Its website is located at <http://www.ghg.net/jlfulcher/ index.htm>. Model number 104-RS55-TBL sells for about $25, and the shipping and handling charge is $17.75 per barrel.

I was recently able to get similar drums from a local soft-drink distributor for only $6 each! They originally contained soft-drink syrup and had to be cleaned out first, but it was well worth the elbow grease. Like everything else, it pays to shop around. Just remember, the longer you wait between now and January 1 to obtain these supplies, the more likely prices will be way up, or the items will not be available at all.

If you plan to store water in fifty-five–gallon drums, think about the best location for the drums in advance. Trust me: Once filled, that drum is not going anywhere (440 pounds of water).

Cisterns

A cistern is simply a receptacle for holding water, especially any tank that catches and holds rainwater. Cisterns are widely used in the Middle East, where rainfall is scarce. Even in the United States, old cisterns dot the property of abandoned farmsteads throughout the midwestern states. Deep well-drilling techniques were not common until the mid-twentieth century, so until that time the only way to save water was in a cistern.

Cisterns are often built right into the ground. This way they can be filled easier and the water remains cool, which inhibits bacterial growth. In the old days cisterns were generally eight to ten feet deep and about three feet across. They were dug by hand, and the interior walls were made of brick and mortar.

Other, simpler designs can also make effective cisterns. Plastic drums or barrels, stainless steel milk tanks, swimming pools, and even a pit lined with a plastic tarp can hold a supply of valuable water. A swimming pool in particular can be a great way to store enormous amounts of water. However, make sure that you treat the water as if it were water from any other outdoor source: filter it and/or chlorinate it. Even if you use chlorine in the water, it's a good idea to rechlorinate it before using it for drinking water since the chlorine you probably put in the pool originally evaporates and breaks down over time.

The roof of an average house (24 feet × 36 feet) has almost 900 square feet of surface area exposed to rain. During a 1-inch rainfall, more than 540 gallons of clean water falls onto this roof (75 cubic feet). Most homes already have a system of gutters and downspouts. The key is to channel the water—using hoses, tubes, or additional sections of gutter—to the cistern. It is advised that the initial portion of rainwater *not* be channeled to the cistern. Let the first few minutes of rain wash the dirt, bugs, and leaves off your roof—kind of like hosing it down. The subsequent rainwater will be much cleaner. You also may want to rig up a screen or cloth to filter out large particles before the water enters the cistern. Of course, any water held in a cistern should be purified before drinking, using one of the methods listed below.

Each person must decide if he or she wishes to create cisterns before Millennium Bug problems occur. Don't forget: January is in the dead of winter, a time when it will be too cold for people in many locations to build cisterns. The ground will be frozen, and any stored water will freeze. But if Y2K disruptions persist into the spring of 2000 and water utilities have yet to restore reliable service (not to mention that stored supplies of water inside even the most prepared homes will be running low), it may be time to start burying drums near the house's downspouts and take advantage of the spring rainfalls.

Purifying Your Water

The only thing worse than not storing water is going through all the trouble of storing it and then getting sick because it wasn't purified properly. There are all sorts of potential dangers lurking in water. After all, water is arguably the most essential ingredient of life, not only for our lives, but for the lives of microscopic organisms—many of which can make us terribly sick. Viruses, bacteria, and harmful protozoa such as giardia and cryptosporidium thrive in water. It is crucial that these hazards be removed from the water you intend to drink.

Water is fairly easy to purify and store, especially when it starts out relatively clean. If you have been drinking the water from your faucet right along without getting ill, you can assume for now that it is clean. If you are forced during an emergency to obtain water from a source that might not be clean, the purifying process is a bit more involved.

Boiling the Water

Boiling water makes it safe to drink because the bacteria and other harmful organisms that can make you sick are destroyed. The water should be brought to a rolling boil for at least ten minutes to ensure all bacteria are killed.

The advantages to boiling water are that it is:

- Fast
- Easy
- Effective

However, there are some disadvantages to boiling water:

- It requires a heat source. In a crisis situation, stoves or other cooking devices may be inoperable, and it may not be possible to start a fire.

- Boiling water removes organic impurities, but it will not remove certain chemical impurities if the water was originally obtained from a polluted source.

- Boiled water tastes lousy. Most people claim it tastes "flat." (You can improve the taste by pouring the water back and forth between two containers. This reoxygenates the water.)

- Some of the water boils off as steam, reducing the amount.

- You have to wait a little while for the water to cool down before you can drink it.

Chlorine

Chlorine is an effective method for purifying water. It is the recommended way of ensuring your supply of bottled water stays clean, as it inhibits the growth of bacteria. Any household bleach containing sodium hypochlorite (5.25 percent solution) will do, as long as it does not have any soap additives or phosphates. Unscented Clorox fits the bill nicely.

The advantages of purifying water with chlorine are that it is:

- Quick
- Easy
- Inexpensive
- Effective at killing harmful organisms

The three primary disadvantages of using chlorine to purify your drinking water are:

- It does not remove heavy metals or other toxic chemicals found in water polluted by industrial waste (see the section on filtration techniques, below).

- Chlorine is essentially a poison. Exposure to high concentrations of chlorine over an extended period of time is not healthy. That's why the Clorox bottle has a warning label. In fact, some water filters are marketed as being able to *remove* chlorine from drinking water. But in an emergency situation, the choice is a "no-brainer." Drinking water with a trace of chlorine in it is much better than drinking water teeming with microorganisms that can make you deathly ill.

- You can taste the chlorine. (You can eliminate this substantially by letting the water stand overnight in an open container or by pouring the water back and forth between two containers.)

Table 5.2 shows how much chlorine to use.[2] For tap water, consider its condition as "clear." For water of unknown quality, consider its condition as "cloudy."

For water that you are going to store, add the chlorine, secure the cap or lid tightly, and store it in a cool, dark place such as a basement (this inhibits the growth of bacteria). Water stored in this way will typically be drinkable for years afterward. Do not store water near chemicals or petroleum products, like paint thinner or gasoline. The chemical fumes can work their way through the plastic bottles over time and affect the taste and quality of the water.

For water you want to use immediately, mix thoroughly after adding the bleach. Let the water stand for at least thirty minutes before drinking it. The water should still have a distinct chlorine taste or smell. If you cannot detect the chlorine smell, add the same dose of bleach to the water and let it stand for an additional twenty minutes.

Iodine

Tincture of iodine (2 percent solution) can also disinfect water and make it safe for drinking. The advantages of using iodine to purify water are that it is:

- Quick
- Easy
- Inexpensive

There are certain drawbacks to using iodine, and certain precautions to take:

Table 5.2:
Amounts of Bleach Required to Treat Various Amounts of Water

Water Quantity	Water Condition	5.25 Percent Sodium Hypochlorite
1 quart	Clear	2 drops
1 quart	Cloudy	4 drops
1/2 gallon (or 2 liters)	Clear	4 drops
1/2 gallon (or 2 liters)	Cloudy	8 drops
1 gallon	Clear	8 drops
1 gallon	Cloudy	16 drops
5 gallons	Clear	1/2 teaspoon
5 gallons	Cloudy	1 teaspoon
35 gallons (small food-grade drum)	Clear	3.5 teaspoons
35 gallons (small food-grade drum)	Cloudy	7 teaspoons
55 gallons (large food-grade drum)	Clear	10.5 teaspoons
55 gallons (large food-grade drum)	Cloudy	21 teaspoons (almost 2 ounces)

- Iodine has a distinctive odor and taste that some people simply cannot stand. They may gag while attempting to drink the water.

- Water treated with iodine may be harmful to pregnant or nursing women.

- People with thyroid problems should not consume iodine-treated water.

- It is recommended that only small amounts of water be treated with iodine; therefore it is not an ideal long-term solution.

Table 5.3 shows the amount of iodine needed to disinfect water.[3] Again, consider pre-Y2K tap water "clear," and any water of unknown quality "cloudy."

After adding the iodine, mix the water thoroughly and let it stand for at least thirty minutes before drinking. As with the chlorine treatment, the presence of the iodine taste or smell (no matter how unpleasant) is a sign of safety. If you can't taste or smell the iodine after the water has been treated, don't drink it! The iodine may be so old or weakened by excessive heat that it is no longer effective. It is much better to remain thirsty for a little longer while a different disinfectant method is used than to drink unsafe water and be stricken with a severe gastrointestinal illness.

Aerobic Oxygen

Many experts consider aerobic oxygen the most effective method for treating potable drinking water for long-term storage. Aerobic oxygen is produced when oxygen is stabilized in a nontoxic liquid form. When added to water it kills all anaerobic (infectious) bacteria, while the bacteria that is harmless or good for us is left untouched. It

Table 5.3:
Amounts of Iodine Required to Treat Various Amounts of Water

Water Quantity	Water Condition	Quantity of 2 Percent Iodine
1 quart	Clear	3 drops
1 quart	Cloudy	6 drops
1/2 gallon (or 2 liters)	Clear	6 drops
1/2 gallon (or 2 liters)	Cloudy	12 drops
1 gallon	Clear	12 drops
1 gallon	Cloudy	24 drops

also aerates the water—adds oxygen to it—which keeps harmful bacteria from growing. The advantages of using aerobic oxygen to purify water are that it:

- Is easy to use
- Purifies effectively
- Produces high quality oxygen-rich water
- Has no chemical taste/odor

The primary disadvantages of using aerobic oxygen to purify your drinking water are:

- Expensive
- Not easily found in supermarkets
- May be difficult to obtain after Y2K

Aerobic oxygen can be purchased from a company called Watertanks via the Internet (<http://www.watertanks.com>). A two-ounce bottle will treat fifty to seventy-five gallons of water, and sells for $13.95. Request item number AO18.

Watertanks also sells aerobic oxygen in many other sizes of bottles, including a sixty-four–ounce container that sells for $269.95. In addition, the company sells other emergency water supplies, such as storage containers—from one-gallon and five-gallon bottles, all the way to huge vinyl "water bags" that hold thousands of gallons. It's an interesting and informative website to check out.

Filtration Techniques

Filtering water is an effective way of removing impurities. The reason well water is generally pure is that it has been filtered through many feet of earth before reaching its underground destination, the aquifer. As the water molecules squeeze past billions of grains of sand, clay, and earth, impurities are extracted.

Treating water with heat (boiling) or chemicals (chlorine or iodine) will kill dangerous bacteria and generally make the water safe for drinking. But if heavy metals or other hazardous chemicals are present, they will remain in the water. As we all know, many of our streams, rivers, and lakes have been polluted over the years by industrial waste. And don't forget, the chances of a hazardous spill will increase significantly when Y2K failures hit high-tech processing facilities. It is quite possible that in an emergency situation some people may be forced to obtain water from a source containing these industrial pollutants. Water filters are capable of removing most of these hazards.

Carbon Filters

There are various types of filters available. Many water filters use carbon as the main element for removing impurities. Amazingly, one ounce of porous carbon has about one square mile of surface area. A lot of chemicals will cling to the carbon surface as it passes by. But as water expert Stu Campbell explains, "Carbon filter technology has only been around since 1956, and it's proving *not* to be the wonder cure we'd hoped. Carbon filters are not completely effective in removing chemical pollutions from water—though many health authorities… insist they're one of the best solutions available."[4]

The problem is that at a certain point the carbon cannot accept any more pollutants, and poisonous substances pass through. The filter must be replaced.

Many homes already have carbon water filters installed under the sink or attached to the faucet, especially in regions where the regular tap water has a strange odor or color. But these devices are not practical for Y2K preparations since drinking water in an emergency will likely not come through your home's plumbing system.

A company called PUR makes a line of portable water filter units that combine carbon filtration with an iodinated resin element. They effectively filter out bacteria, viruses, and giardia. The model I recommend is called the "Scout," which sells for $89. It cleans approximately one liter of water per minute, and each filter is good for up to four hundred liters. Replacement filters cost $44.95. You can obtain further information and order this filter at the following websites: <http://www.backcountrygear.com> or <http://www.ewalker.com/adgear/h2opur.htm>.

Ceramic Filters

Another type of water filter uses a ceramic material containing microscopic pores no bigger than 0.2 microns (0.0002 mm). Water molecules can squeeze through these pores but chemical impurities and microorganisms cannot. The Katadyn line of portable ceramic water filters is probably the most popular ceramic filter available. Using the hand pump at the top of each unit, you force water through the ceramic filter, and clean water pours from a tube into your bottle or canteen. These Swiss-made devices have an excellent reputation among campers and hunters who need to convert stream, snow, or pond water of unknown quality into healthy drinking water.

The model Y-KF-61-PF "Pocket Filter" can purify approximately one quart of water per minute. The ceramic element can be removed, cleaned, and reinstalled up to three hundred times. The service life of this model is about 13,000 gallons. It sells for $269.

The model Y-KF-MINI-CER "Mini Filter Ceramic" has an output of approximately half a quart per minute. It is designed for short-term emergencies and has an estimated service life of two thousand gallons. It sells for $138.

These products are usually available at many camping supply stores—although because of Y2K, they may not be as easy to find. You can also order by visiting the website at <http://www.y2ksupplies.com>, or calling toll-free (877) 580-7844. Be advised, however, that back in December 1998, shipment of these filters was already backlogged for four to six weeks.

Another ceramic option, and frankly the one I prefer, is the British Berkefeld water filter. This is a gravity-operated system and looks much like an industrial-strength coffee maker. It is made of high-grade, stainless steel for maximum corrosion resistance. Each filter can provide up to twenty-one gallons of safe drinking water each day.

One interesting feature of the Berkefeld is the silver-impregnated ceramic elements. The silver prevents the growth of bacteria. The filter has been testified and certified by Spectrum Labs, the University of Arizona, and Clare Microbiological. It has been widely used by the Red Cross and other emergency relief agencies. It will remove E. coli, klebsiella, cholera, shigella, salmonella, guinea worm, giardia lambia, and cryptosporidium.

Each filter will produce well over 2,600 gallons and is easily replaced. The unit sells for $259 and comes standard with four filters. You can order the Berkefeld from:

Noah's Pantry
902 W. First Street
Claremore, OK 74017
Toll-free: (888) 925-6624
Fax: (918) 342-4675
Internet: <http://www.noahspantry.com/filter.htm>

Distillation

Another effective method for purifying water is distillation. As you may remember from high school science class, distillation is the cycle by which water is converted to gas (evaporation or steam) and then through condensation changes back into liquid form. Distillation is the process by which we get most of our drinking water. Water evaporates from the oceans and lakes, condenses in the atmosphere, and falls to the ground in the form of rain.

Distillation produces clean water because the impurities remain behind when the water vapor rises away. A commercial water distiller recreates this process. Water is heated in one chamber, the steam is made to pass over a refrigeration coil in another chamber, and the clean water that results is collected. There are two major drawbacks with these units: (1) they are pricey, anywhere from $1,300 to $3,000 for a quality device; and (2) they require electricity.

If you have a reliable, alternate source of electricity during a blackout and are interested in purchasing a commercial water distiller, visit <http://www.radiant health. com> for further information and ordering instructions. If you are interested in building your own passive solar distiller, visit <http://www.epsea.org/stills.html>.

Water can also be distilled using less sophisticated methods. Simple distillation kits are part of the equipment on life rafts. Most emergency survival manuals explain how to create a primitive water still, including one of the books I recommend for your Y2K library, John Wiseman's *The SAS Survival Handbook*.

However, distillation is complicated, it requires heat to boil the water, and it doesn't produce clean water in abundance. It's a good survival technique if you are in the military or enjoy jungle safaris. But since Y2K problems will not catch us by surprise, I recommend that you focus on some of the other, easier water purification techniques.

Self-sufficient Water Sources

With enough effort and determination it is certainly possible to create a large water supply in your home that will keep many people alive for quite some time during an emergency situation. But each gallon of water you consume means there is one less gallon in your finite supply. There is only so much room in your home to store clean water. If Millennium Bug problems disrupt municipal water companies and the electrical power industry for a long period of time, eventually it will be necessary to secure a new source of clean water.

Wells

Although most families these days get their water via a municipal water company, many rural and suburban homes still have wells. The problem is that in virtually every case, electricity is required to run the water pump, and as we all know, reliable electrical service is something we should not count on after December 1999.

But there are nonelectric methods for getting water out of a well. With shallow wells, a bucket and rope or a manual pump will work. (Some people have built well buckets out of PVC pipe. Once you affix a cap on one end and a rope on another, it becomes a narrow "bucket" that can be lowered down a well casing.) But most wells today are deep-drilled—sometimes hundreds of feet below the surface—and these simple manual methods are not strong enough to raise the water that far. Other, more sophisticated methods are required.

Wind-powered pumps are effective if you live in a region that is breezy. The Jade Mountain website offers two attractive models: the "Rancher," which can pump water from a well as deep as three hundred feet, and sells for $1,550; and the "Homesteader," which can pump water two hundred feet, and sells for $1,250. The website is located at <http://www.jademountain.com>. Keep in mind that a structure with big propeller blades spinning in the wind is quite conspicuous. If you want to keep a low profile during an emergency and not advertise to the whole world that you've got plenty of water, maybe you should consider an alternate method.

Solar-powered well pumps are also an option. With these devices, photovoltaic solar panels convert the sun's energy into DC current that powers a pump. The amount of water you can pump, obviously, depends on how much sunlight you receive. Dankoff makes three different types. They have a life expectancy of about twenty years and come with very easy-to-follow installation instructions. There are three basic types:

- The Solar Slowpump, which draws water from wells up to 450 feet deep, but is suspended in the well above the water table.

- The Solar Sunrise Submersible Pump, which can be submersed and can be placed in deeper vertical wells.

- The Solar Force Piston Pump, which draws surface water from shallow wells, springs, ponds, rivers, or tanks.

Each of them comes in several models with different voltages and flow rates. You can get more information from Y2K Approaches at:

Y2K Approaches
P.O. Box 888
Gambrilla, MD 21054
Toll-free: (888) 925-8801
Internet: <http://www.y2kapproaches.com/products/
        solar_products/water/solar_pump.htm>

For the most part, the best way to get water from a well in a Y2K emergency situation is to have access to an electric generator. Some people with wells purchased generators long before Y2K was an issue. Being unable to get water for even a day or two because of a storm-related power outage was all it took for them to take action.

Many other people have purchased generators since learning about the Millennium Bug. Some people plan to use their generators *exclusively* for pumping water. They will use other methods to provide heat and light, thus conserving the precious fuel needed to power the generator. Which brings us to the Achilles heel of generators: fuel. Gasoline or diesel fuel is needed to run a generator. These products, like all others we take for granted, may be in short supply—or not available at all—if the Y2K Crisis is severe.

If you plan on using a well as a self-sufficient source of water, you must consider the following points:

- The location of the well

- How to retrieve water from the well during a power outage

- How to ensure the power outage–proof retrieval method will work indefinitely

To use a well, you must first have access to one. Does your home have a well? If not, do you have a friend or relative who has one? A major theme with Y2K preparedness will be friends and families and neighbors pulling together and pooling their resources. But to do that you must plan ahead and offer to work together, perhaps trading something in return for water—food, fuel, money, labor, or whatever special skill you may possess.

Can you get the well water if the lights go out? This usually means a generator is needed. Test the generator. Throw the circuit breaker, disconnecting the house from the power company, and fire up the generator. Make sure it is wired properly and strong enough to drive the pump. (Don't laugh. I have a friend who purchased a small campsite-size generator to run his well pump. The only problem is the pump requires 220 volts and the generator puts out only 110, so he could have run, say, his coffee maker but not have been able to put any water *in* the coffee maker.)

Again, the major risk with generators is the fuel supply. Make sure you and your friends/family/neighbors have a plan to store enough fuel to power the generator for many weeks or months. Be advised that the quality of gasoline begins to deteriorate after about six months in storage (not to mention that it is extremely flammable and should never be stored inside your home).

Springs, Streams, Lakes, and Snow

Other self-sufficient sources of water are the various bodies of water nearby your home. Springs, streams, and lakes are all freshwater sources—except for those streams so close to an ocean that the water is brackish (partly fresh water, partly salt water). These water supplies most likely will not be pure—and even if they are, always be cautious and assume they are not. The same goes for snow.

Use the filtering and purification methods described above to prepare this water for drinking. Also, don't forget that water is heavy. How to transport the water from its source to your home will be a major consideration.

Hidden Sources of Water in the Home

There are some hidden sources of water contained in the average home. If during an emergency your stored water runs out and you are still trying to find a new source, you should check the following places in your house:

- *Water line into the house.* This pipe can contain several gallons of water. It's important, however, to close the main valve at the start of a crisis so contaminated water does not flow into your home.

- *Plumbing system.* Pipes in your kitchen and bathrooms also contain drinkable water. Access the water via the lowest faucet in the house. If water does not flow, open the highest faucet in the house to let air in and break the suction.

- *Hot water heater.* Depending on the size, hot water heaters can contain fifteen to forty gallons of drinkable water. Open the drain faucet at the bottom of the heater. Some sediment may first have to be screened out before using this water.

- *Toilet tanks.* Toilet tanks (not the bowls!) contain five to seven gallons of water. Always boil or treat this water first before using. (It is exposed to sewer gas every time the toilet is flushed.) If any commercial disinfectants or cleaners have been used in the toilet tank, you *cannot* use this water.

- *Freezer.* Ice cube trays or other items in your freezer may contain small amounts of water.

- *Water beds.* The water contained in water bed mattresses is most likely not suitable for drinking, no matter how you boil or treat it. This water often contains an algae inhibitor solution that is toxic. The only safe way to use water from a water bed mattress is if you plan in advance to use it: use only a new mattress, add 2 ounces of bleach per 120 gallons of water (no other chemicals!), rotate the water at least yearly, and test it four times a year for algae and toxins. And even then, you would have to boil it thoroughly before using. This water should be used only for certain cleaning chores or toilet flushing.

Final Thoughts About Water

The fact of the matter is, most of us never think about water. It is simply there, ready to serve us whenever we wish. Our technological know-how has made us the first generation in recorded history that does not have to spend a significant portion of the day securing the clean water we need to survive.

Ironically, the technology that has allowed us to be complacent about so many things is the very technology threatened by the Millennium Bug. Our generation may suddenly find itself faced with the problems our great-grandfathers had to face—except we will be lacking great-granddad's wealth of common sense and practical experience.

If the Y2K Crisis disables many of our primary utilities—even for a short while—our society will be cold, dark, hungry, and unable to communicate. But all of these problems will seem minor compared to a lack of clean drinking water.

When drinking water is gone, drinking water is the only thing on a person's mind. Trust me, I know. That thirty-minute boat ride years ago was an awful experience. And I *knew* that plenty of clean water was only minutes away, as soon as we got back to the marina. If Y2K disruptions are severe, we really won't have any idea when things will return to normal. Just think of how frightening and helpless people will feel—especially people without a supply of water.

Clean water is by far the most important item to have during an emergency. It is also the cheapest item to store… before the crisis arrives. Afterward, it will be the most costly commodity, if it can be obtained at all.

I sincerely urge you to take action now to secure an emergency source of water. Make water one of the pillars of your Y2K preparedness program. It is truly a matter of life or death.

Y2K PREP TIP #5
Stock Up on Two-liter Soft Drink Bottles

Regardless of how grandiose your Y2K water plans are—whether you have secured a self-sufficient well or are storing thousands of gallons in a heavy duty, vinyl water bag—you should begin collecting two-liter plastic soft drink bottles.

Obviously, two-liter soft drink bottles can't match fifty-five–gallon drums, cisterns, and swimming pools for sheer volume. You would not want to make pop bottles your *only* method of water storage. But soft drink bottles do have three outstanding features: they are *cheap*, they are *convenient*, and when filled with clean water in a post-Y2K world, they will make excellent *gifts* and *barter items*.

You can acquire two-liter plastic bottles today for nothing—or next to nothing. If you currently buy soft drinks in cans, switch to plastic bottles and save the empties. When you're visiting someone's house or are at a party, ask for the empty bottles. To other people, the bottles are trash. They'll be happy that you are taking the bottles off their hands.

I have a friend who lives in a state that imposes a five-cent deposit on all cans and bottles to encourage recycling. He recently went to the supermarket, and, as people brought bags full of empty bottles in to be redeemed, he offered them a couple of bucks for the whole bag. In ten minutes he filled up his station wagon with plastic soft-drink bottles. Total cost: $6.50.

With a little thought and ingenuity, you can accumulate dozens of plastic bottles. If you have children, challenge them to think of creative ways to obtain bottles (pay them, say, a dime apiece). Just make sure they don't hijack one of those recycling trucks.

Plastic soft drink bottles—properly filled with clean water, four drops of Clorox, and sealed tightly—are convenient to store. They can be placed in all sorts of nooks and crannies around your house. They are also convenient to use once a water emergency occurs. Young members of the family can handle them, and they will probably turn out to be the easiest way to transfer water from your large storage source into your kitchen and bathroom.

Finally, two-liter soft drink bottles filled with water will be a precious commodity if the Millennium Bug becomes severe. What a great gift to give to a friend! Also, they will make a great barter item. In an emergency, people will gladly exchange food, fuel, or other valuable articles for safe, clean water.

While building your collection of bottles, don't forget to buy a bottle of unscented Clorox. And whatever you do, don't forget to fill the bottles while clean water is still flowing from the faucet.

Y2K PREPAREDNESS CHECKLIST					
Level	*Action Step*	*Qty*	*Unit Price*	*Total Qty*	*Total Price*
1	Collect empty 2-liter bottles.	50	$0		
1	Buy bottles of unscented Clorox and an eyedropper.	N/A	$5		
1	Fill 2-liter bottles (plus 4 drops of bleach); store in a cool, dark place.	N/A	$0		
2	Purchase 55-gallon food-grade drums.	N/A	$43		
3	Purchase Katadyn ceramic water filter (long term) or a British Berkefeld, or...	1	$279		
3	Purchase Katadyn filter (short term).	1	$87		
3	Set up cisterns near house downspouts.	N/A	N/A		
4,5	Locate a self-sufficient water source (well, spring, stream, etc.).	N/A	N/A		

Chapter Six

Acquire a Basic Selection of Tools

It's better to have it and not need it than to need it and not have it.
—James Talmage Stevens

I f the Y2K Crisis has a devastating effect on the nation's electrical power grid, as research and investigation by some of the nation's leading electrical industry experts and government analysts indicate, we will all be left without one of the most basic needs for our modern society—electricity. Without electricity, few things can function. One of the few things that you can have on hand that do not require electricity is a good selection of reliable nonelectric hand tools for making minor repairs around the house and in your community.

You may be asking, "Why do I need to stock up on hand tools? My handyman is Y2K-compliant. He'll be over here in a jiffy if I need him!" And you're mostly right. Your regular handyman—and your plumber, yardman, and roofer—doesn't rely on a lot of computers to do his job. But, do remember this: Your handyman probably has a family—a family that might be as desperate and as in need of comfort as you are.

Wouldn't it be beneficial, then, if you knew how to make repairs yourself *and* had the tools with which to do them? You should be thinking of the different types of day-to-day repairs that are common around your home and how you can plan ahead and be ready to handle any situation that comes along after January 1, 2000.

Your Y2K Toolbox

Now is the time to take inventory and see what you need.

To have an effective Y2K Tool Kit, you will need an assortment of tools, which I've divided into four separate categories: tools for working with wood, tools for all-around maintenance, tools for gardening and yard work, and tools for fastening.

Working with Wood

During the course of the Y2K Crisis, you will undoubtedly need an item that you don't currently possess and you can't get somebody to build. This could be anything from a new doghouse to a storage shed to an outhouse. No matter what the project is, you will complete it quicker and more soundly if you are equipped with the proper tools for the job.

Wood. If you've got the storage space, you might consider stocking up on a good supply of 4 foot × 8 foot plywood and some 2 inch × 4 inch lumber, which can be used in a variety of projects, including boarding up doors and windows in the event of a severe storm or constructing a composting area in your backyard. Make sure you store your wood in a cool, dry place to prevent it from warping and rotting.

Saws. A traditional handsaw will be useful for cutting kindling, trimming lumber, and clearing brush, among other things. Handsaws vary from fourteen to twenty-five inches in length, the smaller of which will fit nicely into a small toolbox. Cost: usually under $15.

Drills. A handheld manual drill (not a corded electrical one) will be useful for predrilling holes for large screws or for other woodworking, such as making furniture. Cost: under $10.

Chisels, rasps, and planes. These are all handheld devices for shaping wood, rounding edges, and eliminating splinters from woodworking. Also include packs of high-quality, fine sandpaper for treating rough edges and preparing bare wood for stain or paint. Cost: under $15 each.

Hammers. A high-quality, steel-head hammer is a necessity. Get a twelve-ounce hammer for small jobs and a twenty-two–ounce hammer for heavy-duty construction; or split the difference and buy an all-purpose sixteen-ounce hammer. Cost: about $15.

Screwdrivers. Buy a set of assorted sizes. You'll never know when you need to fix a bike, your glasses, or one of your child's toys. Different sizes will make the job a lot easier. Cost: a good twenty- to thirty-piece set will run about $30 to $40.

All-around Maintenance

No one really knows what is going to happen during the Y2K crisis. You may find yourself becoming the neighborhood handyman with both the know-how and the tools. You might need to cut off a neighbor's water or natural gas, or you may be set-ting up your community's fresh water distribution system. In any case, here are some all-around tools that may make any of these jobs easier, more effective, and more efficient.

Hacksaw. The difference between this saw and a handsaw is that this one has a smaller metal blade on it with finer teeth for cutting plastic tubing and metal pipe with extra precision. This will be useful for cutting plastic PVC pipe, which is often used to carry fresh water. Cost: about $20.

Wrenches. Wrenches are available in a variety of sizes and are another one of the fundamental basics of any tool kit. They will be useful for fastening and unfastening bolts, removing your car battery, or shutting off your natural gas or water lines. You will also want one or two plumbing wrenches. Remember to have the right size for those specialty jobs—check in advance. Cost: about $60 to $70 for a good quality twenty-piece wrench set.

Pipe cutter. Who knows, you may have to be the plumber during the Y2K crisis. But, if so, you will be prepared with a good pipe cutter. Cost: about $10.

Pliers. Another essential, especially if you're working with electrical wires. While you're at it, get a good set of wire cutters. Cost: under $5.

Crowbar. If you've locked your keys in the house or lost the keys to your shed, a crowbar might be handy. It also makes a good defensive weapon. Cost: $10.

Axe. How else would you chop wood for the fireplace or wood stove? Keep one side sharp for cutting down fresh wood and the other side less sharp for splitting wood. Cost: for a good double-edged axe with a fiberglass handle (lifetime warranty) from Sears, $30.

Gardening and Yard Work

Shovel. If you can afford it, get a shovel with a straight-edge and one with a rounded tip. Try to get a shovel with a fiberglass handle and a lifetime warranty. Cost: variable.

Weed-digger. Once you've planted your garden, you will have to maintain it. Too many weeds will thin your harvest out quickly. So, pick up a basic weed-digger (there are several available) to keep tabs on your vegetables. Cost: under $10.

Hoes. Hoes loosen hard soil and provide aeration for plants' roots. Cost: about $10 to $20, depending on quality.

Shears and clippers. Cost: together, about $30.

Lawnmower. To be exact, your existing lawnmower will be functioning properly. But, will you have enough fuel on hand to power it for a whole week, month, or year? Maybe you will. As an alternative, you can purchase a Craftsman 18-inch hand-pushed reel mower from Sears. Remember these? My grandfather used to cut his lawn with one. I haven't seen one in years, but Y2K may take us all "Back to the Future." Cost: $99.

Fastening

In my home, it never fails. When one of my girls needs me to repair a toy or something, I find myself digging through drawers and toolboxes, looking for glue or a few nails. By organizing your fasteners, you can be prepared to fix anything the kids (or your neighbors) have that needs fixing.

Nails. Pick up a gross or so of the common-sized nails, like eight-penny or ten-penny (for big jobs). They are inexpensive and take up little storage space, but they are invaluable when you need to hold things together. Cost: about $15.

Screws. Again, same song, second verse. Just pick up an assortment of common sizes and weights. Cost: about $15.

Staples. Staples might be a better idea than screws or nails. Staples hold strongly and can be inserted into a low-cost staple gun. Cost: staples and gun, $20.

Duct tape. Duct tape is the ultimate in fastening. Take it from a construction-challenged yuppie: There aren't many things you can't fix with duct tape. And it's inexpensive. Cost: $4 to $5 per roll.

Rope and wire. Get a couple of spools of each in case you need them to run a clothesline or hang a tarp. Cost: under $15.

Glue. Make sure to have supplies of wood glue, white glue, super glue, and even rubber cement or epoxy. Cost: under $20.

The Know-how

These tools won't do you a lot of good if you don't know how to use them. Visit your local bookstore and add titles on furniture repair, electrical wiring, and plumbing to your Y2K Emergency Preparedness Library. Stores like Home Depot also have a wide-range of do-it-yourself manuals written in easy-to-understand, step-by-step formats—perfect for someone like me.

Another good buy is *The Foxfire Book Series* by Elliott Wigginton. This ten-book series looks in-depth at homesteading, gardening, and furniture-making from Appalachian Mountain customs in the era before modern tools. It is definitely an interesting read and highly recommended. These books are available on the Internet at <http://www.amazon.com> or by special order from your local bookstore. Even my local Barnes & Noble had several volumes.

Specialty Supplies

The Swiss Army Knife. Manufactured exclusively by the Swiss cutlery company Victorinox since 1891, the Swiss Army Knife is actually issued to the Swiss military as an all-purpose tool for almost any small job imaginable. The flagship knife in the Swiss Army line is the SwissChamp, which costs about $65. The features of the SwissChamp include both a large and small blade, a bottle opener, a screwdriver, a wire stripper, scissors, a metal saw with a metal and nail file, a wood saw, a wood chisel, a hook, pliers with a wire cutter, a toothpick, and a set of tweezers. All of this packs into a single knife small enough to fit in the palm of your hand. Simply put, it's like an entire toolbox that you can fit into your pocket. A must for your Y2K Tool Kit. As an alternative, you can buy a Leatherman "Super Tool," which contains seventeen different tools and is guaranteed for twenty-five years.

The Craftsman 12-in-1 Multipurpose Tool. Similar to the Swiss Army Knife, this product, which is offered exclusively through Sears, is a small set of pliers that encases several other small tools inside the handle. Features of the 12-in-1 include needle-nosed pliers, three screwdrivers, a knife, a ruler, two files, an awl, a can/bottle opener, and a key ring. The whole device weighs less than a pound and attaches easily to any size belt. And, like all Craftsman products, it's guaranteed forever. Cost: $39.99.

The WonderWash. This incredibly useful contraption is a small washing machine for clothes. Using a unique pressure system that causes hot water to heat trapped air inside, the WonderWash forces water and soap at high speed through fabrics when you manually rotate the washing barrel. You get super-clean clothes with only a tiny amount of detergent. The only energy it needs is the motion of your hand turning the crank. It holds up to 4.8 pounds of clothes and uses very little water. It's not as easy to use as an electric washer, but it sure beats the old-fashioned washboard and wringer for cleaning clothes. The WonderWash is available through Jade Mountain, (800) 442-1972, and costs $45.

The Mag-lite. This is my personal choice for your Y2K flashlight. It uses three standard, off-the-shelf, D-cell batteries and is the most powerful flashlight for the price.[1] I personally feel that it merits stocking up on D-cell batteries. Not only does the Mag-lite project a powerful beam that can be adjusted from pinpoint brightness to a wide angle lamp to fill an entire room, its weight (about four to five pounds) and hardness make it a formidable defensive weapon in the event of an emergency. Also, the Mag-lite is equipped with high-quality O-rings in the cap to make it waterproof. Cost for the Mag-lite itself: about $20. As for battery usage, James Stevens discusses D-cell battery usage in his book, *Making the Best of Basics.* He shows that intermittent use of flashlights will lead to a life of about seven to eight hours for each battery.[2] Although every Mag-lite comes with a spare bulb in the butt cap, you'll want to store some extra bulbs along with your batteries.

Starlight. If you really want a nonconventional flashlight that doesn't use batteries, try the Starlight flashlight. Amazingly, the flashlight gets its energy from motion—you simply shake it. The light will work indefinitely but isn't as bright as a Mag-lite. Still, you never have to worry about batteries. It sells for $79, and you can order it from:

> Applied Innovation Technologies
> P.O. Box 754
> Fort Lupton, CO 80621
> Toll-free: (888) 828-1405
> Fax: (303) 975-5133
> Internet: <http://www.innovativetech.org>

Solar Lantern. Yet another option for lighting is the Real Goods Solar Lantern. This innovative product features a five-watt fluorescent flood light, a powerful flashlight, and a red-lens flashing warning light. The built-in NiCad battery pack will run the fluorescent lamp for more than four hours, the flashlight for eight hours, or the warning light for forty hours. Solar recharging takes eight to ten hours in full sunlight. The unit sells for $69.95. You can order it from:

> Real Goods Trading Corp.
> 555 Leslie Street
> Ukiah, CA 95482-5507
> Toll-free: (800) 762-7325
> Internet: <http://www.realgoods.com>

Oil lantern. This old camping stand-by is a perfect answer to the day-to-day lighting needs of the average family. All of the components of this piece of equipment are inexpensive, the fuel is nonperishable and long-burning, and the product is safe enough for every member of the family. According to Stevens, using the lantern at the rate of five hours per day, and with the knowledge that the oil burns at a rate of about one ounce of fuel per hour, it would only take twenty-five gallons of fuel to last an entire year for every lantern that you use.[3] Ounce for ounce, it's the best. Cost: lamp and fuel for a year, $75.

Sewing supplies. I have no doubt that some of us will need repairs to items of clothing sometime during the Y2K crisis. Don't forget to pack a sewing kit with needle and thread, patches, extra buttons, and scissors. Cost: less than $10.

Tarps. If you ask a camper what his most useful piece of equipment is, he will probably tell you about his trusted tarp. Tarps could be very useful during the year 2000 for repairing leaky roofs, keeping the sun off your area, or hiding supplies. It is a good idea to invest in a few large, good-quality, multipurpose tarps. You might also want to buy some inexpensive plastic drop cloths or sheet plastic. Cost: depending on size, $20 to $100.

Chainsaw. A chainsaw uses very little gasoline—ten to fifteen gallons, along with a bottle of two-cycle engine oil, should be enough to last through the winter at least. Where I live, when a bad storm blows through, downed trees are everywhere. With a good chainsaw and a little fuel, you could become the neighborhood hero, clearing roads and removing fallen trees from cars and property. Plus, think of all the free firewood! Cost: for a Craftsman with a 2.8 cubic inch motor, $169. For a more heavy-duty model, $299. In my opinion, it's a worthwhile investment.

Y2K PREP TIP #6
Use Alternative Energy to Recharge Batteries

Just because the power is out for a while doesn't mean that you can't use power tools during the Y2K crisis. In fact, you have lots of options if you are willing to invest a little time and money in your project.

There are lots of rechargeable batteries on the market right now, including all brands and sizes of conventional batteries. However, there are some manufacturers, such as Craftsman and Black and Decker, who produce power tools that use rechargeable batteries in a multitude of products. For example, Black and Decker's VersaPak series of products includes drills, screwdrivers, circular saws and jigsaws, and several other items, including a flashlight, a weed trimmer, and hedge trimmers. All of these products run off the same model battery. If you could operate the battery recharger, you could have enough batteries to run several power tools every day.

Did you know that you can convert the energy from your car battery into twelve-volt power to use in your home? With a few supplies from your local Radio Shack, you can run two wires from your car battery inside your house and into a plug-in outlet for your appliances. So, by running your car (thereby charging the battery via the alternator) you can power a twelve-volt outlet inside your house for as long as your car has gasoline. This makes for a great temporary solution, provided you plan ahead and purchase the supplies beforehand.

As a second option, you could plug your recharger into a generator to charge the batteries. Remember to be careful when working around generators, and not to overload them with power drains. They have been known to kill if not used properly! (See Chapter 9 for more details.)

One final option is solar power. Charlie Collins, founder of Do-It Homestead and president of Mr. Solar Alternative Energy, has created a solar energy panel recharger kit specially made for the Black and Decker–type products that recharge power tool batteries in a central charger. Since most products take two batteries, I suggest you buy three packs of batteries and rotate them. Use one while the rest are charging. The cost is around $350. For more information, you can contact Charlie at <CharlieCollins@mrsolar.com>.

	Y2K PREPAREDNESS CHECKLIST				
Level	Action Step	Qty	Unit Price	Total Qty	Total Price
1	Make a checklist of what tools you need for your Y2K Tool Kit.	N/A	N/A		
3	Purchase all the tools you lack.	Varies	Varies		
3	Study how to use all of the tools.	N/A	N/A		
3	Purchase a repair manual for your Y2K Emergency Preparedness Library.	1	Varies		

Part Three

Shelter

Chapter Seven

Evaluate Your Current Location

Location, location, location.
> —The three most important considerations
> when choosing a place to live

The residents of South Central Los Angeles know they live in what most people would call a "rough," inner-city community. They know crime and drugs are commonplace, and that it is unwise to venture alone into unfamiliar neighborhoods—especially at night. They also know that most residents in the community are law-abiding people trying to lead decent lives and be productive citizens. Many churches, shops, and businesses can be found in South Central Los Angeles. The people living there call it home.

Despite their street-wise awareness about the hazards of inner-city life, the residents of South Central Los Angeles were completely unprepared for the lawlessness that erupted when the verdict in the Rodney King trial was announced. Impromptu street protests accelerated in mayhem and destruction within minutes. When the police, realizing they were outmanned and outgunned, decided to pull back and regroup, all hell broke loose.

Rioting and looting raged for days. People lost their lives, billions of dollars in property was destroyed, and the heart and soul of a community was forever scarred.

But don't forget that in recent years we have seen civil unrest around the globe: riots in Indonesia, violence in Palestine, atrocities in Bosnia, and even widespread destruction in sophisticated Montreal as residents "celebrated" the hockey team's Stanley Cup victory.

But if there was ever an event that could spark civil unrest, it's the Millennium Bug. Try this mental exercise: Imagine what it would be like to live in your current neighborhood without electricity, water, or the benefit of police protection. Also imagine that surrounding neighborhoods, communities, states, and even nations are experiencing the same thing and cannot offer any help.

Would you and your family survive? For how long? How would you heat your home? (Don't forget, the Y2K crisis will begin in the dead of winter.) Where will you get water? How will you protect yourself?

What will happen when people are cold, hungry, thirsty, fearful, and angry?

Or think about this: How vulnerable is your neighborhood to looters? Don't make the mistake of thinking that looting is just an urban phenomenon. What happens when the inner cities have all been looted? Where will the looters go next? Would your subdivision, apartment complex, or neighborhood be an attractive target?

The Y2K crisis could force unpleasant choices. Probably the most difficult is: Should we uproot our family and move to a different location?

Risks and Benefits of Your Current Location

The first calculation is estimating the severity of Y2K disruptions. A Level 1 crisis (seventy-two hours) requires less drastic measures than a Level 5 crisis (one year or longer). The other major factor in where you live now.

Urban Locations

In an urban setting, even seventy-two hours of Millennium Bug disruptions (Level 1) will be very dangerous. Rioting and looting can break out within minutes. If the police are paralyzed by either communications breakdowns or a lack of manpower (cops will likely choose to stay home and protect their families rather than report for duty), street unrest could quickly spiral out of control.

Urban locations are the most dependent on our high-tech, modern infrastructure. Public utilities provide the electricity, natural gas, water, and sewer service that people need. Y2K breakdowns could cause all of these services to cease. Still, proper preparation and stockpiling of supplies should allow many urban dwellers to survive a seventy-two–hour crisis. But it might be impossible to provide heat and sanitation in some urban developments.

All urban areas are completely dependent on transportation and distribution networks to provide the steady flow of food and other goods that cities need to survive. If Y2K problems shut down these operations, food will disappear from store shelves within hours. No new supplies will be forthcoming. Even those distribution companies that can still operate will be reluctant to send their trucks into urban areas where crime or rioting becomes a factor. If they can move any goods at all, they'll send them to safer suburban stores.

For any level of Y2K crisis beyond Level 1 (that is, anything lasting longer than seventy-two hours), it will be virtually impossible to live safely in an urban area. Am I saying that everyone in an urban area will die if Y2K disruptions last longer than three days? No, but I am saying that the safety and health of everyone in an urban area will be genuinely threatened. Even wealthy people and high government officials will be in danger. Disease can spread quickly if water, sewage, and garbage disposal services break down. Illness can strike anyone, regardless of status. Fires may rage out of control. Hazardous materials may be released into the environment. Flames and fumes can harm both rich and poor.

If you currently live in an urban area and you think there is a chance that Millennium Bug chaos could last longer than a few days, my urgent advice to you is to move from the city before the new century arrives.

Suburban Locations

There are countless types of suburban communities, each with its own unique set of risks and benefits. For Y2K purposes, the primary considerations are:

- Climate
- Proximity to urban areas
- Proximity to water supply
- Proximity to food supply
- Character of citizenry

Climate is a big factor. Many parts of North America are extremely cold in January. Do you have an alternate form of heat if your current method is disabled by Y2K? When the temperature is hovering around zero, even the best-insulated home will become an icebox in a matter of hours. The more northerly your address, the more important this climate consideration becomes.

How close you live to an urban center is also important. Some idyllic residential neighborhoods are within walking distance—or at least a short drive—from teeming inner-city areas. Other suburban communities are hundreds of miles from the nearest city. Is it logistically possible for roving mobs of desperate predators to appear on your street within a few hours or days of Millennium Bug breakdowns?

Your proximity to a supply of clean water is a major factor. For example, tens of millions of people live in lovely southern California. But the region is actually a desert. The water supply is brought in from out of state. If Y2K problems disrupt this flow of water, or if the neighboring states decide they no longer want to share their precious commodity with California, millions of people will be in dire straits. Also, in some suburban towns virtually every home is connected to the municipal water company. In other towns most homes have their own well. Y2K glitches could contaminate the entire municipal system, while each well—despite the possible loss of electricity—will still be a potential source of clean water.

The proximity to a food supply should be a big component in your decision-making. Suburban neighborhoods located close to farmland will have a much better chance of obtaining food in a prolonged crisis, while those with food supplies trucked in from hundreds of miles away could be in real danger.

The character of the people within your suburban community is another key consideration. Some towns have a strong community spirit—the residents respect each other and wouldn't hesitate to help one another in an emergency. Other suburban locales are (let's face it) populated with self-centered, pampered yuppies who don't really care about their neighbors—and wouldn't know how to help in an emergency situation anyway.

In short, if the Y2K crisis turns out to be only Level 1 or 2 (seventy-two hours to one week), most suburban dwellers will be fine with some minimal preparation focused on food, water, and heat.

If the emergency is a Level 3 (thirty days), then much more significant preparation is required, not only regarding food, water, and heat, but also waste disposal, medical care, and self-defense.

With a Level 4 crisis (three months), tremendous preparation will be required. A sizable stockpile of food, water, fuel, medicine, and hand tools will be needed. Local community or neighborhood support groups will have to deal with self-defense, transportation, communication, and medical emergency issues.

If the Millennium Bug causes a Level 5 crisis (one year or more), you will need to be almost entirely self-sufficient in your current location. It is possible to stockpile a year's worth of food (which I highly recommend). But it will be very difficult to store up a year's supply of water and fuel. If you believe Y2K disruptions could last up to a full year, make sure you have access to a dependable source of clean water and fuel to heat your home.

Of course, Y2K may prove to be the most cataclysmic event of our lifetime, disrupting society on a long-term basis, in which case you will need to be *fully* self-sufficient in your current location. No matter how much food you stockpile before the year 2000, at some point it will be used up. Do you have access to enough productive farmland to allow you and your family to survive a long-term crisis? If not, and if you truly believe Y2K will devastate our societal infrastructure for years, your present location is not acceptable.

Rural Locations

If you currently live in a rural location… congratulations! All the city slickers are green with envy right about now. Of the three primary categories—urban, suburban, and rural—rural locations are by far the best able to deal with Millennium Bug disruptions. This is because, generally speaking, the more urban the location, the more dependent the citizens are on modern technology and complex social systems. Conversely, rural locations are less dependent on these modern systems and are less likely to be devastated by Y2K failures.

But aspects of your location still need to be evaluated even if you live in a rural area. Many rural homes are just as dependent on electricity and natural gas as urban homes. A prolonged power failure or gas shutdown would cause severe hardship. Living in a rural area does not exempt you from the threat of Y2K. Extensive preparations must still be made.

Most rural areas have access to adequate water and firewood, but food could be a problem. Most rural locations are in or near farm country, and if this is the case for you, definitely stay put. If sophisticated transportation and distribution systems break down, the best place to be is close to the source. Some rural locations, though, are not very close to farmland or an adequate food supply. Even very isolated areas have become dependent on produce that is trucked in from far away. If this is your situation, relocating might make sense.

Pros and Cons of Moving

Pros

Safety. The most obvious reason for relocating to a more rural community before the year 2000 is safety. If Y2K disruptions are severe, certain areas—especially urban areas—will be unsafe. As already discussed, infrastructure hazards (loss of power, water, sewer, and food supply) and human hazards (rioting, looting, and lawlessness) could erupt and put people's lives at risk. A less populated area is simply safer in an emergency situation.

Health. Many potential health hazards could be caused by Y2K failures. Unsafe drinking water, improper sewage and waste disposal, and toxic chemical spills are just some of the dangers. The greater the population density, the greater the odds that these problems could occur.

Impetus for desired change. A lot of people dream of making a major move. Fed up with corporate ladder-climbing and the urban rat race, these folks sincerely wish to make a career change. But the security of a steady paycheck and familiar surroundings often keeps them from seizing their dream. Y2K offers a reason to move.

Less stressful lifestyle. Even if the Y2K crisis turns out to be a "bump in the road" (downright impossible in my view), you might still be glad you moved away from the city. Living in a small town is usually cheaper and less stressful than living in a bustling metropolis. And just maybe, with a little planning and creativity, you could keep your present job by negotiating a work-at-home arrangement with your employer. With the advent of high-speed telecommunications, faxes, e-mail, and the Internet, many people have been able to set up offices and perform most of their duties right at home.

Cons

Loss of current job. Not all occupations lend themselves to a work-at-home arrangement, and some employers refuse to consider it as an option. The stark fact of the matter is, most people who move because of the Millennium Bug will have to quit their current job. It is certainly not easy to walk away from your source of income and, in many cases, your health insurance and pension benefits.

Traumatic experience. Even under normal circumstances, moving to a new location can be a traumatic event. I have a friend in his early thirties who swears that the next time he moves it will be to either a nursing home or the cemetery.

Economic loss. Besides the likelihood of losing your job, other economic factors are involved in a move. A lot of real estate was overpriced in the 1980s and early 1990s. You may be forced to sell your present home for less than you paid for it. And as we move closer to December 1999, it may become difficult to sell an urban area home at any price. The same economic factors may work in reverse for rural properties. As the year 2000 looms and concern and possibly panic among the population grow, the price of homes in small, quiet communities could skyrocket.

Unfamiliar surroundings. Leaving your home and friends to move to a new area can be intimidating and lonely. There is also the possibility that because of Y2K, residents of small communities might be slow to warm up to you as the number of urban emigrants increases. It will take extra work on your part to get to know and win the trust of your new neighbors.

What to Look for in a New Location

There are two primary considerations you should address in choosing a location: the ordinary issues about moving and the Y2K-specific extraordinary issues.

Ordinary Issues

People move to new locations every day. They moved long before anyone ever heard of Y2K, and they surely will move long after the Millennium Bug is relegated to the history books. In normal times people choose a location based on a handful of fundamental factors: employment opportunities, nearness to relatives, climate, quality of the school system, tax rates, and cultural considerations.

Even if your move is prompted by Y2K concerns, you should still address these issues. But be aware that school systems and taxation structures might be forever altered in the wake of Y2K. The other issues of climate, region, and culture are important. For example, if you've lived your whole life in Brooklyn, New York, it might be a major culture shock if you suddenly relocate to rural Mississippi. Or if you're a native Texan currently living in metropolitan Houston, you might be more comfortable steering clear of the French-speaking regions of northern Maine. Let common sense be your guide.

Y2K Extraordinary Issues

If you are going to take the major step of relocating your family, you don't want to choose a location that is highly vulnerable to societal breakdowns or critical shortages when Y2K hits. The issues addressed throughout this book must be factored into your decision: water, food, heat, sanitation, and self-defense, among others.

Will your new community be able to fend for itself if major breakdowns occur? Are there reliable sources of water? Nearby agricultural and livestock farms? Woodland areas for firewood? Citizens willing and able to assist one another and defend their community from violent outsiders? Chemical or other manufacturing facilities nearby that use hazardous materials?

Does the community depend on nuclear-generated electricity? Is it downstream from a computer-controlled dam?

These Y2K-specific issues, combined with the normal issues of everyday home-buying, should help you make the best choice for you and your family. Keep in mind, of course, that time is short and it might be impossible to select the ideal location. One thing is certain: The longer you wait, the fewer options you have.

Other Considerations

There are those who advocate that we should "head for the hills." There are others who say that this is "cowardly" and that we should stay and help our neighbors. I believe the right answer depends on your particular situation. The following items must be taken into account:

Resources. For many people, moving is simply not an option. They don't have the resources. This is especially true of those on fixed incomes and those who cannot drive long distances to their existing employment. If you're in this situation, take responsibility for what you can control and work with neighbors to build community support.

Motivation and commitments. The Millennium Bug forces us to contemplate some of the "big picture" questions we can so easily ignore in our fast-paced, live-for-the-moment society. Questions such as: What is my duty as a citizen? What kind of example should I set for my children? Am I really my brother's keeper?

Calling. Because I'm a Christian, it ultimately comes down to what I believe the Lord is leading me to do. In the influenza epidemic of the early twentieth century, some Christians in Memphis, Tennessee, decided to stay in the city and minister to those who were sick and dying. Many of them paid for their decision with their lives. But, as I have often said publicly, as important as survival is, there are other, sometimes more important, values to consider.

If Moving Is Not an Option

If Y2K-related infrastructure failures and societal breakdowns hit your community, you and your family will have a greater chance of being safe if you prepare in advance. Having a supply of food and water will allow you to stay off the streets and out of harm's way. The following suggested steps can also increase the odds that you do not become a Millennium Bug victim.

Install new locks and security devices. How easy is it for someone to break into your home right now? Will one swift kick send your front door flying open? If law enforcement collapses and thugs are on the prowl, you want to give criminals a good reason to go elsewhere. Make your home not worth the effort. Install dead bolts on the doors and bars or boards nailed across the windows. (Don't bother with electronic security systems—they require electricity and 911 service.) Do whatever it takes to increase the chances that a thug will think, "This place is a pain. I'll break into the building down the block instead."

Make your home as inconspicuous as possible. Along the same line of thinking, you don't want to tempt or encourage law-breakers to attack your home. An acquaintance of mine was recently bragging about the diesel generator and extra fuel tanks he installed. "If Y2K knocks the power out," he said, "I'll have the only house with lights. At night people will see my house from miles away and be green with envy." I reminded him that some of those people may not sit back politely and stare wistfully at his house. They may decide to take what he has. Any outward sign that you have prepared for disruptions (a visible supply of food, fuel, water, and, of course, lights) will be a magnet for thugs. Evaluate the appearance of your home. Make sure you're not presenting an inviting target. Give the appearance of being as down and out and desperate as the law-breakers.

Defensive weapons. Criminals generally prey on defenseless victims. If they think that they might meet some resistance that could put their own lives or health at risk, they will choose a different victim. If your self-defense philosophy includes firearms, be sure you're properly trained to use them. Large dogs have also been known to steer looters to a different target.

Show of force. You really don't want to get into a shoot-out with a criminal unless it's absolutely necessary to preserve your life or the life of a loved one. You have no way of knowing what kind of firepower the thug has, nor whether a mob of his friends is about to arrive to join in the battle. The best way to defend your home with a gun is to show the hoodlums you have one and are willing to use it if necessary. As mentioned earlier, your main goal is to steer the troublemakers away from your location.

Group/community efforts. A single person showing that he is armed and willing to protect his home can be an effective show of force. But *many* people showing that they are armed and willing to protect their homes will be many times more effective. If you go it alone, you've still got to sleep sometime. And what if a mob approaches your home? Neighbors who pull together, organize themselves, and make it clear that they will defend their homes and families by whatever means necessary have the greatest chance of avoiding Y2K misfortune. There truly is strength in numbers. But just remember: New Year's Day 2000—as the power goes out and frightened mobs take to the street—is not the best time to begin discussing community defense plans with your neighbors. This is a subject that must be discussed, coordinated, and planned in advance. We hope it will never have to be put into practice, but you must broach the subject with your neighbors soon. Be as low-key and matter-of-fact as possible. You don't want to get labeled as a dangerous looney if your neighbors do not yet understand the grave risks of Y2K.

During rioting in Miami a number of years ago, two men set up lawn chairs at t he entrance of their trailer park. They sat with .22 caliber rifles clutched in their hands (not very powerful weapons, actually). All night long looters came running by, ready to enter the park. But with one glance at the two sentries, the looters kept running to find easier prey elsewhere. Not a shot was fired, and no damage was done to those trailer homes. A show of force, rather than the use of force, was effective protection.

Sometimes in a crisis situation a little common sense, preparation, and plain old courage can make the difference between triumph and tragedy. The major problem with the Millennium Bug is that we simply do not know in advance how bad the crisis will be. Courage and preparation may not be enough if the social order breaks down. You and your family must ultimately make the momentous decision about whether to relocate before the Y2K disruptions hit. Whatever the decision, it is likely to be the most difficult choice you have ever faced.

Y2K PREP TIP #7
Devise a Half-way Relocation Plan

For many people, moving is not an option. They may truly want to get out of harm's way before Y2K disruptions occur, but for a multitude of reasons it might be impossible. If you are in this particular situation and are convinced your present location will be too hazardous when the new century arrives—regardless of how many self-defense and community planning steps you take—you should investigate what I call the "half-way relocation" option.

Essentially this plan means you must find a friend, relative, or coworker who lives in a safer location and make arrangements to spend the century rollover period at his home.

For a lot of people this will be rather easy. I know one city-dweller whose parents have *ordered* him, in no uncertain terms, to bring his family to their house for Christmas 1999 and stay for as long as needed—even permanently if necessary.

For other people who don't know a single soul outside their urban neighborhood, this will be an extremely difficult plan to accomplish. If you don't know anyone at all in a less dangerous location, now is the time to find one. Church groups often have contacts with other communities. Coworkers may live, or know others who live, in rural areas. Talk to people in your congregation or at work—subtly and low-key, yes, but persistently, too. This certainly could be awkward, but let's not lose sight of what we are talking about here. The risks of Y2K are real. This could be a matter of life and death. The health and safety of your loved ones may depend on whether you successfully accomplish this plan.

The first step is to identify someone who could make an acceptable host. First and foremost, his location should be safer than yours. Also consider whether your personalities and views are compatible, and, of course, there should be at least a remote chance that he will agree to this plan before you approach him.

When you do approach him, don't present yourself as a helpless charity case. Make your potential host see an advantage to having you at his home. Offer something in return—food, fuel, money, labor, a special skill or talent. Make him *want* you at his place during a crisis.

If you are able to arrange a "half-way relocation," you will be abandoning your current residence for an unknown period of time. It might be in pretty bad shape when you return. But your life and health are much more valuable than property or possessions. Psychologically and emotionally, be prepared to lose it all. Possessions can always be replaced—your life cannot.

I admit this Y2K Prep Tip is drastic. But drastic situations call for drastic measures. The Y2K Crisis has the potential to be the most drastic experience we have ever faced.

	Y2K PREPAREDNESS CHECKLIST				
Level	*Action Step*	*Qty*	*Unit Price*	*Total Qty*	*Total Price*
1	Do a mental exercise: Imagine your neighborhood without electricity, water, and police protection. Honestly assess how your family would fare.	N/A	N/A		
1	Have a long talk with spouse and/or family about this issue.	N/A	N/A		
1	Determine if you can keep your present job if you move (work-at-home arrangement or commute).	N/A	N/A		
2	Investigate job/real estate markets in more rural locations.	N/A	N/A		
2	Meet with real estate agent—assess the value of your present home.	N/A	N/A		
3	Make the decision to move or stay.	N/A	N/A		
3	If you stay, make self-defense plans with neighbors.	N/A	N/A		
3	If you stay, arrange "half-way relocation" plan... just in case.	N/A	N/A		
3	If you move, get to know new neighbors and become part of your new community.	N/A	N/A		

Chapter Eight

Secure an Alternative Source of Heat

Everybody talks about the weather, but nobody does anything about it.

—Mark Twain

The rain had been coming down for almost two days when the first explosion rattled the frigid air. Darkness had already enveloped nine-year-old Nathan and his family, and they were in the process of looking for their flashlights when the transformer just outside their house gave resounding notice that the electricity would not be on again anytime soon. As evening turned to night, and the freezing January air became even colder, the boy and his father decided to go out for a walk and admire the gleaming coat of ice that blanketed just about everything. Their journey through the darkened streets of their hometown in northwestern Maine was punctuated from time to time with spectacular fireworks of blue, white, and green; transformers were exploding at a stunning rate all across the landscape.

Flickering candles welcomed them home, but as they stripped off the damp outer layers of their clothing, Nathan noticed that three of his fish had already succumbed to the cold. Looking at the lifeless creatures floating silently on the surface of the aquarium, the boy's father began to wonder just how long their own descent into the freezing darkness would last. He knew one thing: With no way to heat the house, they wouldn't be able to stay there long.

Farther to the north, in his chalet-style home east of Montreal, Robert Plante was beginning what would become thirty-two straight days without electricity. "Leaving was out of the question," he said in early February, just before power crews finally switched off his generator and started the electricity flowing once again. "And why leave? I had heat and plenty to eat." Stored food, a wood stove, and a generator kept this feisty seventy-two-year-old safe and happy, sleeping in his own bed, while many of his Canadian neighbors were forced to flee their homes for shelters with heat and supplies.

For hundreds of thousands of people across eastern Canada, and tens of thousands more in the United States, the ice storm of 1998 tested their mettle as few things ever had. For those who were prepared, staying in their own homes and helping others were viable options.

The year 1998 provided three different glimpses of life without electric power. Auckland, New Zealand, went dark for more than two months due to a mechanical failure. January's ice storm interrupted electrical delivery for as many as thirty-two days in Canada and the northeastern United States. And San Francisco, California, was out for the better part of one day because of human error and failed back-up systems. While each of these provided an interesting preview of life when the Millennium Bug sinks its teeth into the power grid, each was only a warm-up act for the Main Event.

⌨ ⌨ ⌨

Whenever I think about Y2K, the one thing I keep coming back to is the possibility of *power outages*. I've been through a few—one that lasted for three days—and they are never a pleasant experience. When you really get down to it, there is nothing we are more dependent on than electricity. (Without electricity we can't even keep the computers going to continue working on the Y2K problem!) Not only does it animate our toys and creature comforts, it also makes possible most of our necessities, including heat. And, to add insult to injury, Y2K is scheduled to begin in the dead of winter. For most people in the northern hemisphere, this is a bone-chilling time of year. At best, trying to get along without heat could be uncomfortable; at worst, it could be life-threatening.

I continue to be concerned about the lack of progress being made by the electric power utility companies. All of them are telling us not to worry. The only problem, in my opinion, is that most of them are *not* making adequate progress. For example, at the time of this writing in early 1999:

- Not one publicly held electric utility is Y2K-compliant (this is according to the utilities' own 10-Q filings with the SEC).[1]

- By the end of 1998 these same publicly held utilities had spent only 30 percent to 35 percent of their Y2K budgets.[2] If you "follow the money," this does not bode well for finishing on time.

- Energy companies like Chevron, Exxon, and Mobil are also behind schedule.[3] These companies provide the fuel for many power plants.

As a result, I believe it is highly probable that we are going to have regional brownouts—and likely some blackouts—in many parts of the country. The one thing I know for certain is that we don't have enough evidence at this point to believe that we won't. Anyone who is making statements to the contrary is "spinning the truth" for some other purpose. As a result, the only prudent thing to do is to assume there will be outages and plan accordingly.

As an additional worry, in each of the examples I cited above—whether eastern Canada, Auckland, or San Francisco—regions around the affected areas had ample power, and people were able to relocate temporarily to carry on daily life. Also, when it came to the longer outages in New Zealand and Canada, the rest of the infrastructure—and other communities—remained in perfect operating order and were able to assist with emergency relief. In other words, these were *single system failures*. Y2K has the potential to disrupt everyone, everywhere, at just about the same time. It could thus produce a *multiple system failure* in which no one is unaffected, no one can come to the aid of others.

Therefore, unless you live in south Florida, you probably need to consider some form of back-up heating, other than natural gas and electricity. Obviously, if the electricity goes off and your home relies on electric heat, you've got a problem. What may not be so obvious is that electricity is necessary for most natural gas heaters as well.

According to *Y2KWatch News*, a free weekly e-mail newsletter dedicated to educating people about Y2K and helping them prepare:

> Most, if not all, forced air natural gas furnaces these days use electricity for three major purposes in the furnace. First, the thermostat uses electricity to turn on the heat. The second use is the igniter which starts the flame. No power, no flame. The third use is the blower motor. If the thermostat is bypassed and the electrically controlled valve is bypassed, and the furnace is lighted manually, it still cannot be run for any period of time as there is no forced air to propagate the heat and cool the furnace enough to keep it from overheating.
>
> And that isn't the end of the problem. Natural gas suppliers depend upon the power grid to provide the pressure and to keep the larger gas valves open. Without power, the valves close, stopping the gas. I suspect that most consumers have not thought about the cascade of events that happen based upon the grid failing.[4]

There are a number of possible alternatives, including fireplaces, fireplace inserts, wood stoves, and space heaters. I'll also discuss some alternative options for cooking, along with the safety issues you need to consider. Finally, we'll look at obtaining some extra clothing and beefing up your supply of blankets in order to keep everyone warm when the sun goes down.

Home Is Where the Hearth Is

Many of us in colder climates have experienced temporary power outages, in which everyone gathers in the family room in front of the fireplace, huddling close and trying to keep warm. Often the time begins with nervous laughter as family members, who usually spend their time with electronic distractions of one sort or another, are actually forced to sit in the same room and talk.

Often that laughter turns to grumbling when it becomes apparent the power won't be coming on before it's time for bed and people have to decide whether to shiver between their own cold sheets or pull out the sleeping bags and snooze in front of the hearth.

Unfortunately, if you have a typical fireplace you know that when it's really cold, and the power is out, you almost have to sit on top of the flames to feel the warmth. Simply put, most fireplaces today are made for decoration and ambiance, rather than as a true heat source. Many of them have a heat-efficiency rating of somewhere between 15 and 20 percent—not exactly the best situation to be in when the temperatures are hovering near zero and the power might not be turned on for a day or two (or three, or four... or thirty, or sixty).

So what can you do? One answer is to get a *fireplace insert*. Vermont Castings has a couple of models with efficiency ratings near 80 percent. What that means is that you get four to five times more heat from the same amount of wood burned in the average fireplace—a huge improvement.

An insert fits easily into the opening for your existing fireplace, turning it into a more efficient source of heat. Vermont Castings calls its insert series "Winter Warm," and it has two different sizes. The small unit (suggested retail starts at $1,199 for "classic black") will heat an area from 500 to 1,000 square feet, while the large one ($1,839) heats from 750 to 1,500 square feet. You can view these items for yourself on the company's website at <http://www.vermontcastings. com/products/woodinserts.htm>. Please note that each of these inserts, and the wood stoves mentioned below, require certain accessories (connectors and/or stove pipe) at additional cost, for complete installation. Also, Vermont Castings does not sell directly to the public, so you'll need to call to find retailers in your area who carry its products. To do so you can call its Dealer Information Line at (800) 227-8683.

Though I hate to state the obvious, please remember if you choose one of these inserts (or a wood stove), you'll need a good supply of firewood. A few other things to keep in mind with regard to wood:

1. Buy seasoned hardwoods. Ask when the wood was cut. Ideally, you want wood that is at least a year old. In addition, you want hardwood like oak or maple. It will burn longer and more evenly than the softer woods.

2. Make sure that you get what you pay for. I've been shorted on more than one occasion. I don't know if it's because the supplier thought I was a "city slicker" and wouldn't know any better or he didn't know himself, but inspect your order before you pay for it. Remember a "cord" is 4 feet × 4 feet × 8 feet. A "rick" is half that size: 2 feet × 4 feet × 8 feet. Some suppliers don't even know the difference!

3. Buy more than you need. You can always give it away to others who run out or barter it for items you didn't remember to get. You might want to run a test to see how much wood you burn a day. Then multiply that amount by the number of days you think you might be without power. It's better to have more than you need. Give yourself a margin for error.

4. Figure out a way to keep it dry. Take it from firsthand experience: Wet firewood is hard to light. Place your firewood in a tool shed, a garage, or under a tarp or plastic drop cloth. You might also want to elevate it on some wooden skids or packing crates. If you are using a tarp or drop cloth, make sure the edges are secure and won't blow away in a high wind.

5. Keep it out of sight. After January 1, 2000, firewood may become a prime target for thieves or desperate neighbors. While I don't mind sharing—provided I have enough for my family—I don't like making an involuntary donation! Like almost everything else you are storing, it is better to keep a low profile and not draw attention to yourself.

A Better Way to Stoke a Fire

While a fireplace insert is better than a fireplace, a wood stove is the best of all. It is more efficient than either one, and—as an added bonus—you can usually cook on top of one as well. Wood stoves are also aesthetically attractive and light up a room in a way that makes it warm and inviting. Depending on your budget, I recommend two sources for wood stoves: Vermont Castings and Vogelzang.

Vermont Castings produces six models, each of them featuring glass doors for viewing the fire, and all but one coming in a variety of decorative, enamel colors.

Vermont products are among the most efficient you'll find, and their cost is comparable to stoves without equally stylish features. You can see them online at <http://www.vermontcastings.com/products/woodstoves.htm>.

The least expensive model from Vermont Castings, the "Dutchwest Federal Convection Heater," comes in three different sizes (the other five come in only one size), with heating capacity between 700 and 2,400 square feet. Suggested retail for these three ranges between $909 and $1,249.

Vogelzang, on the other hand, provides the heat and function you need at an economy price. Its six models provide a wider range of styles from which to choose (from a low-profile "Boxwood" stove, to a "Pot Belly," to a three-door "Kitchen Stove"), and some can burn wood, coal, or even charcoal. The company's website contains pictures and complete descriptions at <http://www.vogelzang.com/index.htm>.

Vogelzang has recently been developing channels to direct-market these stoves to the public through its website and a toll-free number, but I encourage you to check local retailers for the best prices. In late December a friend of mine picked up a "Deluxe Boxwood" stove—suggested retail at the time of $449.50—for just $199.99 through his local True Value Hardware outlet. Other retailers carrying Vogelzang include Ace Hardware, Damark, Northern Tool and Equipment, and Target (a more complete listing can be found online at <http://www.vogelzang.com/dealer_info.htm>).

I found another great deal through Northern Tool and Equipment. At the time of this writing, that company was offering the basic "Boxwood" model for $139.99 (suggested retail $249.50) and the "Pot Belly" (suggested retail $599.50) for $299.99. If you're at all interested in a wood stove, there's no time like the present—meaning right now!—to give Northern a call. You can reach Northern at:

> Northern Tool and Equipment
> (800) 533-5545
>
> Cast Iron Boxwood Stove, Catalogue #172891-C134, $139.99,
>   plus shipping
> Cast Iron Pot Belly Stove, Catalogue #172892-C134, $299.99,
>   plus shipping

According to an official at Vogelzang—for the first time in its history—the company ordered a dozen cargo containers of stoves to arrive in early 1999, typically the "off-season" for wood stove buying. It plans to keep a close watch on demand as the year progresses, and hopes to keep product in stock—although for obvious reasons it can offer no guarantees. Also, whereas its most expensive model (the "Kitchen Stove") is usually a slow seller, it booked two full containers because demand for that particular design has been especially high. To order directly from the American importer, here is the information:

Vogelzang International Corporation
400 West 17th Street
Holland, MI 49423
Toll-free: (888) 229-6905
Voice: (616) 396-1911
Fax: (616) 396-1971

Space—The Final Frontier

For many people—especially apartment dwellers—fireplaces, inserts, and wood stoves are not an option. In those situations, one option is a kerosene space heater. Even if you do have a fireplace or wood stove, a kerosene space heater can come in handy if you plan to spend any time working out in the garage (perhaps splitting some of that nicely seasoned wood to use in your fireplace insert).

The first decision you'll need to make is how powerful a space heater to purchase. Jeffry Manning of MSI in Saratoga, Indiana, has been in kerosene heater sales and service for more than twenty years, and he says there are two basic sizes: approximately 10,000 BTUs (British Thermal Units, a standard heating measurement that is also used for wood stoves), and around 20,000 BTUs. The smaller one will heat an area of about 420 square feet, while the larger can tackle an area twice that size.

While many people are quick to choose the most powerful model available, Manning cautions that there are serious drawbacks to getting a unit that is too potent. One factor you need to consider is that most kerosene space heaters do *not* have a thermostat; the heater is either all the way on or completely off. Since heating up and cooling down are the roughest times on a space heater—and since those are the moments when virtually all of them emit somewhat unpleasant odors for five to ten minutes—it's best to pick one that won't need to be turned off very often. Given those cautions, I recommend you take a long, hard look at the 10,000 BTU-size.

If you're in the market for a space heater, give MSI and Jeffry Manning a call. MSI has been in business for more than fifty years and is quickly becoming a nationally recognized leader in kerosene heater sales. You'll find its products listed on the Internet at <http://www.msiwix.com>. Two models you should preview while you're online are the Toyostove "Radiant 41" (RC-41, $179.95), among 10,000 BTU models, and the Kero-Sun "White Clean 105" (WC-105, $199.95) at 23,000 BTUs.

The Radiant 41 is, as the name suggests, a radiating heater (heat comes out in only one direction) and will keep you warm for up to twenty-four hours on a single tank of kerosene—1.24 gallons. This is one of the easiest heaters to use, and it comes with a unique "lift out" fuel tank. This means you don't have to lug the entire unit out to the fuel source when it's time to refill; you just pop out the tank, refill it, and drop it back in. This is a nice safety feature too, since you can fill the tank in a separate location from the heating unit itself.

For larger heating needs, the White Clean 105 warms 950 square feet for up to sixteen hours on two gallons of kerosene. In contrast to the Radiant, the WC-105 is an *omni*-directional unit, providing convection heat in all directions. MSI does sell a high-end model, the "Double Clean 100," that comes with a dual-adjustable flame to provide either 11,200 *or* 17,500 BTUs. Flexibility has its price, however; the DC-100 sells for $299.95.

> Manning Service, Inc. (MSI)
> 101 East Washington Street
> Saratoga, IN 47382-0027
> Toll-free: (888) 537-6786
> Voice: (765) 584-2041
> Fax: (765) 584-4055
> E-mail: mail@msiwix.com

When it comes to buying kerosene, you have several options. The best thing to do is look in the yellow pages under kerosene and talk with a couple of dealers. Make sure you get K-1 kerosene. This is the type for burning indoors and doesn't give off an odor. When you go to buy it, ask twice to make sure you're getting K-1. Sometimes a dealer will call it K-1 when it's not, and you don't know the difference until you light it and have to deal with the smell.

In my neck of the woods, kerosene is typically stored in fifty-five–gallon drums. (You can also use plastic gasoline containers. However, be aware that gasoline is always stored in red cans and kerosene in blue ones.) The drums cost anywhere from $15 to $20 plus tax. You'll also need a pump. These cost anywhere from $20 to $30. (If your local kerosene distributor doesn't carry them, you can usually find them at a hardware store.) At the time of this writing, kerosene was selling at about $1.10 per gallon. According to most of the sources I checked, kerosene will keep indefinitely, as long as you keep it uncontaminated and free from moisture. But some kerosene heater manuals say that you should begin each season with fresh kerosene and not use any kerosene that is older than six months. I have been unable to verify this elsewhere. My guess is that the six-month recommendation is simply a safety precaution. But it's your equipment, so you be the judge.

It would be a good idea to have some plywood, plastic sheeting, and duct tape on hand in the event a window breaks or you need to wall-off part of the house to keep one room warm. If you do determine to shut down part of your house, make sure that you don't let your pipes freeze. Turn off the main supply valve to the house (usually in the basement or in the crawl space under the house), then open all the faucets, especially the lowest ones in the house, and let the pipes drain. You will want to collect this water in suitable containers so you can use it for your other needs. For drain pipes, you can pour a cup or so of automotive antifreeze down each sink or toilet.

Cooking Up a Storm

Regardless of what you use to heat your home in an emergency, you also need to think through alternatives for cooking. Of all the options I have discussed above, a wood-burning stove is the only option that can perform double-duty in cold weather, both heating your home and providing a surface for cooking. If you want to get really sophisticated, you can buy a wood-burning cook stove that provides even more surfaces for cooking and even sports an oven. But they are not cheap; most models I found are about $3,000 and up. If you choose one of the other options—a fireplace insert or a kerosene space heater—you will also need to come up with an alternative for cooking or warming your food.

If you do any camping, you may already have one of the best alternatives: a one- or two-burner camping stove that runs on propane, white gas, or even the same unleaded fuel you use in your car. No need to get fancy here, check out what's offered at your local Sam's Club, Wal-Mart, K-Mart, or specialty camping store. Most likely you can find something that fits the bill for $100 or less. I bought a three-burner Coleman model for $90. You may want to consider a model that runs on more than one kind of fuel just in case one or more types are unavailable, or simply hard to get, in 2000.

Yet another cooking option is an item called a "Volcano Stove." It is advertised as "the world's most efficient Dutch oven cook stove you've ever seen." This type of stove must be used outside or with sufficient ventilation, but works effectively on a very small amount of charcoal. Because of the stove's design, one Volcano and about 300 to 500 pounds of charcoal briquettes will last a family of six for about a year. In addition, the outside and bottom of the stove stay cool to the touch when it is in use. There are several models available. Prices start at about $79.95. You can reach the company at:

> Volcano Corporation
> 3450 West 8550 South
> West Jordan, Utah 84088
> Toll Free: (888) 532-9800
> Fax: (801) 566-1993
> Internet: <http://www.rmvolcano.com>

Finally, you may want to explore a solar cook stove. I haven't personally tried this, but if it works, it is certainly a low-cost alternative. You can build it for less than $10 and get the plans free at <http://www.accessone.com/~sbcn/cookit.htm>. You can also read all about solar cooking at the Solar Cooking Archive on the Internet at <http://www.accessone.com/~sbcn/index.htm>.

Another source of heat for cooking, which you may remember from your camping days, is Sterno. Sterno is gelled ethanol that comes in a can and is almost always found in the same retail stores as other camping supplies. Just light a match, touch it to the gel, and you have a flame over which you can suspend a pan of food. Not too fancy, but it gets the job done, so long as your cooking needs are not elaborate. In difficult situations Sterno also performs as a simple hand warmer, but be careful not to get your sleeves or other clothing too close to the flame.

Finally, for those who are chemically proficient and have access to a few items, you can actually make your own gelled ethanol. The recipe is found several places on the Internet, including <http://chem.csustan.edu/chemistry/stkrm/RECIPES/RECIPES-_sterno_.htm> (note: this link is case sensitive).

Beware the Silent Killers

At 6:30 AM Sue Hogan awoke and knew instantly that something was wrong. Very wrong. By now she had become accustomed to the chill that had hung in the house ever since the ice storm had knocked out power to her family's Ontario home, but today she sensed a more oppressive atmosphere—smoke. She quickly roused her husband Dave, who bolted downstairs to check on the oil-and-wood stove that had been their only source of heat for many days. He immediately yelled for Sue to get their three boys out of the house. The Hogan family slipped their bare feet into boots and then rushed outside with only that footwear and their pajamas. Within three minutes the home was ablaze, and by the time it was over, a lifetime of memories had been turned to ashes. "We feel very, very lucky we're all still here," said Sue later. "If we'd slept five minutes longer, we might not be."

While no one in the Hogan family had done anything wrong, what happened that January morning should be a firm reminder to us all about the dangers of warming our homes with fire. According to the National Fire Protection Association, America has the second-highest rate of death by fire in the industrialized world. And that's in a time when most people are not using items like wood stoves as their primary source for heat! Please, if you buy any of the wood-burning devices I've mentioned here, have your equipment installed and inspected by a professional. There are too many little mistakes that can be made, and too much is at stake, to cut corners on installation.

If you use space heaters, keep them at least three feet away from anything combustible, and teach your children to stay back at least that far. If you have to put a space heater on while a child sleeps, it's best that you sleep there, too. Children may attempt to get warm quickly, pulling the unit too close to the bed and risking combustion. The phrase "better safe than sorry" could not be more true when it comes to our loved ones.

In addition, you should have a good, high-volume fire extinguisher in every room where you plan to have something burning. You cannot be too careful when it comes to fire prevention. This is particularly true after January 1, 2000, when some of the emergency response services we take for granted could be operating at less than full capacity—if they are operating at all.

Moreover, flames are not the only killers. While the Hogans survived their brush with danger, at least three other Canadians perished from carbon monoxide poisoning.

Carbon monoxide is produced whenever any fuel such as charcoal, gas, kerosene, oil, or wood is burned. As long as the appliances using those fuels are maintained and used properly, the level of carbon monoxide is not usually hazardous. But if your wood stove, space heater, or other appliance has a problem, dangerous levels of carbon monoxide can result. And the consequences can be deadly. Between five hundred and seven hundred people a year die of carbon monoxide poisoning, and many others become sick and sometimes suffer permanent damage.

Carbon monoxide mimics the behavior of oxygen in the body, while withholding its benefits. Traveling through the bloodstream, it actually starves the body's tissues instead of feeding them. That's why it's so important for you to recognize the symptoms of carbon monoxide poisoning when you're spending time around any type of heating unit:

- Headaches
- Difficulty breathing
- Fatigue
- Confusion
- Nausea
- Vomiting
- Dizziness

If you think this sounds like what you experience with a typical case of food poisoning or the flu, you're right. That's why many people don't realize what's happening until it's too late. As carbon monoxide levels increase in the bloodstream, a victim's blood pressure begins to rise, often causing his skin to become pink, or reddish. If not recognized, this progression can lead to loss of consciousness, brain damage, and even death.

If you think you or someone else is experiencing carbon monoxide poisoning, go outside *immediately*. Open the doors and windows to the house to get fresh air. And, finally, visit a doctor as soon as possible.

Thankfully, there are a variety of reliable carbon monoxide monitors on the market today that can detect carbon monoxide before it reaches dangerous levels. You will find a number of models from makers such as First Alert at your local discount store for $40 or less. Depending on the size and layout of your home you may need to purchase more than one. Make sure, however, that the one you buy will run off batteries. (An electric one won't do you any good if the grid goes down.) First Alert makes two battery-operated models: the First Alert Replaceable Battery Carbon Monoxide Alarm and the First Alert Combination Smoke and Carbon Monoxide Alarm. Both run off a single 9-volt battery. The first one comes in a model that requires no installation; it simply sits on top of a tabletop or shelf.

Don't skimp on something that could save your life and the lives of your family. You can read many more safety tips from the Chimney Safety Institute of America at <http://www.csia.org>. This website discusses everything from chimney safety to choosing and storing firewood. It is an excellent resource.

Your First Line of Defense

This chapter would not be complete without discussing the need for accumulating adequate clothing. In truth, it is your most important weapon in the war against hypothermia. As you look ahead to the century rollover, and the unknowns it will bring, make sure every member of your family has several layers of warm clothing.

Obviously, you'll want to begin with an ample supply of underwear. Keep in mind that it may be very difficult to wash clothes regularly with all of the other new tasks you'll be doing and with the probable need to conserve water. In addition, long underwear is a must in colder climates.

Extra socks will also come in handy—you can wear two or three pairs at a time in extreme conditions—as will all the extra T-shirts, shirts, and sweaters that you can find. Finish off with a warm, weather-proof jacket or two, insulated gloves, a sturdy pair of insulated boots, and a number of hats and ski masks, and you're about ready for anything. Even if you have no way to heat your home, you can still survive in most climates if you have sufficient clothing.

Perhaps you're thinking: *Where am I going to find the money for all this stuff?* This is where you have to be resourceful. For example, I have a good friend who boasts that he gets everything he wears from garage sales. Not long ago he sat in his office pointing to his fifty-cent pants; no one would have ever known. Obviously the area in which you live is important to what you can find, but make it a habit to go in search of garage sale bargains. You'll especially want to watch for sales on the "other side of the tracks" where wealthier people sell once-worn outfits at pennies on the dollar. Also, don't be afraid to stop in at thrift stores and the local Goodwill. You never know what treasures you'll find in someone else's castoffs. Get creative, expend a little effort, and I think you'll be pleasantly surprised. You might also consider paying $1 to $2 extra for four more shirts to share or barter.

One task that will take a little more planning on your part is providing for your growing children. Make it a top priority to have shoes, boots, and warm winter coats that will fit your little ones this year—and next. The last thing you want to do is get to the year 2000 and discover that the supply chain is disrupted and that there's no way to get junior's size 6EEEE shoes. Think ahead and anticipate what you will need several months down the road.

Keeping Warm Between the Sheets

When it comes to bedding, much of the same common sense applies. The best option—if you can afford it—is to buy good down comforters for everyone. Ever since we bought ours I have been amazed at how much colder we can keep the house at night and still stay warm and toasty inside our bed. As a result, we have installed comforters on every bed in our home.

Velux blankets are another option, but any thick blankets will do—and the more the merrier! Search the house, find out just how many you have, and then seek to supplement your cache during those same visits to garage sales and second-hand stores while you're picking up surplus clothing.

You may want to consider buying a sleeping bag for every member of your family. These come in handy if you all have to sleep in the same room as your heat source.

There's nothing more difficult than getting up for a hard day's work after a sleepless night shivering in bed. You may have to fight the cold during the day, but you shouldn't have to at night, so make sure your bed will be warm enough.

🖥 🖥 🖥

Sue, Dave, and their three boys watched helplessly as their home burned completely to the ground. Yet even while firefighters were fighting a losing battle, a growing crowd surrounded the Hogans with offers of food, a place to stay, and clothes to wear. Those who had prepared were able to share their provisions. "It was just amazing," Sue remembered later. "Neighbors, friends, even people we didn't know. It takes something like this to show how blessed you are."

Miles away, Montrealer Jennifer Lynn reflected upon what she'd been through: "When the temperature is minus-eighteen at night (or lower), it's just too cold to stay in your house unless you're fortunate enough to have a fireplace or wood stove. Nobody will ever take electricity for granted again after this—especially in the winter!"

Y2K PREP TIP #8
Set Up an Emergency Survival Shelter

If you ever get stuck without heat, you may find yourself in a survival situation within your own home. If it's cold enough outside, if you've run out of fuel, or if your house somehow becomes damaged, you can literally freeze to death in your own home. What follows are just a few tips for surviving when your heat sources are few or weak.

1. Line your clothing with something that insulates. Survival-school instructor Susan Conniry says the pages of a phone book work very well. Put them as close to the skin as possible. Then put on as many layers of clothing as you can.

2. Find a small room that is relatively free of wind drafts. Make a shelter in a corner using the two walls of the room, plus a couple of mattresses to form two more walls. Essentially you're making a room within a room.

3. Make a "nest" in which to keep warm. Find every pillow, blanket, towel, and article of clothing you can, and create a pile or nest. If there are only two or three of you, you can get between the two mattresses on the floor like a sandwich and fill the edges with your nesting materials.

The key to keeping warm and surviving is to prepare as best you can, and *whatever* happens, think of ways to use what you have for your own good, and the benefit of others. No matter how ill prepared you are, there are ways to conserve what little warmth you have, even in the worst situations.

	Y2K PREPAREDNESS CHECKLIST				
Level	Action Step	Qty	Unit Price	Total Qty	Total Price
1	Purchase extra underwear for every member of your family.	N/A	N/A		
1	Purchase long underwear, if appropriate for your climate.	N/A	N/A		
1	Purchase extra socks for every member of your family.	N/A	N/A		
1	Make sure you have a sufficient number of jackets, hats, gloves, and boots for every member of your family.	N/A	N/A		
1	Purchase a down comforter or extra blankets for every bed in your home.	N/A	N/A		
1	Purchase a sleeping bag for every member of your family (optional).	1	$50 to $300		
1	Purchase fire extinguisher(s).	1	Varies		
1	Purchase carbon monoxide monitor(s).	1	$40		
1	Purchase waterproof matches.	1	Varies		
1	Purchase a Coleman cook stove.	1	$50 to $100		
1	Purchase some Sterno as a back-up.	1	Varies		

(Continued)

	Y2K PREPAREDNESS CHECKLIST *(Continued)*				
Level	*Action Step*	*Qty*	*Unit Price*	*Total Qty*	*Total Price*
2	Purchase a fireplace insert, or...	1	$1,200 to $2,000		
2	Purchase a wood stove, or...	1	$200 to $1,500		
2	Purchase a kerosene space heater.	1	$180 to $300		
2	Purchase firewood (price per cord), or...	1	$120		
2	Purchase kerosene (price per 55-gallon drum, including the drum).	1	$80		

Chapter Nine

Develop an Alternative Source of Energy

But you can be absolutely certain that your power will be off for one reason or another, when you least expect it.... And when it does, you can suffer along with the unprepared crowd, or you can take some steps so that you are merely inconvenienced or have no discomfort at all. It all depends on what you do next, right now, and in the way you think and plan.

—Anita Evangelista,
How to Live Without Electricity—and Like It

Residents of Pulaski, Tennessee, received an unwelcome early Christmas present in 1998, when, at about 9 PM on December 23, the electricity went out, plunging the region into darkness. Many people didn't get their power restored until the day *after* Christmas, turning many families' plans into what one resident termed a "disaster."

Yet for Stan and Tammy Pierchoski and their family, Christmas 1998 was as bright and warm as any other. In their sprawling 4,100 square-foot home, December 25 found the lights glowing as colorfully as ever on the tree, the turkey cooking in the oven, and all electrical appliances functioning as well as it did on any other day.

How? Simple: Stan operates his own "power company," using an ingenious combination of solar panels, a diesel generator, a small hydroelectric set-up, and a room full of deep-cycle batteries. The Pierchoskis' home operates only on the power they produce themselves.

Stan's concern about the stability and availability of electric power in the United States grew out of his fifteen years as a nuclear power engineer. As the 1990s dawned he became convinced he would live to see the day when electric power was the sole possession of the very wealthy, or of no one at all. Excessive regulation was making it harder and more expensive to construct new power facilities, and he could foresee the day when some major event would create a crisis.

Today, seven years since moving to a 140-acre farm in Middle Tennessee, he believes he sees the catalyst for electrical chaos: Y2K.

"When I first began to construct all of this everyone was telling me I was crazy," says Stan, "but I felt I needed to do it." Even Stan's wife Tammy wasn't too sure about the wisdom of his obsession at first, but after researching the Millennium Bug, "She was hugging my neck when she realized we're ready for Y2K."

Many older Americans still remember the day their home was finally hooked up to electrical power. It's not uncommon to find people over sixty-five who spent up to ten years of their lives in a "powerless" state. In one respect, that's a tremendous encouragement because it demonstrates that it's *possible* to live without electricity. Unfortunately, modern America has become so dependent on a diet of cheap and reliable power that going "cold turkey" would undoubtedly cause severe hardships. Some younger members of our society might even "starve" without their daily dose of MTV.

Unless you're independently wealthy, it's highly unlikely that you can maintain your current lifestyle in the absence of a monthly electric bill. It is unlikely that you will be able to power air conditioners, heat pumps, water heaters, electric stoves, and the rest. But with careful planning and action, you *can* generate enough power for lights and a little convenience. By using renewable energies like solar, hydro, and wind power—either by themselves or in combination with some form of fossil-fuel generator—you can produce adequate power in the event of Y2K-related utility failures. And when it comes to creating light to dispel the darkness, we can hearken back to tools our grandparents used, and that are still in use in the homes of many Mennonites and Amish today.

The bottom line? If you want an alternative source for light and power, you can have it… but you'll need to do some planning and take action *today*, before the supply problems get any worse. One thing you notice quickly when you research the alternative energy business is that it's largely a cottage industry, often run by husbands and wives out of their homes. This means just about all of the long-time suppliers are *very* busy right now. It's a good pay-off for their years of effort, but a difficult situation for you and me if we want back-up power when the Bug bites.

One more note about what follows: Unlike the vast majority of items discussed in this book, there are almost endless combinations of equipment that can be assembled to create your own unique power system. "One-size-fits-all" may sound nice when you're overwhelmed with preparations, but taking the easy way out in this category can leave you with serious regrets, and a severe dent in your pocketbook. Yes, you need to move ahead if you're going to develop an alternative power system, but without proper information you can spend a great deal of money very quickly and not get the results you need.

How Much Power Do You Really Need?

"Need" has become a horribly abused word in America. Nurtured by Madison Avenue, we have succeeded in elevating countless nonessential *desires* to the level of needs. But when it comes to alternative power you'll have to rediscover the true meaning of "need"—as in "necessity," "essential," and "absolute requirement."

Solar power, wind power, and hydropower are best suited for light- to medium-duty tasks such as lighting, small pumps and motors, and electronic equipment. Larger units that take care of heating and cooling, including electric space and water heaters, cooking ranges, and most conventional refrigerators, consume far too much power to be cost-effective. If you have an extra $50,000 to $80,000 to spare, you may not have to worry about cutting back on too much. If not, you likely have some tough decisions to make.

Although I will suggest a number of businesses that can help you design a complete renewable energy system, there are at least three bits of homework you need to get out of the way before you make a phone call. Not only will these exercises save time, for both you and the supplier, they could also save you literally thousands of dollars.

Lighten Your Load

Congratulations, you're about to start your own power company! Of course power plants are expensive to build, so you don't want to make it any larger than is absolutely necessary. The demand on a power plant is called the "load," and it's important to identify every possible way to lower the amount of power you'll need to produce, thereby lowering the cost of constructing your power plant.

For example, did you know that the common light bulb devours most of its wattage producing heat and not light? You can now buy compact fluorescent light bulbs that provide as much light as a typical 100-watt bulb while consuming only 28 watts of power. Imagine the savings you can realize over just a couple of years by replacing all of the bulbs in your house, saving 75 to 80 percent each. Lights of America produces these new bulbs, and in addition to saving power they last thirteen to sixteen times longer than an incandescent light bulb—up to 10,000 hours. Although several models won't fit certain lamps, I recommend the company's new

"Twister" bulbs, which produce as much light as 60-, 75-, and 100-watt incandescent bulbs (model numbers 2415, 2420, and 2425) while consuming only 15, 20, and 25 watts of energy, respectively. The Twister (named for its interesting shape) is available in many home centers, hardware stores, and major retailers. Check local stores for price and availability. Twister bulbs typically retail for around $10 each, but you may find them on sale directly from the manufacturer. These products can be viewed on the Internet at <http://www.lightsofamerica. com/product/electronic.htm>, but to ask about current phone specials you'll have to call its Energy Saving Products Service Center at:

> Lights of America
> Energy Saving Products Service Center
> (800) 377-4545

If you're in the market for a major appliance, check the power consumption levels of competing units. Though it used to be very cost-effective to spend up to $3,000 or more on a special low-energy refrigerator, some recent tests have shown that today's standard models use only marginally more power than the ultra-expensive ones. It's a matter of weighing the additional cost of a specialized appliance versus the cost of expanded solar, wind, hydro, or generator capacity.

Measure Your Load

Now that you've found ways to save on energy consumption, you need to make a list of all the items you'll want to power with your own system. Remember, unless you have a lot of money to spend, be as conservative as possible. Table 9.1 is an example to help you create and complete your own.

Begin in the left-hand column by listing all of the electric devices you'll need and want to operate during a brownout or blackout situation. Next you need to identify just how much energy each item demands. Somewhere on the back or bottom of the unit should be a panel or sticker displaying how many watts, volts, and/or amperes the device uses. Your goal is to learn the wattage, so if listed, write it down in the proper column.

If you can find only the amps and voltage, multiply those two numbers and the answer is the wattage (for example, my laptop is 3.5 amps and 18.5 volts; multiplying the two tells me that my computer uses 64.75 watts per hour). Next you multiply the watts per hour by the number of hours you'll use the item on an average day, and voilà, you have the daily watt-hours for that device. Add up everything you want to be able to use, and you'll have a watt-hour total. The only thing left is to multiply the total watt-hours by 1.3 (some experts advise 1.5 to be conservative) and it provides you with a total watt-hour figure. This is how much power you'll need to

Table 9.1:
Measuring Your Electric Demand

Electric Appliance or Device	Watts (Amperes x Volts)	Hrs/Day Usage	Watt-Hours (Watts x Hrs/Day)	Total (Rounded)
Laptop Computer	64.75	6	388.5	389
Stereo	100	4	400	789
Microwave Oven	1200	.2	240	1029
Dishwasher	1500	.5	750	1779
Toaster	900	.05	45	1824
Iron	1000	.1	100	1924
Electric Clock	3	24	72	1996
Kitchen Light (fluorescent)	30	4	120	2116
Washing Machine	500	.5	250	2366
Color TV (27-inch)	180	4	720	3086
Total Watt-Hours:	(inverter loss) x 1.3			4012

generate each day in order to keep everything going. Please realize as you make your usage estimations that some items will be used more in one season than another (for instance, you'll use more lighting in the winter, when days are shorter).

With these two steps complete, you can call a dealer and discover what power inverter and batteries are best for your needs, but I want to take you through one more exercise before we pause for a brief explanation of the various components in a renewable energy system. One question we have yet to answer is how we're going to generate the power that will be stored in those batteries.

Identify Your Resources

The final step before calling a solar equipment dealer is to identify what source or sources of energy are most plentiful in your particular location. If you're settled in the Arizona desert, it's a good bet that solar will be your best choice. On the plains of Wyoming, you might choose wind power. And if your property has a swift stream or creek flowing through it, you may be able to generate electricity using hydropower. In many locations a combination of resources will exist and you'll need to make a choice whether to go with one type, or more.

1. Solar Power. This is perhaps the best-known renewable energy source, but it's certainly not the least expensive. Estimates are that it costs around $6 for each watt of solar—or photovoltaic (PV)—generated power. Solar power is collected by panels that soak in the sun's rays, turning them into energy that can be used immediately, or stored in batteries for use later. If you live in the Deep South, or in the southwestern United States, solar power is probably a good source of energy for you.

Ask your dealer about the "insolation" rating for your area when you speak with him. This is a measurement of just how much sun power is available in your region, largely measured between the hours of 9 AM and 3 PM. Less sunshine during peak hours means you will need either to get more panels or to find a way to supplement this method of capturing energy.

2. Wind Power. Wind generation has been around for a long time in America. According to *Home Power* magazine, more than eight million mechanical windmills have been installed in the United States since the 1860s, some of them having operated for more than one hundred years. Windmills finally fell out of favor when the government subsidized the construction of fossil fuel power plants and utility lines in the 1930s.

If you have a good supply of wind (averaging at least eight to ten miles per hour) then your property is a candidate for a wind turbine. Wind energy does tend to follow seasonal variations, generally providing more power in the winter, whereas solar is better in the summer. Because of this, many people are combining the two for the best of both seasons.

3. Hydro Power. If you have a river, stream, or creek not far from your home, hydropower can be the most effective source of all. Solar panels can collect energy only while the sun is shining, and wind turbines when the wind is blowing, but if you have a healthy body of water you can make power twenty-four hours a day. All that is needed is a volume of water that is falling (flowing downstream) at a rate sufficient to drive your water turbine. The complicated formulas needed to make these measurements are included in materials from several of the suppliers I'll recommend below.

See It to Believe It

If you are interested in a renewable energy system and would like to see each of these systems in action, get the *Power House* video and workbook ($149 + $5 shipping and handling) from Power House, <http://www.powerhouse2000.com>. In the video, Stan Pierchoski demonstrates the system he uses to power his middle Tennessee home, imparting many of the lessons he's learned along the way. Watching this video and using the workbook will almost certainly save you time and money in constructing your own system. And, if you purchase a generator from the supplier listed in his workbook, it will refund the total price of the video and seventy-two–page workbook.

Stan Pierchoski
Power House
P.O. Box 725
Pulaski, TN 38478
(checks or money orders payable to: Roberts & Roberts Brokerage, Inc.)
Credit Card orders: (877) 363-9117 (9 AM to 9 PM Central Time)
E-mail: <tlmorey@usit.net>

The Parts of the Whole

There are a couple of more items in an alternative power system with which you should have at least a basic familiarity. While most people see only the items that actually generate the energy you need, the heart of your system, whether you use solar or hydro or wind power, is the inverter and the batteries. The batteries are the collection point for the energy you generate.

Without batteries, you would have power only when the sun is shining, or when the wind is blowing strong, or when the stream is flowing at a good rate. It is the task of the batteries to store excess power for a rainy day (or a windless day, or when the stream dries up). If you're going to skimp somewhere in your system, the batteries are not the place to do it. The more batteries you have, the more power you can store for those days when you can't generate it.

There are different types of batteries on the market today, and each has its advantages and disadvantages. What is right for your system and in your location may be entirely wrong for mine. Again, this makes it virtually impossible to recommend a specific product, though I can provide some brief background.

Lead-Acid Batteries

These are the most common batteries in the world. The battery in your car is a lead-acid battery, though with a very distinct difference when compared to those designed for use in alternative energy systems. A car battery is a "shallow cycle" battery, while those used in home power systems are called "deep cycle." Shallow cycle batteries are designed to supply a large amount of current for a short period of time. The drawback that makes them entirely unsuitable for use in power systems is that they can't tolerate being deeply discharged. If a shallow-cycle battery is repeatedly discharged more than 20 percent, it will have a very short life.

Deep-cycle batteries, on the other hand, are made to be repeatedly discharged by as much as 50 percent of their total capacity. They will last longer if discharged in only a shallow manner, and their performance will be severely affected if they are not immediately recharged. Another factor in the performance and life of these batteries is temperature. Lead-acid batteries lose 25 percent of their capacity at forty degrees Fahrenheit and 50 percent when the temperature reaches zero. If allowed to freeze, a lead-acid battery becomes virtually useless. The great advantage to lead-acid batteries is that they come with the lowest initial price tag, and when cared for, will last up to twelve years.

Similar to your car battery, these do need a bit of attention every three months to check the level of distilled water in the battery. This is another problem that can severely impact battery life if it is not closely monitored.

Among these the Trojan L-16 is highly regarded and recommended by a number of the sources to whom we have spoken.

Gel Cell Lead-acid

These batteries use a similar chemical reaction to produce their power, and because their contents are in a gel form, rather than liquid, they can be stored just about anywhere, at any angle, and with no possibility of being harmed by freezing. One caution about the gel batteries is that they are very sensitive to overcharging and excessive discharging. This means you need a good regulator to ensure long battery life.

Nickel-Cadmium Alkaline

NiCads are well suited for all power systems, and they last about five times longer than typical lead-acid batteries. Although the initial cost for a NiCad is much higher, you're able to use a higher percentage of its stored power without harming it, and thus you can afford to buy a smaller battery than you could with the lead-acid type. Depending on your unique electrical loads, and local weather conditions, the size needed could be as much as 30 to 50 percent smaller. One further benefit of NiCad alkaline batteries over lead-acid is that you can add to your battery bank without harming those already in use (experts warn that connecting new lead-acid batteries to others that have been used for more than six months often leads to rapid deterioration of the entire bank).

Nickel-Iron Alkaline

Nickel-Iron batteries are workhorses for a system that uses a lot of power in smaller loads. Dependability is the name of the game with these batteries; some made fifty years ago in the United States are reportedly still in use and working fine today. The alkaline electrolyte solution inside the battery makes this battery, like the NiCad, able to withstand extremely low temperatures.

So, which battery is right for you? That's a question only you and your solar consultant can truly answer. Cost, reliability, climate, and most importantly your specific usage will have a great impact on which type performs best in your system.

Inverted Power

When your solar, wind, or hydro system harnesses power and puts it into your batteries, it stores it as direct current, or DC power. However, virtually all of the appliances and devices in your house run on alternating current, or AC. An inverter provides the solution to this problem.

There are a wide variety of inverters on the market today, but be sure to get one that doubles as a battery charger as well. Your inverter should be able to operate automatically in an inverter-only mode (providing power to your appliances), in a charger-only mode (storing generated power in your batteries), or in an inverter/charger mode (doing both tasks at the same time). Those who have lived with these systems say you have no idea how important all of that is until you've lived with a system that requires some form of manual switching to go from one task to another.

When you size the inverter for your system, use the total wattage figure you developed earlier and find one of a similar size (you can spend more on one with greater capacity if you plan to expand your system at a later time). You also need to consider one more factor: surge power. If the inverter is expected to run an induction motor—like those found in washers, dryers, dishwashers, and large power tools—it must be designed to surge to help these motors get started.

Feel the Power: Fossil-fuel Generators

One more way to generate electricity, either as a stand-alone system or part of a more diversified renewable energy set-up, is by adding a fossil-fuel generator. This can be used as a direct power source for equipment, and as an alternative form of energy with which to charge your deep-cycle batteries.

While gasoline generators are undoubtedly the best known among the general population, they may or may not be the optimum source of back-up power for your home. Below we will compare the advantages and disadvantages of both gasoline and diesel generators. Consider these factors when choosing which generator is best for you and your particular situation:

- *Price.* If cost is a major concern, a gasoline generator may be your only choice. Though there are many good reasons to try and step up to one of the higher priced diesel engines, that simply may not be possible on your budget. Gasoline generators from our preferred supplier start at around $529 for 2,500 watts of power and go up to $3,699 for 11,000 watts. Diesel units, on the other hand, begin at $4,400 for 8,000 watts and move up to $5,990 for 16,000 watts.

- *Portability.* Whereas diesel generators are larger and must remain in a fixed location, most gasoline generators can be moved from place to place without any problems. The models I recommend either are small enough to carry or come with wheels that make moving them around a snap. If you need power on the go, gasoline may be the best bet.

- *Versatility.* If you believe you won't have a need for back-up power once the Y2K crisis has passed, smaller gasoline generators are more easily converted to alternative uses. You can put them to work yourself for recreation (camping, for instance), construction, or other uses around the home when a plug is not accessible, or you can simply sell them to someone else for one of these uses.

- *Fuel availability.* If the Millennium Bug disrupts all fuel sources, it makes sense that the first to be brought back online will be the one used in most applications. Undoubtedly, there would be an all-out effort to restore gasoline and diesel supplies to get as many vehicles as possible back on the road. But if fuel supplies are disrupted, you could use a simple siphon hose to get gas from your car's tank. Taking the last bit of gas from your car isn't ideal, of course, but the Millennium Bug may force us to make some tough decisions.

- *Long-term reliability.* Although Honda gasoline generators are the choice of an overwhelming majority of professional users, there is really no comparison when compared with the reliability of diesel generators. While Honda performs better than many, the average gasoline engine must be overhauled after around fifteen hundred hours of operation. Diesel generators, on the other hand, often produce for more than twenty thousand hours before needing major work.

- *Fuel storage.* Here again diesel has distinct advantages over gasoline. Untreated gasoline begins to break down between six months and a year. Using fuel additives or stabilizers (such as Sta-Bil), found at most automotive and hardware stores, can extend the life of gasoline up to a total of eighteen to twenty-four months. Diesel is less flammable than gasoline and can be stored untreated for up to twenty-four months, and treated for as long as ten years or more. To find a tank storage dealer in your area, look in the Yellow Pages under Petroleum Products Suppliers, or something similar. Many of these companies can sell you not only tanks but also the fuel.

Gasoline Generators

You're probably at least somewhat familiar with the gasoline generators found in most hardware stores and warehouse home centers. These typically supply from five hundred to five thousand watts of electric power using a gasoline-powered motor that is then connected to equipment, or sometimes even right into your home's wiring system. (Note: Always make sure your home is completely disconnected from the local power grid *before* plugging a stand-alone generator into your system. If you have any doubt about safety, consult an electrician.)

Should you choose to go with a gasoline generator, the smallest I recommend is an entry-level 2,500-watt Honda EN2500 ($529), or the deluxe EM2500 ($1,049), which are enough to run your refrigerator, a radio, and a few high-efficiency fluorescent lights. You could also replace the refrigerator with a microwave or other device for short intervals. The key is to use the generator for brief periods of time in order to cool down your refrigerator and run some essential devices and then shut it off until the next day. Small generators are simply not built for constant use over many days or weeks. Adding a furnace fan and perhaps a water well pump to your power load takes you up to the next level, a 5,000-watt Honda EZ5000 ($1,269) or the fully loaded EM5000 ($1,959).

Once you've calculated the number of watts you want to use simultaneously, go to the Mayberry Sales and Service site on the Internet, <http://www.mayberrys.com>, and choose its page on Honda generators. Once you're there, you'll find models that fit just about any level of back-up power generation and that fit most every budget.

Mayberry's is a family business that's been operating for nearly forty years, and it is a leading Honda distributor. When a couple of my friends ordered generators late in 1998 they were pleased with the prompt, professional service they received.

Mayberry Sales & Service, Inc.
232 Main Street
Port Murray, NJ 07865
Toll-free: (877) 41-HONDA (414-6632)
Voice: (908) 689-3310
Fax: (908) 689-3342
E-mail: <sales@mayberrys.com>
(Please include the brand, model number, and your zip code.)

Diesel Generators

After carefully researching the marketplace, I'm convinced that diesel generators offer the best quality and features for the money. They are safer, more durable, and more reliable than gas generators. They can also handle larger loads. If you are serious about getting off the power grid, diesel is the way to go.

The problem is that, because of Y2K, many diesel generator manufacturers have been absolutely swamped with orders. Some have stopped promising delivery times. I searched long and hard for one that I felt good about. I even had an energy consultant review the various specs and do the leg work. Based on that research, I recommend the Lister-Petter Generator. These generators come in a variety of sizes, starting at 7.5 KW all the way up to 20 KW. They are also water-cooled, which, from my perspective, is a nonnegotiable. As a bonus, they are made in America.

The best prices and service I have found on these units are from RJK Power, North America. (This is the company I bought from). When you place your order, RJK Power gives you a "delivery guarantee" with teeth in it—the company shaves an additional amount off the price for every day the delivery is late. You can't beat that! You can contact the company at:

RJK Power, North America
7607 W. 61st Street
Overland Park, KS 66202
Toll-free: (888) 436-0172 x925
E-mail: <skylar@unicom.net>
Internet: <http://www.rjkpower.com>

Make sure you mention this book; RJK Power will give you an additional discount off its already great prices.

When it comes to fuel storage, make sure that you check your local ordinances. Many cities have strict laws about fuel storage. You need to be familiar with how to store various types of fuel, whether gasoline, diesel, or kerosene. You can read a thorough treatment of this topic on the Internet at <http://www.4unique.com/storage.htm>.

One final note. It is possible to spend an inordinate amount of time researching generators. Unfortunately, you don't have much time. Already, supply lines are thin. My advice: don't let the best become the enemy of the good. Something is better than nothing, and if you delay too long, you may well end up with nothing. You need to make a decision and just live with it.

Contacting a Renewable Energy Dealer

There's much more to be learned, but you should now be ready to contact a renewable energy dealer and identify more accurately what you need, and how much it's going to cost. If you're new to the renewable energy scene, it's sufficient to acquaint yourself with how the systems work, go through the three steps outlined near the beginning of this chapter, and get on the phone to talk about what system will best meet your specific needs. Then, if you learn that your appetite for power was a bit bigger than your financial resources, you can begin to economize some more until you reach an acceptable cost.

Northwest Energy Storage. Rob and Jean Shappell of Northwest Energy Storage come very highly recommended. If you're looking for someone with excellent prices and a willingness to help, it's hard to beat Northwest. The company has an extensive website you can browse at <http://www.nwes.com/index.html>. Also, it has an extensive catalogue you can order that walks you through the basics of renewable energy, in language anyone can understand. Whether you're looking for solar, wind, hydro, or generators, Northwest can help from A to Z. It has equipment packages listed on its site as examples, but the company will want to help you specially design a system that is absolutely the best for your location. You can contact Northwest at:

Northwest Energy Storage
P.O. Box 137
Colburn, Idaho 83865
Orders: (800) 718-8816
Fax: (208) 265-3677
Tech Support: (208) 263-6142

Mr. Solar. "Mr. Solar," Charlie Collins, has lived "off the grid" since 1974, and he's put together probably the most extensive website in the world on renewable energy. If you like to get lost while learning new things, here's where you can do it: <http://www.mrsolar.com>. If you want to design your own system, Charlie's site has everything you'll need. If you're looking for something easier, they have a large number of basic systems specially designed with Y2K in mind. Pricing begins at just over $1,400 for a system with inverter and batteries only, and rises to $54,000 for a system that could keep your home lit and buzzing all day and night long. Check out the complete systems at <http://www.mrsolar.com/Solarkitcabin.html>. Mr. Solar also produces newspaper columns on alternative energies, and you'll find a large number of them archived on the site. No matter what you're looking for, Mr. Solar seems to have it all. You can contact him at:

DO IT Homestead, Inc. (Mr. Solar)
P.O. Box 852
La Verkin, UT 84745
Voice: (435) 877-1061
Fax: (435) 877-1070
E-mail, orders only: <MrSolar@netins.net>
E-mail, questions: <CharlieCollins@MrSolar.com>

Note: Please be aware that mail is by far the slowest way to correspond with Mr. Solar.

Abraham Solar Equipment. Mick Abraham is an innovator. His operation is not large, but he specializes in developing highly organized, self-contained solar power units for people who don't want to hassle designing their own. Oh, he'll do that too, but it's his interesting systems that have gained him fame. Not the least expensive source, but a good one nonetheless. You can contact him at:

Abraham Solar Equipment
P.O. Box 957
Pagosa Springs, CO 81147
(800) 222-7242

Solar Extreme. This is another company that has taken some of the sweat out of designing a system by providing standard packages for Y2K. You can view these packages, and request a free e-mail of its report "Off the Grid in 2000 and Beyond" by visiting its site at <http://www.solarextreme.com>.

SolarExtreme.com
c/o Telemagic, Inc.
P.O. Box 6848
Thousand Oaks, CA 91359-6848
Voice: (805) 299-9365
Fax: (805) 299-9379
E-mail: <info@solarextreme.com>

While alternative energy is in most cases not absolutely essential to your survival, there are some things no one wants to live without. Renewable energy is certainly the power of today, and tomorrow, but in some cases Y2K preparation means returning to the wisdom and technology of yesterday.

Light in the Darkness

There has always been something romantic about turning off the lights and putting a match to a few candles. That flickering orange glow has a special attraction, but soon, if enough utilities malfunction in the year 2000, that flickering glow may be the only thing that provides light after the sun goes down.

If you're like the many people who won't be able to afford an extensive alternative energy system, unless you want to live by candlelight you need to come up with a way to create light in the nighttime. One choice I highly recommend is an Aladdin kerosene lamp. There are many lamps on the market today, but the reason I have chosen Aladdin is because their patented burner assembly is clearly the leader in producing the greatest amount of light, without a lot of sooty smoke. The Genie II (C6106-kerosene) provides the same illumination as a 60-watt incandescent bulb. This is their least expensive model (retail $59), the glass chimney brings the height of the lamp to 20 inches, and it includes a beautiful thick glass base. You may also want to look at the Watchman Aluminum Lamp (retail $75, though it's not uncommon to find them for less in many stores).

You may order directly from Aladdin, from one of their many retailers around the country, or from Y2K Prep. In addition to the lamps, you should also consider getting some extra wicks (N230) and additional mantles (R150). Call Aladdin for a free catalogue and additional information at:

Aladdin Mail Order
P.O. Box 100960
Nashville, TN 37224
Toll-free: (800) 456-1233
Fax: (615) 748-3105

If you choose to order from Y2K Prep,* you can contact that company at:

Y2K Prep
251 Second Avenue South
Franklin, TN 37064
Toll-free: (888) 925-2844
Fax: (615) 794-8860
Internet: <http://www.y2kprep.com>

---

*As noted earlier, I have a financial interest in this company, because I found that it offers the best value at the best price and has one of the shortest delivery times available.

Charging into the Future

No matter what small, battery-powered devices you have, you must address how you're going to keep those gadgets going when your batteries wear out. One answer is to get rechargeable batteries using the same Nickel-Cadmium technology we talked about earlier in renewable energy batteries. Of course you may be wondering: How do I recharge them if the power isn't working? It's a good question, and I have an answer.

An Internet site called Y2K Approaches offers a number of solar-powered battery chargers that can keep batteries for your radio and other equipment charged and ready. I suggest you order the Universal Solar Battery Charger, which lists for $29.50 and can charge any size battery from AAA to D. You can order from <http:www.y2kapproaches.com/products/solar_products/univbc.htm>. It's a great product.

What's even better is that the site's creator, Chris Root, has offered to give readers a 10 percent discount just for mentioning this book when you order. So click on over to his site and browse for awhile. In addition to some very simple solar fans for the house, he also has one that is installed in a safari helmet to blow cool wind in your face as you plant those nonhybrid seeds.

Y2K Approaches
P.O. Box 888
Gambrills, MD 21054-0888
E-mail: <webmaster@y2kapproaches.com>
Internet: <http://www.Y2Kapproaches.com>

Summary

If you are going to install alternative energy devices, you need to think seriously about holding "trial runs," where you actually try to live without electricity for a short period of time. If you do this now, while you still have guaranteed access to electricity, you will have the opportunity to correct any problems and make it much easier on yourself later. You will also learn a great deal about those areas for which you are prepared and those on which you have additional work to do.

Y2K PREP TIP #9
Pool Your Resources with Others

Although the media have enjoyed conjuring up images of the lone survivalist, isolated two hundred miles from the nearest living soul, one thing we all need to come to grips with is that we really need each other. If the division of labor truly breaks down in the coming months, the most important people in our lives—after our immediate family members—will be our neighbors and others with whom we have connections.

Though it's possible that a few rugged individualists here and there can survive on their own, the vast majority of us can only (to paraphrase the Beatles) get by with a little help from our friends. One of the best things you can do now is to begin informing those who live in your area about your concerns, identifying those who will be immediate allies in your preparations.

Being able to divide research categories and tasks among several people will give you the edge you need right now to make speedy progress. As an example of how this applies, let's look at how pooling resources can help when it comes to alternative power, specifically generators.

Generators are a great source of back-up energy, but they aren't much good if you don't have adequate fuel to make them run. Before you spend thousands of dollars on a generator, think through how you're going to stockpile enough gasoline, diesel fuel, or propane to keep it running for as long as you think you'll need it.

If you're planning to remain in an urban or suburban environment the first things you'll need to research are your local ordinances on fuel storage. Many locales have laws forbidding the installation of large fuel tanks, often for good safety reasons. If this is the case where you plan to ride out the Y2K storm, you need to consider alternatives that will allow you to obey the law, while still being able to accumulate enough fuel to provide power for your needs.

One good possibility is to find someone in your church, neighborhood, or community group who owns a rural or farm property, within a reasonable distance, where zoning ordinances allow for large storage tanks. Consider pooling financial resources to accomplish more than any one person could do on his own. Perhaps you can convince a local church to prepare its building as an emergency shelter with heat, light, and a usable water well in case the surrounding neighborhood falls victim to the Bug.

Remember, those who live near you who cannot or will not prepare are the first ones who will be at your doorstep when they realize that you have power (or food, or heat, or anything else they need) and they don't. Forming alliances and pooling resources now will enhance your ability to help yourself and others when the need arises.

	Y2K PREPAREDNESS CHECKLIST				
Level	Action Step	Qty	Unit Price	Total Qty	Total Price
1	Decide whether you have the resources to pursue alternative energy and how much you have to spend.	N/A	N/A		
1	At the very least, come up with an alternative source of light.	N/A	N/A		
3	Assuming you are going to pursue alternative energy, determine how you can "lighten your load."	N/A	N/A		
3	Fill out a chart similar to Table 9.1 in order to determine your electric demands.	N/A	N/A		
3	Identify your resources.	N/A	N/A		
3	Order Stan Pierchoski's *Power House* video tape.	1	$154		

Part Four

Money

Chapter Ten

Build an Emergency Cash Reserve

Ah, take the Cash, and let the Credit go.
>—Omar Khayyám, "The Rubaiyat"

In the fall of 1998 I was invited to be one of two keynote speakers at a state-wide Y2K Community Briefing. The other speaker was a well-known, highly visible Y2K expert, who had been—and continues to be—widely quoted by the media. Though we had not had the opportunity to meet, we were each familiar with the other's work. I was looking forward to the evening, hoping to engage in a little behind-the-scenes "shop talk" with the other speaker, but immediately after I introduced myself he began to take me to task. He had heard that I was publicly encouraging people to set aside an emergency cash reserve fund equal to a month's worth of living expenses. At that time the Federal Reserve had just announced that it was stockpiling an additional $50 billion in the event of Y2K-related bank runs. I thought it was only prudent that private citizens engage in a similar kind of cash contingency plan. My fellow speaker vehemently disagreed.

"What you are advocating is *completely* irresponsible," he chided, poking his finger into my chest.

"How so?" I asked.

"If everyone follows your advice, it will cause a banking collapse," he continued with great intensity.

"Perhaps, but I don't think everyone *will* follow my advice, so it's kind of a moot point," I argued.

For the next twenty minutes we went back and forth, until I finally blurted out in exasperation, "Okay, so what are you going to do *personally*? Are you going to leave your money in the bank?"

Without missing a beat, he exclaimed, "*Of course not*, but I'm certainly not going to advocate it publicly!"

I couldn't believe my ears. I looked at him in disgust, shook my head, and walked away.

Unfortunately, since that time I have met and talked with many so-called "Y2K experts" who are espousing one thing in public and another in private. I am not going to give you the public "spin" on banking that is so often set forth by many Y2K pundits. To the best of my ability, I want to provide you with the facts and the truth. Moreover, the recommendation I am going to give is the same one I offer in public *and* private. More to the point, it's what I am *personally* doing.

In order for you to understand the recommendations I will be making at the end of this chapter, you need to understand the nature of modern money and the fragility of the entire monetary system. *Don't let these things scare you—read on!* You need to understand this in order to be sufficiently motivated to take the appropriate action. I will try to keep it as simple as possible.

The Coming Monetary Collapse

Just as blood transmits food and oxygen in mammals, *money* is the lifeblood of any economy. Not only does money transmit information about present and future consumer needs and wants, it enriches us all by providing for the division of labor. Rather than every person learning how to do every possible task, we each specialize in what we do best, and others pay us to do those jobs for them.

Today, however, the money we use has no value in itself, and nothing stands behind it but the public's confidence that other people will accept it for food, groceries, and gas. Money is now mostly electronic—bank deposits, credit cards, debit cards—other than the little bit of paper money and token coins made of copper and nickel.

But what you must understand is that *without electricity and computers, today's money ceases to exist.*

In order to plan for the future, we must take into account three possible phases in the breakdown of money:

> *Phase 1: Electronic money dies.* But the inertia of the public continues to support the paper currency and coins for six months or so.

> *Phase 2: Paper currency dies.* After a while, people begin to refuse paper currency and ask for barter, such as aspirin, matches, salt, coffee, ammunition, antibiotics, and even food.

Phase 3: A new standard emerges. A monetary system must have some foundation of value. Gold and silver, which have been regarded as money for forty-five centuries, are the most likely candidates for rebuilding the system.

Each of these phases requires a different strategy if you are to survive. In this chapter I will deal with Phase 1 and the need for stockpiling cash. In Chapter 11 I will deal with Phase 2 and the need to collect items to use as barter. Finally, in Chapter 12 I will discuss Phase 3 and the need to radically alter your long-term investment strategy by moving into assets that hold their value through crises and over time.

The System Is Inherently Fragile

In order to understand the nature of our modern monetary system, you need to grasp two things: the role of *public confidence* and the nature of the *fractional reserve banking system* itself. When you mix these two ingredients, you have a recipe for disaster. The problem is not that Y2K could *cause* a monetary collapse; it's that it could be the *catalyst* that pushes an already fragile system over the edge. Let's look at these one at a time.

Public Confidence

In trying to understand money, the first thing you need to ask yourself is: "What makes money valuable?" *Modern Money Mechanics*, a booklet published by the Federal Reserve Bank of Chicago,[1] explains how the banking system works. In it, the authors begin by answering this very important question:

> In the United States neither paper currency nor deposits have value as commodities. Intrinsically, a dollar bill is just a piece of paper, deposits merely book entries. Coins do have some intrinsic value as metal, but generally far less than their face value.
>
>   What, then, makes these instruments—checks, paper money, and coins—acceptable at face value in payment of all debts and for other monetary uses? Mainly, it is the confidence people have that they will be able to exchange such money for other financial assets and for real goods and services whenever they choose to do so [emphasis added].[2]

Very few Americans understand that their banking system has such a thin margin for error, or that it rests entirely on confidence.

Ask your friends what they think backs up U.S. currency. Some will say the gold in Fort Knox; a few may mention the government's silver stockpile. The truth is, *nothing at all stands behind U.S. currency*. It is, in the words of John Exter, former vice president of the Gold Operations for the New York Federal Reserve, an "I.O.U. nothing." It is a note, a "promise to pay," but the only thing the government or Federal Reserve will pay is another bill just like it.

Because gold and silver are inconvenient to transport, especially in large quantities, private banks long ago began issuing paper money as a kind of "warehouse receipt." Soon, people began trading the receipts rather than the commodities they represented. The bills were redeemable for silver or gold *upon demand*. The currency was thus backed by the silver and gold sitting in the banks' vaults.

It didn't take long for some bankers to realize that if they could ever separate the receipts (bills) from the metals they represented (gold and silver), they could print money with abandon and make themselves rich. This is exactly what happened in 1933, when the United States went off the gold standard. Consequently, we now have a fiat monetary system that is based on nothing but the public's willingness to accept these Federal Reserve notes as payment. These notes are no longer warehouse receipts. The warehouse is empty and the money is gone. All we have left are pieces of paper with pictures of dead presidents on them!

The real problem is that this *confidence* is a human phenomenon—a psychological phenomenon. For example, you might go in to work one day after a good night's sleep and a good breakfast and have a lot of confidence in yourself. Or, you might go into work after having had an argument with your wife that morning, worried about a presentation you didn't spend enough time on, and have very little confidence in yourself.

Confidence works the same for crowds. When the entire crowd decides at the same time that it doesn't have any confidence in the banking system anymore, you have a panic and a *bank run*. But it's actually worse than that. Not only are the gold and silver gone, but the paper money isn't there, either.

The Fractional Reserve Banking System

Banks around the world operate on a *fractional reserve system*. That means that the banks keep in reserve only a *fraction* of the money that they owe to depositors. When a customer deposits $100 into his savings account, the bank does not pull down an envelope, write the depositor's name on it, stick in the $100 bill, and place the envelope on a shelf in the vault. Rather, it credits the depositor's account and gets busy loaning out his deposit to borrowers. Bankers know that not every depositor will ask for his money at the same time, so they need to keep only a *fraction* of his deposit *on reserve*. Most people think this system is okay—*until they find out how tiny the reserves are*.

Even people who understand the system don't seem to grasp the reserves' minuteness, measured against the whole system. If you ask them, they typically guess that banks must keep a 10 percent reserve, or perhaps 20 percent, against deposits. That isn't even close.

How much money does the Federal Reserve keep in reserve against deposits? If you call a Federal Reserve bank and ask an economist, you will get a fascinating answer. In November 1998, when I went through this exercise for myself, here's what I discovered.[3] (You can follow along with Table 10.1: "Currency Banks Hold in Reserve.")

- First, you have to understand how much the banks owe to depositors. To get this number you add *Total Checkable Deposits* to *Total Time Deposits* to get the *Total Deposit Liabilities* for the banking system. As of November 1998, that amount was $3,772.4 billion (or roughly $3.8 trillion).

- Second, you must understand how much cash (currency) the banking system has on hand to cover these liabilities. As of November 1998, the Fed had $42.53 billion in *Required Reserves*. In other words, against the $3.8 *trillion* the banking system owes depositors, it is required to keep only $42.53 billion in reserve.

- Now, to see how low this number really is, divide the *Required Reserves* by the *Total Deposit Liabilities*. This results in 0.0113 or *1.13 percent*!

Here's what that would mean in real life. If everyone went to the bank to get their money, only two things could happen. Either the first 1.13 percent of the people in line would get all their money and the rest would get nothing, or every person in

Table 10.1:
Currency Banks Hold in Reserve

Total checkable deposits	$ 622.8 billion
Plus total time deposits at all depository institutions	$3,149.6 billion
Equals total bank deposits	$3,772.4 billion
Required reserves, not adjusted for changes in reserve requirements	$ 42.5 billion
Total required reserves divided by total bank deposits	1.13%
Implied multiplier equals the reciprocal of reserve percentage	87.59

line would get $1.13 for every $100 he had deposited. I can't get really excited about either one!

Mix the Two

When you take the reciprocal of the reserve requirement (3,722.4 billion/42.5 billion) you get the "multiplier." That tells you how many dollars the whole banking system can *and will* create from a new dollar deposited. That number is $87.59. In other words, for every $1 deposited, the banking system can create $87.59 in loans. For every $100 deposited, it will create $8,759. This is called *leverage*.

It also works backwards, however. For every $1 withdrawn from the banking system, the banks must reduce loans by $87.59. This is called *deflation*.

But there's another problem. Withdrawing cash from the banking system to stuff in mattresses waiting for Y2K reduces the *velocity of money*. Money passing round and round in the system slows down, effectively reducing the money supply. This, too, is called deflation.

Is the picture taking shape? Unless the Fed can slam reserves into the deflating system, the money supply collapses (except for those people holding cash outside the banking system, whose cash becomes more and more valuable). Borrowers default, loans go sour, and the money supply shrinks further.

Don't forget, this is the "scientific" system that the Federal Reserve Act foisted on us. The fragility and vulnerability of this system has not recently emerged under the threat of Y2K—*it has always been there*. It is the nature of a fractional reserve system. Without fooling the public—without the public's confidence—it dies.

We're right back where we started. When the confidence disappears, so does the banking system. And the money. That's why you must act quickly. There is simply not enough money in the system to meet the demand that will be generated in a crisis.

The Money Supply

Okay, so what exactly happens when the public's demand for cash rises suddenly, for instance, because they're concerned about Y2K? How much currency exists in the country to satisfy that demand? (You can follow along with Table 10.2: "Domestic Currency in Circulation.")

As of November 1998 the Federal Reserve of St. Louis reported $502.66 billion in currency issued. First, not all of that currency circulates *domestically*. From total currency in circulation you must subtract the currency in banks (not in the public's hands) and currency circulating overseas. Since the U.S. dollar is the world's reserve currency, *about two-thirds of the issued currency circulates outside the United States*. Subtract currency in banks ($44.1 billion) and currency circulating overseas ($335.1 billion) from total issued currency, and we find that only about $123.4 billion circulates

Table 10.2:
Domestic Currency in Circulation

Total currency in issue (circulation)	$502.7 billion
Less vault cash used to satisfy reserve requirements	($ 35.3 billion)
Less reserve balances with Federal Reserve Banks not adjusted for changes in reserve requirements and not seasonally adjusted	($ 8.8 billion)
Less 66.6 percent of currency circulating overseas	($335.1 billion)
Total currency in domestic circulation	$123.4 billion

inside the United States. That's all the "cash" available to support an economy of $8.4 trillion!

What does that mean for you and me? For 270 million Americans, that works out to $457.04 per head. How much currency is that for each of the roughly 100 million American households? About $1,234. (See Table 10.3: "Currency Available Per Person or Per Household.")

How long will that currency last each household? The average household enjoys an income of about $35,000 a year, or $2,916.67 a month. Divide $1,234 by $2,916.67, and *surprise!* there is enough U.S. currency in domestic circulation to provide each and every American household with 42.3 percent of a month's supply—enough to last from the first of the month until the thirteenth. Sorry, you won't be eating dinner on the thirteenth, or on any other day during the rest of the month.

But don't despair yet. In August 1998 the Federal Reserve announced (along with New Zealand, Australia, and Great Britain) that it would increase currency to

Table 10.3:
Currency Available Per Person or Per Household

Domestic currency in circulation divided by 236 million Americans equals currency per head, in dollars	$ 457.04 per head
Domestic currency in circulation divided by 100 million households equals currency per household, in dollars	$1,234 per household
Currency per household divided by average monthly income equals months of median household income in domestic currency circulation	0.423 months

accommodate the demand from Y2K (see Table 10.4: "Impact of Increased Money Supply"). To the $123.4 billion estimated to circulate domestically, the Fed will add its two months' worth of unissued currency—$110 billion—and another $50 billion extra the Bureau of Engraving and Printing (BEP) will print. That raises the total to a hypothetical $283.4 billion in domestic circulation. Give the Fed the benefit of the doubt. Assume (contrary to what we already know) that *overseas* demand from places like Russia, Latin America, and Asia (where local currencies are crumbling) won't siphon off some of that new currency. This is a *great* improvement.

Now, for every American man, woman, and child, $1,049.63 will be circulating. That works out to less than one month's cash supply for every household. Okay, so now you'll eat every day of the first month. Sorry, though, next month, no grub.

Perhaps you're thinking, *Why can't the Fed just* print *the money in the event of a banking panic or the Y2K crisis?* One simple reason: It does not have the capacity.

The BEP has testified to Congress that it prints about nine billion currency notes a year. Even in an emergency it could not double that production.

The BEP expects a one-dollar bill to last about a year before it is worn out and must be removed from circulation. If all of them lasted *two* years, each year the BEP would be printing one-half of the total currency supply. It takes BEP one year to print one-half the currency supply, which amounts to nine billion notes.

So the total *currency* supply must be about 18 billion notes, but the 18 billion notes represents only 8 percent of the total *money* supply, if we add in bank deposits. To cover the rest of the money supply now furnished by bank credit, the currency would have to increase to 225 billion notes (18 billion divided by .08).

Table 10.4:
Impact of Increased Money Supply

Currency in domestic circulation	$123.4 billion
Plus the Fed's two months' of unissued currency	$110 billion
Plus Fed's announced currency increase	$50 billion
Equals total cash available for domestic circulation	$283.4 billion
Future domestic currency in circulation divided by 270 million Americans equals currency per head, in dollars	$1,049.63 per head
Future domestic currency in circulation divided by 100 million households equals currency per household, in dollars	$2,834 per household
Future currency per household divided by average monthly income equals months of median household income in domestic currency circulation	Less than 1 month

Even at *double* the BEP's current production rate, it would need 12.5 years (225 billion divided by 8) to print enough money to cover the entire money supply.

Obviously, we're not even close. There is no way the federal government could supply enough currency in a Y2K emergency to carry on normal business.

On the other hand…

If 18 billion currency notes are going to have to do the work of 225 billion currency notes, then those 18 billion must experience a *substantial* increase in value. Since you can't assume that the mix of the notes ($1s, $5s, $10s, etc.) would be identical between the 8 percent currency money supply and the 100 percent currency money supply, it is mere guesswork to figure out what sort of up-valuation the currency would receive in this emergency. It is certainly possible that if an emergency shut down bank computers, U.S. currency could rise to at least ten times its present value. Or, to put it another way, you suddenly purchase ten times the amount of goods for the same dollar.

The Dominos Are Already Falling

As we have seen, the system is inherently fragile. It is based on little more than public confidence. And at some point, when enough people figure out what is going on, the system will collapse when people utter four little words: "I want my money." The truth is, this phenomenon has already begun.

I Want My Money

In recent years, large amounts of money flowed overseas to the Asian nations, based on an unrealistic estimate of their future productivity and consumer demand. "Hot money" poured in seeking a high return, and, as always happens when a fractional reserve banking system is paid to expand loans, the economies overbuilt their capacity to produce. Inventories started piling up. Suddenly someone got nervous. They said, "I want my money. I don't want any more promises to pay, I don't want any more pie in the sky, I want my money—*today*." And that's why the Thai *baht* had to be devalued in 1998. It spread from there to other parts of Asia and is now spreading like a virus across the globe. *Confidence is collapsing.*

This has set loose a train of devaluation of assets and debt from country to country—a kind of rolling panic. Think of it as "credit-questioning": Is this asset—loan, stock, bond, currency—really worth this much? It starts with the riskiest firms and climbs the ladder of credit-worthiness, questioning the soundness of every debt. It keeps on climbing until at last it reaches *sovereign debt*, the debt of a nation.

In our time, every currency is a derivative of a country's national debt, i.e., the value of the currency depends on the creditworthiness and soundness of that nation's debt. Thus eventually the credit questioning must reach that country's national currency. What we saw in 1998 was that the world economy had blown into a huge and unsustainable debt bubble, and the currency was highly overvalued in such countries as Thailand, Indonesia, Malaysia, Korea, and the Philippines.

Then what happened? The local currencies collapsed, the stock markets collapsed, businesses went bankrupt, and gold rose in terms of those local currencies. In fact, the graph of gold in those local currencies looks like the mirror image of the drop in the currency. Currencies go straight down, gold goes straight up.

What happened? This process of credit questioning is the process of *deflation*, letting down the debt-bubble. It is a rewriting of all the assets in the economy. Again, people are asking the question, "Is it really worth that much?"

Questioning the credit is not itself "monetary deflation." Rather, it is a deflation of *assets* that leads to monetary deflation. Why? Because all modern money is *borrowed into existence*. Banks carry those loans on their books as "assets." They have *created* "money" (bank deposits or "liabilities") against those assets. You could say they have "monetized" assets, and you'd be exactly right.

But when the loan goes bad, the dough disappears. By definition, when debt is cancelled in a system where money is borrowed into existence, an equal amount of money is cancelled. The money supply shrinks: *Deflation is a decrease in the money supply*.

Meanwhile, something else happens. Every loaner loses confidence, whether banker or depositors. When people lose confidence, they run out of assets and into cash. They stop lending, and they stop borrowing. This lowers the velocity of money (deflationary in effect), but it also prevents new money from being borrowed into existence to replace what has been destroyed. Very soon deflation becomes a self-reinforcing cycle.

Global Deflation

Now, the Federal Reserve whines and moans about inflation, which is silly. It doesn't fear inflation, any more than B'rer Rabbit fears the Briar Patch. It knows who creates the money and who controls the interest rates. If it can control money creation and interest rates—which it does—it can control inflation. So, inflation presents no problem to the Federal Reserve.

But it cannot control *deflation*. You don't need to prove that theoretically, because within living memory it has occurred in the United States. In 1929, after a long inflation (engineered by the U.S. Federal Reserve Bank and the Bank of England), there came a point at which someone said, "I want my money." The credit questioning began. The stock market took a big dive, and a terrible depression resulted.

Then came the deflation, the revaluing of every asset, and the writing off of bad debts. The deflation was so mighty that in spite of every measure that the New Dealers tried to use to "reinflate the economy"—and they tried a *lot* of measures—

the deflation got worse. In fact, in 1937 the stock market crashed again, worse than 1929. Only World War II bailed the country out of deflation.

This is not a theoretical proposition but rather something we all know about. We have heard the stories from our parents and grandparents who lived through the Great Depression. Ask them what it was like. They always reply, "We didn't have any money. Money could buy a lot, but no one had any money." That's deflation.

Today things might work out differently in their particulars, but the economic process of deflation has started. Credit questioning continues all the way around the globe and all the way up the credit-worthiness ladder until finally it reaches the debt that claims to be the least risky: *U.S. government debt*. That's ultimately where we are headed.

The Derivatives Revolution

That U.S. government debt has a *derivative*, and we all know what derivatives are because we've read about them in the newspapers. Gold, for example, is *not* a derivative. A piece of gold is a self-validating asset. It's not anybody's debt; it doesn't depend on anybody to make payments to make it good; it doesn't depend on anyone's output, or profit, or confidence, or solvency. It is just gold. It's valuable because everybody wants it.

A derivative, on the other hand, is an instrument that has no value in and of itself, but *derives* its value from some underlying asset. Want an example of a "derivative"? Pull a dollar bill out of your pocket and look at it. That's a derivative.

Since 1980 there has been a *derivatives revolution* in financial markets. The fractional reserve principle has been applied to a vast array of real property and commodities and, especially, *financial assets*, to monetize and securitize them.

Mortgages, for example, *monetize* a real asset. The bank creates money for a construction loan, and every two-by-four, every brick, every light bulb that goes into that building is turned into money. The mortgage is a financial asset, but it is a very illiquid and long-term financial asset on the bank's balance sheet. To liquefy them, mortgages are pooled to form "mortgage-backed securities." Once pools of mortgages have been "securitized," they become *liquid* and can be traded easily. Well, it can be traded easily at least until the market shuts down in a panic, as it did in September 1998.

To reduce risk (economists promised us) you can use derivatives. For example, if you own mortgage-backed securities, you don't want to run the risk of interest rates rising, reducing the value of your security. So you enter into a repurchase agreement with some other bank trading department which obligates them to buy the mortgage-backed security if rates rise, say, one hundred basis points. Now the other bank has a *liability*, a derivative it must make good, but most of the time it doesn't have to make good. Most of the time things flow along pretty evenly (i.e., "low option volatility")—*until you have a panic*. And this, of course, is only one example. Derivatives are as complex and numerous as the mind of man can conceive.

Late in August 1998, there was a panic with the hedge fund Long Term Capital Management (LTCM). Two economists who had won Nobel Prizes for their work with derivatives were running things, and they laid a bet. Not a very good bet, but one that appealed to economists with computers who are used to things flowing along pretty evenly for a long time. They bet that the interest rate differential between low class sovereign debt (say, Russia and Third World countries) and high class sovereign debt (the United States) would narrow. It didn't. The Russians went belly up instead.

On equity (paid up cash money) of $4 billion, LTCM had borrowed $130 *billion* from banks. (Remember "banks," the people who have an interest in loaning as much money as possible, even to excess?) This second level of pyramiding the economists then pyramided into a $1.25 trillion *derivative exposure*. Without warning, suddenly, somebody said, "I want my money." Lights out. End of story. Or at least, *almost* the end of the story.

Options and all sorts of other derivatives, they promised us, would reduce risk. By now everything that could be securitized has been securitized. Today, it is estimated that $132 *trillion* in derivatives float around the world. That represents a vast house of cards of pyramided financial assets—castles built out of thin air resting on thin air. The whole shebang is just begging for deflation, and it has already begun. It has already devastated newly developed Asia worse than our own Great Depression. It has spread to Russia, and now it threatens Latin America and Canada and Mexico. Global deflation is responding to banking and monetary excesses that have continued more or less unbroken since World War II.

If you think it's not serious for us in America because we are not a developing economy, take a look at Japan. The best-known Japanese stock index, the Nikkei, topped in late 1989 at 40,000 points. That was eight years ago. Recently it just broke to new low ground under 13,000! That's about a third of its peak value. For us in the United States of America, a two-thirds plunge from a Dow high of 9,374.26 points would land us at 3,124.76 points.

The Japanese have been trying to get their economy "started again" since 1989. Rest assured, they are smart people; they are *not* stupid. They are not all sitting around asking, "Gosh, why did this happen to us?" They know exactly what happened.

In case you think Greenspan's "cure" of lower interest rates will work indefinitely, look at the Japanese. They have dropped their prime rate as low as one half of one percent—it has even gone *negative*—and still their troubles persist. Their banks have about $1.2 *trillion* in bad debts on their books… still. Put that in perspective: The U.S. savings and loan crisis back in the 1980s was a $500 billion problem—*half* a trillion dollars.

The Stock Market Bubble

We face another problem in addition to global deflation and the derivatives collapse. I am not a stock market prognosticator, but certain events have plain interpretations. In July 1998 the Dow Jones Industrial Average reached a high of 9,337. On August 4, 1998, the Dow Jones Industrial Average signaled a technical trend change according to Dow Theory, a technical system for timing stock market purchases. This Dow Theory trend change signal is very reliable. Since that time we have seen the stock market stumble and fall as low as 18 percent from the high. Recently it has recovered—even made new highs—but neither the Transports nor other indices have confirmed that new high.

Don't believe the seductive voices that promise that the worst is over. You have not yet seen the worst. You haven't even imagined the worst. Down days of 300 or 500 points will turn into down days of 3,000 points. It's coming. Count on it.

For the Dow to return to historic valuations according to price/earnings ratios and dividend yield and book-to-value, it would have to sink to somewhere between 5,000 and 3,000 points, depending on the measurement. If you have stocks or mutual funds, I want to make a radical suggestion: *Cash out completely*. The people who get destroyed in a crash are those who hesitate. If I'm wrong and the market goes up, fine. You can always get back in. What have you lost in the meantime? Whatever appreciation you could have earned and whatever penalties you may have incurred for getting out. It comes back to the issue of risk management. As the old-timers are fond of saying, "It's better to be two months early getting out than a day late."

Just tell them, "I want my money." And don't leave yourself in the position of being a creditor to brokerage houses or mutual funds. When the market melts down, everybody will run for the doors. You can call your broker or mutual fund, but there won't be any answer, because the phones will stay busy for days at a time.

Y2K Could Be the Last Straw

Into the context of an inherently fragile system, a growing global deflation, a derivatives collapse, and a stock market bubble comes the biggest technological challenge the world has ever faced. It is a problem that threatens the integrity of financial data and the viability of electronic currency itself. Every problem I have discussed to this point threatens to reduce the value of your assets and money. *Y2K, however, threatens to make them vanish altogether*. If the computers aren't fixed, and the banking system does not reach compliance, then the world's digital assets go up in smoke. Poof! They're gone... at least for a time.

While it's true that the banking and financial sectors are the furthest along with their Y2K repairs of any industry segment, there are several things you need to keep in mind.

Compliance of a majority of banks is not enough. Although there is not one bank claiming to be Y2K-compliant at the time of this writing, you can expect to see this change as we move through 1999. You should not be surprised when this happens. Even the most gloomy of the doomsayers expects the majority of banks to meet or beat the deadline. The real question is what happens if 5 to 25 percent of them *don't* make it? What kind of impact will the noncompliant minority have on the compliant majority? What happens to our economy? What happens to our way of life? It's anyone's guess, but the high-tech world we live in is an amazingly interconnected tapestry of suppliers, vendors, and customers. Problems with the few can cause serious problems for the many. And not much else will work if there's not a reliable means of completing financial transactions.

Compliance within the banking industry is not enough. Banks are dependent on third-party suppliers and a complex web of infrastructure providers to deliver their services. Unless electrical utilities can keep the juice flowing, the bank's computers cannot continue running, even if they are compliant. Without the telecommunications infrastructure, the banks cannot field customer concerns, complaints, or directives, not to mention complete electronic fund transfers via the phone lines. And if enough businesses fail as a result of Y2K, and especially if those businesses default on their loans, banks could be sucked right down the drain with them.

Compliance of all the banks within the United States is not enough. It goes without saying that we live in a global, interconnected, and interdependent economy. Problems in one part of the world inevitably cause problems in other parts. As much as we would like to "quarantine" noncompliant countries, it's simply not possible. We are as dependent upon them for foreign trade as they are on us. Already, we are experiencing the effects of the Asian economic crisis. If their banks are not compliant, it will only exacerbate the problem for them and for us.

Summary

Based on the discussion above, we can draw several important conclusions that will influence our strategy for the future:

- *Currency may be in short supply.* As we have seen, there isn't close to enough money to cover all the deposits on record. In fact, if only 2 percent of the people attempt to draw all their money out of the bank at one time, the system will collapse. If things start moving in this direction, I fully expect the Federal Reserve—and the U.S. Treasury—to declare a limit on cash withdrawals.

- *The purchasing power of currency may rise in the short term.* Deflationary forces at work in the economy will cause prices to fall. Simultaneously, the lack of available cash will cause the value of dollars—if you can get them—to rise. This is precisely what happened in the Great Depression, and it could happen again.

- *The value of currency may completely collapse in the long term.* For a while, people will continue to use Federal Reserve notes because they are familiar. But eventually, people will lose confidence, and when they do, the bottom will fall out. When this happens—if it does—the current currency won't be worth the paper it's printed on.

A Strategy

It should be apparent by now that a monetary and financial crisis is coming our way. What prudent defensive action should you take? I am not trying to terrorize anyone, and I am certainly not trying to create panic. I *am* trying to motivate you to take action, and therefore I recommend a fourfold strategy.

1. Get into cash—now! I recommend that you shoot for accumulating a cash stockpile equal to at least one month's living expenses for your family and preferably six month's worth. If your gas, groceries, house note, utility bill, insurance, and so on, total $1,500 a month, then you should aim to set aside $9,000 in cash. I know for many people that will simply be impossible. Don't worry about it; do the best you can and leave the rest to God.

2. Acquire both small bills and coins. Up to a third or a fourth of your total stash should be in coin (the currently circulating "token" coins, not gold or silver) and the rest should be in bills no larger than twenties. Get as much as you can in one-dollar bills. The reason is that if the value of currency rises, you will be able to buy more with smaller denominations.

3. Build your emergency reserve incrementally. Get some extra cash every couple of weeks, put it back, and don't touch it. If you have a friend in a business that handles lots of coins, you could buy coins from him. Otherwise, just ask the teller for a couple of rolls of quarters or halves every time you visit the bank—or your local grocery store.

4. Store your money where you have twenty-four–hour access. For most of us, this means our homes. At the very least, it would be a good idea to store it in a fire-proof document box and hide it in your house. Keep bank balances to an absolute minimum. When the door of opportunity finally shuts—whether because of government-mandated control or Y2K—it won't be opening for some time to come. You don't want to get stuck with your assets where you can't get to them. The only place I'm totally comfortable with is in my personal control.

Some have criticized this strategy, echoing the comment of the Y2K expert I quoted earlier: "If everyone follows your advice, it will cause a banking collapse." That's true; as we know, if even 2 percent of the population follows my advice it will cause a banking collapse. But *any* financial recommendation, if followed by everyone, will result in chaos.

For example, let's say that I started telling people that XYZ Company is the stock buy of the century, and that you should immediately cash out of your existing portfolio and put it all in XYZ stock. What would happen if everyone did this? Well, every other stock would crash and XYZ would go through the roof. But guess what? Not everyone is going to follow this advice. In fact, the vast majority will not. Only a few will follow my recommendations, and, as a result, only a few will profit if I'm right, or be hurt if I'm wrong.

Another objection I often hear is that stockpiling money is *dangerous*. After all, if I have $17,000 (more or less) tucked away under my mattress, I will be a prime target for burglars, thieves, and other assorted criminals. Right? Well, possibly. But this assumes that (1) they know I have it, (2) they are willing to risk life and limb to get it, and (3) they can find it once they get there. With a little ingenuity, I can *mitigate* each of these risks—and so can you. Like anything else, all it takes is a little planning and the willingness to take the necessary precautions.

But even if you maintain your privacy so they don't know you have it and buy a dog and a gun to defend yourself if they figure out you've got it, you still can't *eliminate* the risk. Alas, life is fraught with risks. Only you can decide what the greater risk is: leaving your money in the bank in digital form with the possibility of having it evaporate overnight—or stockpiling some cash and risk the possibility of being robbed. It's up to you; I can't make this decision for you.

A Final Warning About Withdrawing Cash

I am concerned about much of the advice I often hear about withdrawing cash (currency). If you are not careful, ignorance and lack of preparation could run you afoul of the cash-reporting regulations and earn you a criminal prosecution.

I am not an attorney, and I won't presume to give you legal advice, but, based on my research, the federal government requires banks to fill out a Cash Transaction Report (CTR) whenever someone withdraws more than $10,000. Shortly after that law was enacted, Congress added the crime of "structuring," i.e., ordering your transactions to *avoid* the reporting requirement. For example, it is the crime of structuring if you intend to withdraw $12,000 in total and withdraw $2,000 a day over six days in "related transactions" to avoid the reporting requirement.

The danger is that federal courts in most jurisdictions have interpreted these statutes and regulations as "strict liability statutes." That means that *intent* is not necessary to break the law—you don't even need to know that it is a crime. Structuring is being interpreted exactly like a speeding law—if the speed limit is 40 miles per hour, and you are driving 50 miles per hour, you're "guilty" whether you knew the speed limit was 40 miles per hour or not.

If you withdraw as much as you can from an ATM in several transactions, when you intend to withdraw more than $10,000 in total, that could be interpreted as the crime of "structuring," even though you have no criminal intent and the money is not the proceeds of some specified criminal activity.

I would suggest that if you want to withdraw sums of more than $10,000, you should approach your bank officer openly. Ask him about the bank's Y2K compliance. Tell him that you are concerned about the Y2K problem and you intend to withdraw some cash for your own protection. You understand the bank doesn't inventory much cash, so what is the best way to withdraw the cash to make things easy on it? (Afterwards you should send a letter to the bank officer memorializing the appointment.) You can expect the bank officer to try to convince you not to withdraw any cash. Be polite, but firm. After all, it *is* your money.

At the appointment you should include one other person (*not* your spouse) with you, to act as a witness. If the banker asks you to fill out a CTR, *fill it out; do not object or refuse*. In any event, the remote danger of filling out the CTR is far, far smaller than the *imminent* danger of a criminal prosecution for structuring.

One lawyer suggests another similar method. Ask your lawyer to write your banker a letter like the one in Table 10.5. Attach supporting articles as you think necessary. Note that I am not giving legal or financial advice. This letter is included for information purposes only. Be sure to consult your own attorney for specific advice for your own situation.

Table 10.5:
Sample Letter to Avoid Structuring

[Date]
[Bank Manager's Name]
[Bank Name]
[Address]
[City, State Zip]

Dear [Manager's Name]:

My clients, Mr. and Mrs. [Your Name], are customers of your bank. They are concerned about the "Year 2000 Computer Problem." Congressman James Leach, Chairman of the House Banking Committee, made the following statement in committee hearings on November 4, 1997:

"Experts also emphasize that the problem must be fixed properly and on time if Year 2000 related problems are to be avoided. I was intrigued by a statement Federal Reserve Chairman Alan Greenspan made a couple of years ago. He pointed out that 99 percent readiness for the year 2000 will not be enough. It must be 100 percent. Thus, the message seems clear: all financial institutions must be ready; federal and state regulatory agencies must be ready; data processing service providers and other bank vendors must be ready; bank customers and borrowers must be ready."

Clearly, bankers, both domestically and internationally, are not ready yet, though I understand they are making good progress. In a Reuters article, "Financial Industry Seeks to Avoid '2000' Timebomb," Edward Yardeni, chief economist for Deutsche Morgan Grenfell, wrote, "It's a trivial problem, but it's overwhelming." Mr. Yardeni has also stated that 5 to 20 percent of banks may fail in the recession which he predicts will accompany the Year 2000 Problem.

Consequently, my clients wish to begin withdrawing cash from their [list accounts and CDs as they come due] to safeguard their hard-earned savings.

As you are aware, federal law requires the reporting of cash withdrawals of more than $10,000. In addition, the federal law prohibits "structuring" or ordering withdrawals so as to avoid this reporting requirement. For example, if an individual withdraws $2,500 per day over five days with the intent to avoid the reporting requirement, that individual is subject to prosecution under the "structuring" statute. The withdrawals are subject to seizure, and, if convicted, the individual is subject to a five-year prison sentence and $250,000 fine.

Federal courts in most jurisdictions have interpreted these statutes and their associated regulations as "strict liability" crimes. This means that the intent (mens rea) component of a crime is not necessary to be convicted of committing the crime. In fact, one need not even know that the action of making such a series of withdrawals is a crime.

My clients wish to comply with the law in every respect and request your assistance to do so.

It is understood that your bank does not keep large quantities of small denomination bills and coin on hand. Please inform me of your bank's policy for making large cash (or periodic $3,000 to $5,000) withdrawals. For example, how much notice is required for you to arrange to have the cash available? On withdrawals of less than $10,000 may the Currency Transaction Report (CTR) be filed immediately or do you request that it be filed each time the aggregate withdrawals since the last CTR exceed $10,000? What security do you provide between the teller's window and your parking lot?

I look forward to your prompt response. If you have any questions, feel free to contact me.

Yours truly,

[Your Attorney's Name]

cc: Mr. & Mrs. [Your name]

Y2K PREP TIP #10
Where *Not* to Stash Your Cash

Okay, so you've decided to stash away a little cash. Good idea. But where do you put it? In general, you want to apply the *twenty-minute rule*: Go through your house and ask yourself, "If I were a burglar with twenty minutes to clean out this house, what would I steal and where would I look?"

There are probably a million and one places to hide your money, but, according to experts, you want to avoid at least four places:

1. Don't put it under your mattress. The image of Grandma tucking a little money away in her mattress for a "rainy day" is almost a cultural icon. This is one of the first places thieves look. Moreover, it's not a very convenient place to put money anyway, so avoid it.

2. Don't put it in your dresser. This is also one of the first places thieves look. People often store cash and valuables there.

3. Don't put it in the deep freeze. The phrase "cold, hard cash" came from this practice. Maybe at the time it was a clever place to put it. But now it is a primary target for burglars.

4. Don't put it in a safe. The problem with a safe is that it screams, "Valuables inside!" Most safes that can be purchased are easily cracked by professionals. If you are going to get a safe, buy a substantial one and hide it behind a false wall or floor.

If you want some ideas on places you can store your cash, see Appendix F, which discusses hiding precious metals and other valuables.

| | | | Y2K PREPAREDNESS CHECKLIST | | | | |

Level	Action Step	Qty	Unit Price	Total Qty	Total Price
1	Start with at least a 72-hour emergency cash reserve fund.	N/A	N/A		
2	Acquire a one-week supply of cash.	N/A	N/A		
2	Determine where you will stash your cash.	N/A	N/A		
3	Acquire a one-month supply of cash.	N/A	N/A		
4	Decide how much more you want to stockpile and begin making incremental withdrawals.	N/A	N/A		
4	Revisit where you are hiding your money; make sure it is as secure as you can make it.	N/A	N/A		
4	If you are going to withdraw more than $10,000 send a letter to your banker (see Table 10.5).	N/A	N/A		

Chapter Eleven

Collect Items You Can Use As Barter

A pessimist sees the difficulty in every opportunity; an optimist sees the opportunity in every difficulty.

—Winston Churchill

Barter is defined as any economic activity without the use of money. It has been around as long as mankind has been around. In many cases, barter is convenient, as between two neighbors who exchange services—say, the use of a lawnmower in exchange for the use of a chainsaw. But in a modern economy, of course, barter would be cumbersome and awkward. (Imagine buying a new car and paying for it with cows, or picking up the morning paper at a newsstand and handing the guy a bag of sugar.)

Even primitive cultures realized early on that money was a lot more convenient for buying, selling, and trading. It spurred economic activity by allowing people to conduct business in more distant regions.

Money works fine for trading goods and services—as long as it represents something of value and all parties using it agree on what that value is. If the supply of money is disturbed, if people no longer trust that the money represents something of value, or if people cannot agree on what it is worth, then the monetary system is in trouble.

Nothing since the 1930s has threatened our monetary system like the Y2K Problem. Most monetary transactions today are processed electronically with computers. If these vast and complex computer networks experience disruptions because of the Millennium Bug, our monetary system could be paralyzed. We may be unable to buy or sell or trade using money. We may be forced to engage in barter to acquire the things we need to survive.

If our monetary system collapses, U.S. dollars could suddenly become worthless. On the other hand, since over 98 percent of all deposits in the banking system exist only in the form of electronic entries, Y2K breakdowns could cause the supply of dollars to shrink drastically. Currency—actual coins and paper notes—could suddenly become extremely valuable (the law of supply and demand).

In times of severe economic crisis, however, governments have been known to issue a whole new currency, so even if the value of cash skyrockets in the wake of a Y2K meltdown, U.S. dollars could be replaced by a different form of currency and eventually be worth nothing more than the paper they're printed on.

It's impossible to predict which scenario will occur. All we know for sure is that our economy and monetary system are threatened by the Millennium Bug. Being prepared to barter is one of the most critical steps you can take to protect yourself and your family.

Valuable Barter Items

Virtually any object can be traded. As long as one person thinks an object has value, and owns a different object of value that he is willing to trade, you can barter the items. But certain items have a much greater value than others—especially during a time of crisis. This is why I have a hunch that if Y2K causes people to become cold, hungry, and thirsty, those hotly traded, high-priced "Beanie Babies" will suddenly have zero value.

In an emergency situation where people are required to engage in barter, the goods that are most valuable fall into three basic categories: gold, guns, and grub. But bartering is not exclusively done with goods and products; services can also make excellent barter items.

Gold

By gold, I mean any item which can be used as a substitute currency. You can't eat, drink, or generate heat with precious metals, but people throughout history have agreed that these metals have value because of their unique properties and scarcity. In times of uncertainty, the value of precious metals rises. The three primary metals are gold, silver, and platinum (see Chapter 12 for details and analysis). These metals are valuable barter goods in the form of either bullion or minted coins, although coins are much more convenient and more recognizable by most people.

Gemstones and other types of jewelry are often less effective barter items because their value is more difficult to determine. They are not as readily accepted as a form of currency.

Guns

The barter category "guns" encompasses all self-defense and personal safety products. In emergency situations the law enforcement and criminal justice systems may be paralyzed or nonexistent. Mobs of lawless thugs could roam through once-quiet neighborhoods, putting the lives, health, and property of others at risk.

Firearms are always valuable items when societal structures break down, and ammunition is usually even more valuable. Ammunition is an excellent barter item because most gun owners keep only a few boxes of ammo on hand. Also, it doesn't take up much space and can be easily broken down into various amounts. You can trade ten rounds, fifty, one thousand, or any other amount. It's almost as easy as making change with money.

Other items could also be included in this self-defense category, such as knives, barricades, fences, and more. But firearms and ammunition are by far the best defensive barter items during a crisis.

Grub

This category includes any consumable product that people need or want. Food, water, fuel, medicine, cigarettes, liquor, coffee, and batteries are just some of the goods that make valuable barter items. If Y2K disruptions make it difficult for people to obtain the basics, then the basics will be in great demand as barter items.

Services

The big question is, what services and skills do you have to offer? In our high-tech, specialized, division-of-labor world, people often have narrow and limited talents. Being able to generate and analyze quarterly sales reports for the West Coast territory may be a skill that a large corporation finds valuable, but in a crisis it is worthless. Trade union skills will be in hot demand: plumbing, carpentry, welding, and car repairs. Doctors, dentists, nurses, and EMTs will be able to barter their services for goods; lawyers, accountants, and bureaucrats likely will not.

This is the time to think about your own talent, experience, education, and hobbies. What can you offer to a low-tech society? What tools are on your work bench in the basement? (Do you *have* a work bench in the basement?) Can you build or repair things? Can you cook or sew, hunt or fish? Can you cut hair? Can you sing or play a musical instrument? If the power goes out for an extended period, the silence will be deafening. All of our TVs, stereos, tape players, and other electronic devices will be useless. People will be starved for entertainment and most likely will trade valuable goods in exchange for a performance. The "troubadour" just might make a comeback.

If you have no valuable skills, then the only service you can barter is basic grunt labor. You may have to chop wood for three days to equal a fifteen minute visit from a dentist. And don't forget, middle-aged sales managers make lousy lumberjacks.

You may not be able to offer your services at all if enough strapping twenty-year-olds are willing to work. If your skills are limited, including your strength and endurance, then it is even more important to stockpile valuable barter items.

Diversity—Spread the Wealth

In building up a store of barter items, you don't want to put all your eggs in one basket. Don't collect a large stockpile of the exact same item. Even if it's one of the historically excellent items, like gold coins, canned food, or ammunition, something unexpected could occur. The government could confiscate gold (they've done it before) or outlaw guns and ammo (they're doing it now). Your stockpile of the same food item may have come from a contaminated production run; many people in your area may not have a taste for it; or the guy down the street may have a basement filled with that same item.

You must remember that in a emergency situation where barter is the main method of buying and selling, your market will be a very limited area. Transportation could be restricted and you may be able to trade only within your community, or just a small portion of your community. You don't want to flood your marketplace with a product—even a valuable product. The law of supply and demand will quickly reduce its purchasing power.

It is much better to make a list of many valuable barter items and build up supplies of each. It will make you a more effective and successful barterer, plus it will be easier to unload any surplus stock once the emergency situation ends.

The following is a list of valuable barter items compiled by Rainer Stahlberg, author of *The Complete Book of Survival*.[1] (Although I would never own some of these items myself, for moral reasons, I am providing the information because these items have a proven track record of being valuable during emergencies. Each person must decide for him- or herself which items to collect.)

- Liquor
- Tobacco
- Soft drinks
- Drugs (including antibiotics)
- Salt
- Chocolate
- Ammunition (mainly .22 LR)
- Matches
- Fishhooks
- Lighters and flints
- Razor blades

- Firearms
- Feminine hygiene supplies
- Birth control pills

Many other products and goods would also make valuable barter items. The list includes: candy, cookies, chewing gum, pocket knives, hand tools, nails, screws, nuts and bolts, lumber, rope, candles, playing cards, soap, toothpaste, disposable diapers, toilet paper, reading materials, pens, pencils, paper, nonelectric appliances, Q-Tips, dental floss, cough drops, and chapstick.

Collect a "Smart" Barter Supply

You want to keep three things in mind when choosing which barter items to collect: potential value, convenience, and post-crisis use.

Potential Value

In our current materialistic society, a cornucopia of goods is available on virtually every street corner. We can go down to the nearest department store, drug store, or supermarket and choose from an incredible array of items. Almost anything we can imagine—whether a necessity, a luxury, an exotic import, or just a frivolous knickknack—can be purchased in our consumer culture at the drop of a hat (or rather, the drop of a credit card).

This remarkable economic engine is in danger of grinding to a halt when Y2K failures occur. In an emergency situation, many items that we now take for granted will become scarce. Think of basic survival items: food, water, fuel, health care, and self-defense. These items will be at the top of people's lists.

But don't stop there. Once people have their basic survival needs met, they will want to recapture some of those old feelings they had before the emergency occurred. What are some simple pleasure and pamper items? What are some products that people don't really need, but really enjoy?

If our modern manufacturing and transportation systems break down, items that are complex to produce or have been brought to us from great distances will become scarce. Take a stroll through a department store, drug store, or supermarket and think about the items on the shelves. Ask yourself, "Do people need/want/enjoy this item? Will this item be scarce in an emergency?"

Convenience

You want to choose barter items that are easy to move and easy to store. Gasoline is very valuable in an emergency. But it's a difficult barter item for the average person, because it is hard to store in large quantities. (I don't recommend that you line your basement with plastic and fill it up with gasoline.) You should try to obtain as much gas as you can safely store before the crisis happens, but unless you have access to special storage tanks, it will not be a good barter item.

As mentioned earlier, ammunition is a very good barter item. It does not take up much space, it doesn't rot, and it is easy to move. Convenience is important. You don't want to do extra, unnecessary work when bartering. You want to make each transaction as nice and easy as possible.

Post-crisis Use

The one thing you do not want to do is stock up on barter items and then be stuck with them if the Y2K disruptions prove to be short-lived. Hand-operated can openers will be very valuable if we experience prolonged power outages. But you are taking a big risk if you invest in thousands of them, figuring that you can corner the can opener market in a crisis. If power failures don't occur or are brief, you will be stuck with items that you can't use and no one else wants.

Before choosing any barter item, ask yourself if you can still use it or sell it after the crisis is over. If the answer is no, don't stock up on it.

Each of my three favorite barter items passes the "smartness" test: coffee, chocolate, and toilet paper. All three will be valuable in an emergency. Although none is essential to human survival, people enjoy these items a lot now and I am convinced they will still want to have them no matter how terrible Y2K disruptions are. Coffee and chocolate originate outside the United States and likely will be scarce if international trade and transportation are crippled.

Each of these three items is convenient. The items store easily, they don't deteriorate quickly, and they are easy to move.

Most of all, coffee, chocolate, and toilet paper will never go to waste if I have a pile left over when things return to normal. My wife will gladly help me drink the coffee; my daughters will gladly help me eat the chocolate; and, well, Mr. Whipple and I have a relationship that goes back many years.

Manufacture Barter Items During a Crisis

Barter items do not necessarily have to be the prepackaged goods that we currently purchase in retail stores. If you are able to make something of value—especially during the midst of the crisis—you will have barter items available even when other people have run out of goods.

Goods produced by baking, sewing, wood-working, and metal-working will be in high demand. Can you make home-made chocolates, cookies, or candy? Can you create (or mend) clothing? Did you know that an inexpensive turret press, available at many gunshops, can be used to reload ammunition? (I didn't.)

If your circumstances make it feasible to produce your own barter items during an emergency, make sure you stock up on the raw materials necessary. For example, if you want to reload ammo, you'll need a supply of powder, primers, and bullets. (Don't worry too much about the brass shells; your customers can collect their spent shells for you to reload.)

Build up an inventory of the flour, oil, sugar, cloth, thread, needles, lumber, metal, and so on for the particular items that you will manufacture. Also make sure you have the proper tools for emergency conditions. Your electric sewing machine, gas oven, or power tools may be useless if major utility services are shut down.

Barter Tactics and Techniques

As with most other human activities, you can improve your bartering abilities with a little study and a lot of practice. Just as certain skills and techniques will make someone a more effective (fill in the blank: police officer, insurance salesman, truck driver, dental hygienist, etc.), certain tactics and techniques will make you a more effective barterer.

Understand the Barter Environment

When a barter economy becomes commonplace, it is usually accompanied by ineffective law enforcement or even occasional periods of anarchy. There will be no Better Business Bureau or Fair Trade laws protecting your interests. It will truly be a "let the buyer beware" situation. You must be extra careful that you are not trading for counterfeit or defective goods. If someone trades you what turns out to be junk, you won't be able to call your lawyer and sue him for fraud.

On the other hand, if you think that you can pull a fast one on some gullible sucker, remember that the lack of normal law enforcement may prompt people to express their displeasure by shooting first and asking questions later.

The need for adequate self-defense is a significant issue in a barter economy. By definition, you're making it known that you possess something of value. You may be meeting with strangers. In a society on the verge of anarchy, people may not hesitate to steal what you own if they think they can get away with it. I'm not trying to say that every barter transaction will be like one of those tense drug-dealer meetings depicted by Hollywood. Simply be aware that the usual rules of civilized behavior may not apply and take the appropriate precautions.

Honesty Is the Best Policy

In a barter situation, you may be able to pull a fast one on a gullible or desperate person. Being well stocked and well prepared for an emergency can offer tremendous leverage in negotiations. If people are hurting for basic necessities, they may trade five gallons of gasoline for one gallon of clean water. They may exchange a new car for a few days of food. You may be able to get away with this type of "price gouging," but please don't do it. It's simply not right, and besides, you won't get away with it for too long.

When societies are disrupted enough to make barter necessary, it usually means transportation is restricted. The only people you may be able to barter with could be right in your immediate vicinity. A barter economy is a local economy. Even if the phones are dead, word will spread quickly. If you take advantage of someone, everyone will hear about it and you will be labeled a sleazy crook. They may continue to barter with you out of necessity, but as soon as another source of goods becomes available, you're history. You'll be blackballed right out of the local market. Your neighbors will take delight in seeing you squirm, too.

Developing a reputation for being a fair and honest trader will be your greatest barter asset. People will *want* to do business with you and seek you out (more potential customers means more demand, which means the price/value of your goods will rise without your even trying to raise them). People will haggle less, trusting that your first offer is fair. Most of all, people will remember acts of kindness and fairness and will be more likely to help you out if you experience some difficulties. (Remember the final scene of *It's a Wonderful Life*, when the townsfolk busted their piggy banks and jukeboxes to raise money for George Bailey/Jimmy Stewart? I know Frank Capra oversentimentalized it, but I truly believe that even in this cynical, selfish age, many people will still assist a person in need—especially if that person was good to them first.)

You may even want to consider offering a potential trading partner a small gift before making your first deal, to show your sincerity and willingness to develop a long-term business relationship. Also, in your very first trade with a person, you could accept less than what you might be able to get. This will make the other person feel good about doing business with you and lay the groundwork for your next deal. Word will spread that you do not take advantage of people.

Avoid Desperation

You don't want to engage in barter when you are desperate. You will not be on an even footing with your trading partner and you may be forced to accept a thoroughly unfair deal. Of course, once you become desperate, what can you do about it at that point? The answer is to prepare in advance so that you do not find yourself in dire straits.

Approach each trade opportunity with the attitude that you will make a deal only if the offer is right. If negotiations are not going well and if the other person refuses to make a fair offer, politely end the discussion. You can only take this laid-back approach if you are well prepared and not panicky.

You also want to be wary of situations where the other person is desperate, and begins to tell tales of woe and puts pressure on you practically to give away your goods. There is a big difference between charity and fair trading. I firmly believe that charity is important, and assisting our friends and neighbors will be a major part of dealing with the Y2K crisis. But if you are there to trade, trade. Don't let the other person shift the discussion to a plea for charity. Word will spread that you are an easy mark, and people will actually come to resent you if you don't continue to "give away the store."

Don't Expose Your Surplus

If, for example, you are willing to trade fifty rolls of toilet paper with someone, don't let him know that you have one thousand more rolls stored in your basement. Psychologically, this knowledge will affect your negotiations. It's supply and demand again. His demand is still the same, but now he knows the supply is much greater and consequently the price ought to be lower. You don't have to lie to him. If he inquires, politely decline to answer. The big thing is, don't show him your surplus or brag about it. Focus on the deal at hand.

Middlemen, Commissions, References

When an economy shifts from money to barter, the method of paying for goods changes, but many typical business structures remain intact. Salesmen and brokers will represent wealthy people or groups of people. Their job is to bring people together to trade, and for this service they expect a fee or commission.

In really chaotic situations, if the government does not restore order, powerful warlords will emerge. Some semblance of order may return, but at a price. The warlords or militia leaders will attempt to monitor economic activity and exact tribute in exchange for "protection." You may have to turn over a percentage of all trades to these people.

As the bartering networks becomes more sophisticated and complex, or if the particular trade you're making is large, you may need to provide references before making the deal. A person that each party has traded with previously can make the negotiations more comfortable. If you use references to make a deal go smoother and safer, don't forget to offer them a gift for their services.

Other Considerations

Bartering is work. To be effective and successful, you need to work hard at it. You need to be industrious and persistent. You need to hustle, utilize salesmanship, and keep good records (of completed trades and potential trading partners). You need to constantly analyze your own needs, your inventory of goods, and any changes in the local market (product surpluses and shortages, new supplies and demands, potential competition, etc.). You've got to plan ahead and be innovative. In other words, bartering is a lot like owning and running your own business… because that is exactly what it is.

* * *

Every Saturday morning across America, countless determined warriors give their equipment one last check, strap themselves into the cockpits of their trusty machines, and take a deep breath. The moment of truth has arrived. At the crack of dawn, wave after wave of these resolute combatants are on the move, traversing the highways and byways of this great land with only one thought on their minds: "Today I shall be victorious!" Yes, the fearsome tag sale brigade is on the march.

Swarming in formation, and ignoring all parking regulations, these heroic gladiators swoop into battle. Minivans and Buicks, Chryslers and pickup trucks, all descend with lightning speed on hapless neighborhoods. The combat is fierce— at times, hand-to-hand. Wrangling, posturing, haggling, bluffing… the struggle rages. Offers, counteroffers, wavering, indecision, retreat, and then… counterattack! Thrust, parry, and finally… victory! A deal! A great bargain! The day has been won!

Those of us who spend our time in office buildings and factories may boast that our efforts are the heart of the nation's economy and that we alone possess the true knowledge and ability to conduct business. But deep down, we are in awe of the skill and tenacity displayed by the driveway deal-makers. If they ever chose to descend on the downtown districts and industrial parks, we would be in big trouble.

If the Millennium Bug causes our monetary system to falter—even for a short time—the skills on display at Saturday morning tag sales, rather than those on display at Monday morning board meetings, will rule the economy. Barter, and the skills needed to conduct it, are foreign to most of us. In a very short while, however, we may have to take a crash course. While we're still learning the ropes about bartering, we should remember to stick close to a decorated veteran of the tag sale wars. It always helps to learn from the masters.

Y2K PREP TIP #11
Sharpen Your Barter Skills

Even with a large stockpile of valuable goods and a basic understanding of how a barter economy operates, you may not be very successful if you do not have good bartering skills. Basic salesmanship and negotiating talents are necessary to make sure you get what you deserve in return for your valuable items.

In our present consumer economy, little negotiating occurs anymore. Items sit on store shelves with the prices stamped on them. The only decision to be made is whether to buy the product or not. If you wish to pay less for an item, you must check the prices in other stores or wait for it to go on sale. You can't walk up to the sales clerk in a Wal-Mart and say, "The price on this toaster is $34.95. I'll give you 20 bucks for it. Whataya say?"

Some people may use negotiation and sales skills in their particular line of work, but for the average consumer it is not a common practice anymore. If Y2K causes us to go to a barter economy for a period of time, these skills will be crucial. Whether you call it haggling, dickering, wrangling, negotiating, or horse-trading, this important talent can be honed and improved with practice.

My Y2K Prep Tip is to go out and get some practice in trading and haggling before the Y2K crisis occurs. Although most prices are pre-set in our modern economy—without any room for negotiating—there are still plenty of opportunities to do business where the price is not firm. A person with good negotiating skills can be very successful.

Flea markets, garage sales, swap meets, second-hand shops, and antique stores are some places where dickering takes place all the time. Most of these transactions are consummated with money, but the skills you obtain will enable you to get the best price if you must barter for goods and services in the future.

I'm not suggesting that you learn how to take advantage of someone else in a negotiation situation. Honing these skills is primarily designed to make sure someone else does not take advantage of you! There will surely be a lot of sharks and con men and smooth talkers doing business in a barter economy. You just want to make sure you can hold your own with these pros.

	Y2K PREPAREDNESS CHECKLIST				
Level	Action Step	Qty	Unit Price	Total Qty	Total Price
2	Make list of "smart" barter items; be sure to diversify.	N/A	N/A		
2	Immediately begin buying some of these items *each* week; do not skip a week.	N/A	N/A		
2	Go to flea markets, swap meets, etc., and sharpen your barter skills.	N/A	N/A		
3	Determine whether you have a valuable skill or service; if so, obtain needed supplies/tools and practice your skill.	N/A	N/A		
4	Determine whether you can manufacture barter items during a crisis; if so, obtain needed supplies/tools.	N/A	N/A		

Chapter Twelve

Change Your
Investment Strategy

Put all your eggs in the one basket and—*watch that basket.*
                    —Mark Twain, *Pudd'nhead Wilson*, 1894

In the summer of 1929 Joseph Kennedy made one of the most important decisions of his life.

An extremely successful businessman, Kennedy had started in banking and then expanded into shipbuilding, movie financing, and ultimately stock market investment. By the time he was forty, he was already a multimillionaire.

He wasn't alone in his stock market success. Everyone in America was "speculating," as they called it. From the sophisticated financiers of Wall Street to the school teachers of rural Iowa, everyone was making money. It was the longest running bull market in history.

But in the summer of 1929, Kennedy became increasingly concerned, as a few financial analysts were predicting a market crash. Analyst Roger W. Babson warned, "More people are borrowing and speculating today than ever before in our history. Sooner or later a crash is coming, and it may be terrific… factories will be shut down… men will be thrown out of work… and a vicious circle will get in full swing and the result will be a serious business depression."[1] For the most part, however, Babson's warning fell on deaf ears. The vast majority of analysts, along with the media, ridiculed pessimists like Babson as "doomsayers." A few sources even accused them of "fear mongering" for the sake of personal gain.

For several months, Kennedy vacillated. He was making more money from his investments than from his business interests, so it just didn't make sense to get out. He wasn't sure what he would do with his money if he did. So, for months, he did nothing, hoping that the few lone voices predicting a bear market were wrong.

Finally, in the summer of 1929, on a visit to Wall Street, he entered one of the brokerage houses and stood aghast at what he witnessed. People were speculating feverishly—all dreamed of instant wealth, and many had already attained it. The scene nauseated Kennedy, who took one last glance and decided to go outside to get his shoes shined.

He soon found a young bootblack who, hoping to garner big tips, gave investment advice while shining his customers shoes. This amused Kennedy, who didn't take it seriously until later that afternoon, when the market performed *precisely* as the lad had predicted. This further unnerved Kennedy, who decided that "if a mere boy could predict the movement of the market... then it was certainly no place for a man with plenty of money to lose. Then and there, he decided to sell his securities."[2]

A few days later he called his broker and uttered four crucial words, "I want my money." His broker desperately tried to talk him out of it, but Kennedy was undeterred. He had decided to get out, and nothing was going to stop him—not his broker, not his friends, not even his wife, who begged him to reconsider. Why? Because Kennedy understood two very important investment principles about the stock market: (1) what goes up must come down and (2) it's better to be two months early than a day late.

So, in the late summer of 1929, he cashed out. At the time, he looked like a fool. But when the market came tumbling down sixty days later, he looked like a genius.

There are strange parallels between Kennedy's time and ours. Whenever I speak on the subject of Y2K, the number one question I get is this: "What do I do with my 401(k)?" It may take a slightly different form (for instance, "What do I do with my mutual fund?"), but it is essentially the same question. People want to know what to do with the money they have in their retirement accounts. For years, their money has been tied up in the stock market, and they simply can't conceive of putting it anywhere else.

Often the people who ask these questions are afraid. They have never seriously considered the possibility that the market could crash. This is especially for babyboomers, who have never known anything but a bull market since they started investing. So, like the proverbial deer caught in the headlights, they stare into the future, unable to act, hoping that the doomsayers are wrong and their earnings will continue without disruption.

Unfortunately, in a crisis, it is the timid—those caught "between and betwixt"—who get hammered. Whether it's a war, a famine, or an economic downturn, those who refuse to act eventually become history's victims. My goal in this chapter is to keep you from becoming one of these people. I want to change your investment paradigm and motivate you to take action now, while you still have a chance of getting out with most of your assets intact.

The Paradigm

For the past ten years, the most important investment question you could have asked was, "How do I *grow* what I've got?" This really is so basic that it hasn't been a question at all. It's been an underlying assumption that goes unquestioned. But unless you are an extremely sophisticated investor with the experience and ability to navigate the turbulent financial waters ahead, this is exactly the *wrong* question. The question you need to be asking yourself now is: "How do I *protect* what I've got?" You must shift from a paradigm of growth to a *paradigm of protection*. To say it another way: You need to shift out of those investments that are *a promise to pay* and into *self-validating assets*.

Promises to Pay

Nearly all conventional investments are promises to pay. They may take the form of a stock equity, a government or municipal bond, a corporate bond, or even a domestic or foreign currency. Regardless, at their core, the thing that makes them all similar is that they are based on someone's promise to pay you at a future date.

Consider stock equities, for example. Almost everyone investing today has his or her investment capital tied up in the stock market. A stock purchase allows you to buy ownership in a specific company or, in the case of a mutual fund, a group of companies in the hope that (1) the company's future profitability will pay you a dividend and/or (2) the company's stock price will escalate, allowing you to sell the stock at a profit. In a stock purchase, you are exchanging the current value of your money in the hope that it will be worth more later. Regardless, your purchase is based on a promise—or perhaps more accurately, a *hope*—to pay.

If an investor believes the market is about to fall, or if the market's volatility pushes him too far outside his comfort zone, he will often move some portion of his portfolio into bonds. Why? Because they involve less risk. The reason for this is that a bond makes you a *creditor* rather than an *owner*. Why is this important? Because typically creditors get paid before owners. As a result, you have a higher probability of getting paid, thus there is less risk.[3] However, risk is not completely eliminated because some borrowers default on their loans. Consequently, bond prices fluctuate, depending on the market's perception of how likely the borrower is to default on the loan.

Of course, all of these bonds trade on the open market. In other words, you don't have to make the loan yourself, you can simply buy a loan someone else has made.

People and institutions buy and sell them all the time. (They are, however, less liquid than stocks.) Because these bonds fluctuate in value, investors can make money by simply selling them at a higher price than they purchased them.

But, whether it is a stock market equity or a public or privately issued bond, it is still a *promise to pay*. As such, it depends on the issuing organization's *ability* to make good on its promise and the public's *confidence* that it will do so. *Y2K puts both of these at risk.*

- If a company experiences Y2K-related disruptions and is unable to operate at full production capacity, this could cut deeply into its profits, causing its stock price to fall or even collapse. This is particularly a risk today when we have a "stock bubble" based on little more than public confidence.

- If a company is sued because of a Y2K-related matter, this could also seriously impact its profits or drive it out of business altogether. Either way, it could have an adverse effect on its stock price.

- If enough businesses go belly-up because of Y2K, it could negatively impact tax revenues. This, in turn, could result in a city having to default on or renegotiate its debt structure, including municipal bonds. As a result, the value of the bond could plummet.

In my opinion, in a crisis you don't want to depend on someone else's ability to pay. There are just too many things related to Y2K that could impair an organization's ability to make good on its promises. But there's another reason—a more important reason—why, in my opinion, you should get out of stocks and bonds.

Digital Assets

Outside of their personal dwelling, most investors today have their money tied up in *digital assets*. Stocks, bonds, and even currencies are, more often than not, nothing more than a digital entry on a computer.

Consider your typical stock purchase. You call (or e-mail) your broker and order a trade. Your broker dutifully makes the trade and calls you back (or e-mails you) with a confirmation. Does he then send you a stock certificate for the particular company whose stock you bought? No! (Okay, he may do it occasionally if you request it, but it is extremely rare.) He simply makes an entry in the computer and assigns the stock to your account. Once a month, he sends you a statement, telling you precisely what is sitting in your account. The same is true of mutual funds and bond purchases.

Consequently, the only proof of ownership you have is what's in the computer.

Now sit down and think about this long and hard: what happens if the data on the computer—your data!—suddenly disappears or is corrupted because of a Y2K-related computer failure.

At the very least, you may not have access to those assets until the computers are fixed. Imagine this: It's the first week of January 2000. The market is in a free fall. You call your broker (assuming the phones are working) and order him to sell. He says, "I can't. The computers are down. I can't make any trades. In fact, I don't even know what you've got in your account!" Is this scenario probable? Perhaps. Is it a remote possibility? Absolutely. (Don't forget: Even if brokerage houses are completely Y2K-compliant, they are dependent on electricity, telecommunications, and other services outside of their control in order to conduct business.)

The question comes down to what you are willing to risk. What will your assets be worth when—and if—the system comes back on line? Will they hold their value? Will they be worth a fraction of what they were before the crash? Will they have disappeared altogether? All of these are possibilities, and you need to consider them carefully.

Perhaps you're thinking, *Yes, but if I have a hard copy of my statement, I can prove what is in my account.* Okay, let's play out that scenario.

You order your broker to sell. He tells you that he can make the trade but he can't verify what's in your account. You say, "No problem, I'll fax you my last statement." (That's assuming the fax machines and the phone lines are working.)

He says, "That won't do me any good. How do I know that you didn't make a big trade *after* you received your statement? I'm sorry, but I can't make the trade until I can verify *on the computer* what is in your account."

You're right back where you started—a digital asset that you can't access.

Self-validating Assets

So if you don't want your money in a digital asset that is based on someone else's promise to pay, where do you put it? I would suggest that you cash out and put your money in *self-validating, hard assets.* By "self-validating" I mean an asset that doesn't depend on someone else's promise to pay—something with intrinsic value. By "hard asset," I mean nondigital, real property.

Basically, five kinds of investments meet this minimal standard:

1. Land and real estate
2. Capital equipment
3. Collectibles
4. Gems
5. Precious metals

All of these assets are self-validating inasmuch as they don't rely on a promise to pay. They are also nondigital. However, we need to apply more precise criteria. Specifically, you should move your money into assets that

- either appreciate or, at the very least, hold their value through an economic crisis;

- are widely recognized for their value so that they are readily accepted by most people;

- are easily converted to other assets so that you have as much liquidity as possible;

- are portable in the event that you have to transport them;

- are durable and cannot be easily destroyed; and

- are easily divisible so that you can actually use them in financial transactions if necessary.

Now let's run each of our five self-validating, hard assets through this fivefold filter.

Land and real estate. The problem with land or real estate is similar to the problem with the stock market: the values are currently overinflated. Historically, no real estate boom has ever survived a stock market crash. They tend to move parallel to one another. My guess is that there will be some enormous bargains *after* January 1, 2000, but that you want to stay away from real estate for the time being. (I have many friends who are actually selling their homes and moving into a rental house. They want to sell at the top of the market and buy at the bottom. They intend to buy another home after January 1, 2000, for what they believe will be pennies on the dollar.) The other problem land and real estate have, especially in a crisis, is that they are not easily converted to other assets. In other words, they have low liquidity.

Capital equipment. Capital equipment can be a good investment, especially if it is in your particular area of expertise or enables you to deliver your goods or services better. Although it is somewhat speculative, I know of people who are trying to anticipate what kinds of things might be valuable after January 1, 2000, and are stockpiling them now to sell later. These include things such as diesel generators, wood-burning stoves, and hand tools. I also know of doctors, dentists, and even lawyers who are purchasing nonelectric or solar-powered tools so they can continue to offer their services in the absence of electricity, should that become a reality after Y2K. Again, the problem is liquidity. Also, these assets are usually not portable.

Collectibles. This category includes things like rare art, stamps, and numismatic coins—perhaps even Beanie Babies! The primary problem with collectibles is that you have to be very knowledgeable about what they are worth. As a result, they will not be as widely recognized for their value as other investments. Worse, they have no practical use in a crisis. You can't eat them, and they won't keep you warm. You can hang on to them and hope that they regain their original value after the crisis. Again, if you wait on these items, you may find some great values after the crisis hits.

Gems. Diamonds, rubies, sapphires, and other precious stones meet several of the criteria. They are portable, durable, and may be divisible. However, they are not widely recognized (as an amateur, how do you distinguish a real diamond from a faux one?) or easily converted. They also don't have much practical use in a crisis. Unless you have a great deal of wealth and are simply looking for a way to diversify your portfolio, I'd stay away from these, too.

Precious metals. Silver and gold, at least in bullion or coin form, meet *all* the criteria. Historically, they have proved to be the best way to transport value over time and through a crisis. They are widely recognized by most people because they are usually clearly denominated based on weight. Once people learn the system, they are able to convert them into other assets. They are, of course, portable, durable, and easily divisible. In fact, if you buy them in coin form, they come divided into a variety of sizes and values that are useful in day-to-day transactions.

Table 12.1 shows how each of the above assets compares to another based on the criteria I set forth above.

Table 12.1:
A Comparison of Self-validating, Hard Assets

	Stability	Divisibility	Recognizability	Portability	Durability
Land or real estate	●		●		●
Capital equipment	●				
Collectibles				●	
Gems		●		●	●
Precious metals	●	●	●	●	●

Get Liquid Now!

It should be obvious by now that I am recommending that you immediately cash out your 401(k), IRA, and mutual funds, *if possible*. I know that this flies in the face of current conventional wisdom. In fact, most people who read these words will *not* follow my advice. They will wait until it becomes obvious that the stock market is going to crash and by then it will be too late. What I am hoping is that you are different, that you will read these words, understand their significance, and take action now while you still have the opportunity.

The most important thing to do—especially if you are unable to cash out (some plans don't allow it)—is to move to a safer harbor. For example, if you are in stocks, move to bonds or U.S. Treasuries. Table 12.2 shows "Concentric Circles of Investment Safety." You have the most exposure on the outermost rim of the model. That's where there is the most risk. Each time you move toward the center of the circle, you decrease the risk and increase your safety. If your circumstances or needs will not allow you to move all the way to the center of the circle (silver and gold), move as far inward as you can.

Can I guarantee that the market is going down? No. No more than any official can guarantee to you that the electricity is going to stay on, the banks will remain solvent, or the Defense Department will be operating at full capacity. Once again, you have to look at the risk of staying where you are versus the risk of changing your

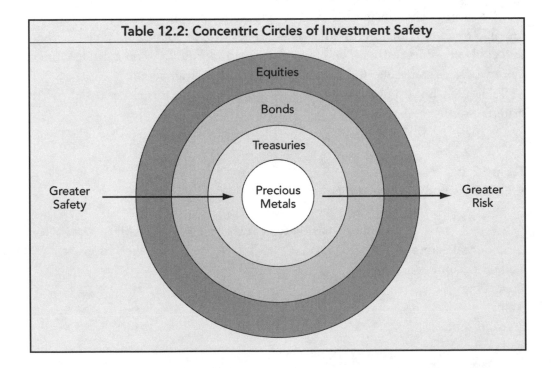

Table 12.2: Concentric Circles of Investment Safety

investment strategy. If you cash out, as I am suggesting, you will probably pay a price. The day after you cash out the market may shoot up. If it does, you will have lost the return your capital could have earned if only you had stayed in the market a while longer. Moreover, you will probably pay a hefty penalty for early withdrawal and face some significant negative tax consequences—assuming the IRS is around to collect. Are you willing to do this to protect *some* of your nest egg?

I don't know about you, but I would rather take a 40 percent hit (or more) and make sure I've got at least the 60 percent in hand than risk the whole 100 percent on the assumption that enough of the computers get fixed to protect my investment. (There may be other ways to get your cash out, depending on the nature of your program. For example, you may be able to borrow against your 401(k) without a penalty.) Call me paranoid. I'll readily admit, I may be wrong. But if I am, the most it will cost me is 40 or so percent. If I stay in the market and am wrong, I could lose *everything*. Is that a risk you are prepared to take? If so, then understand what you are putting at risk.

If you do decide to cash out, be prepared for a fight. Plenty of people will try to get you to change your mind, starting with your broker. Just remember: Your broker has a vested interest in your staying in the game. (This is why most of the people pooh-poohing the Y2K problem are either brokers or bankers.) In most cases he can't make the kinds of investments I am recommending, so there is nothing for him to gain from your changing investment strategies. In fact, there's a good deal to lose.

In addition to your broker, don't be surprised if your friends or family think you're nuts. If they do, you're in good company. (Remember Joseph Kennedy?) I get daily e-mail messages from people who have faced similar opposition. The most important thing you can do is decide what you want to do, mentally walk through the responses you are likely to get, and be prepared to stay the course. You also must be willing to take responsibility if you are wrong.

First Things First

Okay, let's say you're cashed out—you're liquid! Congratulations. It wasn't easy. It may even have been expensive, but you followed through. You're not feeling too sure of yourself, but you've crossed the line, and there's no turning back now. But before you move forward, you need to reevaluate your priorities. Before you call a gold and silver dealer, you need to make sure you are investing in the most important things first.

First, you need to invest in Y2K preparations. Silver and gold won't do you any good if you don't have a way to keep your family warm. It won't do you any good if you can't feed your family and provide a safe, reliable supply of drinking water for them. And it won't do you any good if you can't protect yourself or your family. These items should be your *top* priority. Once you have them nailed down you are ready to move forward—not until. People generally invest for the long term, but there *is* no long term if you can't make it through the short term. The short term is Y2K and the aftermath that may ensue.

Second, if possible, you need to make some provision for others. There are going to be many people—perhaps the majority of people—who either don't have the foresight or the means to prepare for themselves. You may not be able to save the world, but you can help your extended family and perhaps some of your neighbors. As a result, you should consider laying up extra supplies for them. Do you owe it to them? No. But, if you are like me, you believe you are your brother's keeper and have a responsibility to look out for him as well.

Third, you need to make sure you have sufficient cash to get through the early part of the crisis. If you have not yet read Chapter 10, now is a good time to do so. No one knows how long things will be in a mess, but it's a safe bet to think you are going to need some cash to get through the first part of the crisis. If you have cashed out of your stocks, you probably have enough to "fund" your emergency reserve. All you need to do is pull your money out of the bank and get it under your control. Also, you need to come up with a safe place to stash it.

Fourth, you need to collect some items to use as barter. I covered this in the previous chapter, but it bears repeating here. In the event that our currency collapses— and I certainly hope that it doesn't—barter will likely emerge as the transitional "money" until a new standard is established. As a result, you need to set aside some part of your portfolio for barter items.

Fifth, invest in silver and gold coins. Once you have the above items taken care of, you are ready to consider long-term investments and asset protection. Assuming that you have something left, and want to get it from one side of the crisis to the other, I know of no better means that by investing in silver and gold. Let me explain why.

The Ten Commandments of Buying Silver and Gold

Through four-and-a-half millennia of human history, mankind has valued gold and silver. The gold *aureus* or silver *drachma* minted in 100 B.C. have retained value until today. Shares in the *Trans-Imperial Tax Farming Corporation* haven't. Sure, the purchasing power of both metals rises and falls through history, but it still transmits wealth across time. Therefore, it is my contention that there is no safer place to put your money than in these precious metals. With that in mind, let me offer "The Ten Commandments of Buying Silver and Gold."[4]

Table 12.3:

The Ten Commandments of Buying Silver and Gold

1. Remember your purpose.
2. Buy at the lowest price per ounce.
3. Focus on coins.
4. Avoid "numismatics" (i.e., rare coins).
5. Acquire silver first, then gold.
6. Buy small coins first, then large coins.
7. Know your dealer.
8. Protect your privacy.
9. Always take delivery.
10. Keep your valuables safe.

Commandment #1: Remember your purpose. As I have tried to make clear throughout this chapter, your primary goal in acquiring silver and gold is *asset protection*, not *growth*. I happen to believe that silver and gold will grow in value significantly over the next two years, but that is not my primary goal in buying them. My objective is to transport what little wealth I have from this side of the crisis to the other. I know of no better way to do this than through the vehicle of silver and gold. If these two precious metals don't rise in value, I won't be disappointed. I will simply be grateful that I was able to protect most of what I had.

Commandment #2: Buy at the lowest price per ounce. I recommend you buy the most gold and silver you can for your money. Look for the lowest cost per ounce, consistent with liquidity and divisibility. To figure the cost per ounce merely divide the cost of the coin by its content. If a British sovereign (a type of gold coin) containing 0.2354 troy ounce of fine gold costs $90, then its cost per ounce is $90 divided by 0.2354, or $382.32 per ounce. Compare this price to the "spot price" of gold or silver.

The spot price is the market benchmark, the price per ounce for 100 ounces of gold or 5,000 ounces of silver for immediate delivery in New York. However, since you probably can't take immediate delivery in New York, you will have to pay a *premium* over the spot metal value to cover minting, commissions, and distribution costs. Other things being equal, you want to buy the coins with the lowest possible premium. I have an "Axiom of Premiums" you should keep in mind: *Over the long haul, all premiums disappear.*

Commandment #3: Focus on coins. Liquidity refers to how easy it will be to trade metal under the worst possible circumstances. The question you should be asking is, what form of gold and silver will people want most in a crisis?

Historically, coinage was a great technological advance. Instead of having to test every piece of metal for purity and weight, mints stamped pieces with a guaranteed weight and purity. Everyone could be sure they got what they paid for. Coins still offer this security today.

But not all coins have the same liquidity in a crisis. Although there's nothing wrong with foreign gold or silver coins (they were legal tender in this country until 1854), if you live in America you should generally prefer coins minted in the United States, unless you can buy foreign gold coins at an attractive price per ounce. Why? Because unsophisticated vendors or investors will likely trust and accept domestic coins before they accept foreign ones.

The most recognized form of silver is pre-1965 U.S. dimes, quarters, and halves. They are 90 percent silver and are sometimes called "junk silver." Virtually everyone knows what they look like, and if they doubt they are silver, they can check the date on the face. The amount of silver every coin contains can be precisely known.

These silver coins are currently traded in bags of $1,000 face value (that is, ten thousand dimes, four thousand quarters, or two thousand halves). A $1,000 face value bag weighs fifty-five pounds, has the volume of about a gallon-and-a-half of milk, and contains 715 troy ounces of pure silver. With *spot silver* around $5.00 an ounce (at this writing), a $1,000 *face value* bag of 90 percent coin costs about $5,000.

Recognizability is the same reason I recommend the currently minted American Eagle half-, quarter-, and tenth-ounce gold coins. They plainly say on their face that they are United States coin, and plainly state how much gold they contain. However, they also carry high premiums. But since the premium on sovereigns, twenty francs, fractional Krugerrands, and all the other alternatives have risen greatly since the summer of 1997, you have few options. If you want fractionals, you just have to swallow hard and pay the price. Remember, you are buying future flexibility in the number of transactions you can perform.

Commandment #4: Avoid numismatics. A "numismatic" is an old or rare coin that trades at a handsome premium because of its value to collectors. Many sophisticated investors have made a good deal of money from these coins, even when silver and gold were not performing well. However, they are sometimes sold by unscrupulous coin dealers to amateur investors who pay more than they should for them. I strongly suggest that you stay away from these kinds of coins, unless you have a large portfolio (more than $1 million), you know what you are doing, and you have a coin dealer you trust with your life.

In an emergency like Y2K, all values tend to sink to their lowest common denominator. For example, suppose the city is on fire and you're standing on the curb. A man in a Geo Metro screeches to a halt in front of you. "Get in, and I'll take you to safety!" he yells.

How likely are you to look down your nose and sneer, "No, thank you, I'll wait for a Lincoln town car"? Not very, because the only thing that matters is bottom line *transportation*. The same applies to the value of gold and silver coins in a Y2K crisis. Nobody will care about their "collectible" value. They'll ask only one question: How much gold or silver does it contain?

Unfortunately, I have met many people who have suffered at the hands of numismatic sales people. Much to their chagrin, they discovered too late that the coins they bought were worth much less than they were told. They were also given additional reasons why they should buy numismatics; I'll deal with these later in the chapter. Regardless, the best defense is to know what you want and refuse to buy something you don't want or need.

Commandment #5: Buy silver first, then gold. There are a number of reasons why I recommend that such a large portion of your portfolio be in silver. The primary one is because I believe silver will be more useful in the kinds of day-to-day transactions you will likely be making in a transitional economy. Gold is valuable, of course, but, in a crisis, it is often *too valuable* for run-of-the-mill purchases like groceries or household goods.

Moreover, silver may actually rise in value more quickly than gold. The current gold-to-silver ratio (at the time of this writing) is at about fifty-six to one. That means that it takes about fifty-six ounces of silver to buy one ounce of gold. Historically, however, a ratio above sixteen to one is an anomaly. From 1873 to 1939, the ratio trended upward to a hundred to one. But each time it fell, it moved toward sixteen to one. From 1939 to 1968, it trended downward, again bottoming below sixteen to one. In the mid-1970s it turned down again, bottomed below sixteen to one, then turned up into 1991. Since 1991 the ratio has continued to move *down*, meaning that the value of silver is moving up relative to gold. If history is any indication, my guess is that silver may shoot up in the next several months.

The other reason silver may rise in value faster than gold is the *monetary demand*. Increased monetary demand is historically what drives the ratio up; absence of monetary demand is what drives it down. Based on my conversations with coin dealers, there is every reason to believe that there is a movement toward the *private remonetization* of silver. Until recent times, silver has served as mankind's daily "monetary workhorse." If this holds true for the future, we can expect the price of silver to rise more quickly than gold.

Commandment #6: Buy small coins first, then large coins. Divisibility means that you want pieces small enough to trade. You don't want to go shopping for a loaf of bread with a 400-ounce bar of gold. It's much easier to offer several small coins than to try and divide one large one.

When it comes to silver, this means that you need to start with dimes, move to quarters, and then finally fifty-cent pieces. With dimes, there are fourteen transactions to an ounce. This decreases as the denomination increases (for example, there are roughly six transactions to the ounce with quarters and three transactions to the ounce with fifty-cent pieces).

Because fractional gold coins carry a larger minting premium than the one-ounce coins, save yourself a little money by buying one-ounce coins *after* you have a reasonable stock of fractional coins.

Commandment #7: Know your dealer. I don't know of any more important advice to give you than this. I have had contact with many people who did business with the wrong dealer and lived to regret it. The best way to avoid this is to get a recommendation from a friend you trust. But since you may not have many friends that have purchased silver and gold, it may not be that easy. Therefore, I want to get you started. One coin dealer I can recommend without qualification is Franklin Sanders. He is knowledgeable, experienced, and honest. I have sent literally thousands of my readers to him and never had a *single* complaint. (I don't receive any financial compensation from him; I'm just a happy customer.) You can reach Franklin at:

> The Moneychanger
> P.O. 341753
> Memphis, Tennessee 38184-1753
> Voice: (901) 853-6136
> Fax: (901) 854-5138
> Internet: <http://www.the-moneychanger.com>

Commandment #8: Protect your privacy. Because they are concerned about the government seizing gold, many investors are worried about the "paper trail" of their purchase. Face it: In America today, you have almost *zero* financial privacy. Government agencies can go to your bank and get your every financial record *without ever informing you.* Does the person who sees your Visa or MasterCard or checking statement know everything about your finances? Of course he does. About the only way you can buy gold and silver and preserve anonymity is to buy in the name of another entity, like a trust, corporation, or LLC. If you have significant assets, it's definitely worth consulting with a professional for the best way to do this, given your unique circumstances.

You should also forget buying with cash. Every gold and silver dealer is scared to death that the government will set him up on money-laundering charges. If you walk into his shop, as a stranger, and offer to buy six or eight thousand dollars worth of gold or silver for cash he will escort you to the nearest exit. Can you blame him?

So don't spend too much time worrying about the paper trail. Just take whatever precautions are necessary to secure your family's survival, buy what you need, and trust God to protect you.

However, just because it is difficult to keep the government from knowing about your silver and gold purchases does not mean that everyone else has to know. The last thing you want to do is become a *target* for criminals. To avoid this, do not tell anyone, including your children, that you are buying silver and gold. Many people operate under the assumption that "keeping a secret" means you can tell only one person at a time. If that person happens to be the *wrong* person, you could be putting yourself or your family at risk. As a former navy friend of mine is fond of saying, "Loose lips sink ships." Thus, the best policy is to stay tight lipped—no exceptions!

In addition, don't make the stupid mistake I made when I ordered my first bag of silver. I had the bag shipped by UPS to my front door. Worse, the return address on the shipping label had the name of the gold dealer! The best thing to do is have your coins sent to a mail drop. The clerk may figure out what's in the box, but he won't know where you live, if you are careful. You should also have the coin dealer omit the name of his or her company on the return address or use an alias. Any decent coin dealer should be using this as part of his standard operating procedure.

Commandment #9: Always take delivery. This commandment is, I hope, self-explanatory, given the nature of the Y2K crisis. If all you have is a silver or gold certificate, then, once again, all you are holding is a "promise to pay." It is a piece of paper, which, in a crisis, will likely be worth nothing. You want to own your assets, and you want to have them under your *exclusive* control. Therefore, take delivery. Do not put your coins in a safety deposit box or in any other place that may prove inaccessible when you need them.

Commandment #10: Keep your valuables safe. Obviously, you will want to store your valuables in a place that is known to you but unknown and inaccessible to others, especially thieves and burglars. See Appendix F: "Where to Stash Your Cash and Other Valuables" for a laundry list of ideas on where to hide your silver and gold.

What About Platinum?

Although in recent years many national mints have begun issuing platinum coins, platinum has never been widely used as a monetary metal. Still, it has a high value-to-weight ratio and can be a convenient way to store wealth.

Platinum's supply and demand are both quirky. Most of the world's platinum comes from just two places: southern Africa and Russia. Both are sources subject to political disruptions, and that makes platinum's price volatile. Platinum demand is quirky, too, because very few substances behave physically as platinum does, so in some industrial applications it is nearly irreplaceable. "Industrial" is the key word here. Will Y2K choke industrial demand down so low that platinum prices drop? Or will Y2K demand for portable, small wealth storage raise its price? It's anyone's guess.

That's why I don't recommend you buy platinum unless you invest at least $75,000 in metals. Then, for diversification, you can put up to 10 percent of your investment on platinum. You should stick to platinum coins such as American Eagles, Maple Leaves, Nobles, or Koalas.

Some Thoughts on Numismatics

When you begin shopping for gold and silver, many coin dealers will try to convince you to buy numismatic or rare coins. Many gold and silver dealers specialize in numismatics and use bullion coins only as a "loss leader." Their intention is to "upsell" you on the coins that pay the biggest commissions.

Generally speaking, they base their recommendation on three arguments:

1. Numismatics are exempt from government confiscation.
2. Numismatics have no reporting requirements.
3. Numismatics are better investments.

I want to dismantle these arguments one at a time, so that you can keep from being sold something you don't want and likely don't need. Please note: I am not against all numismatic purchases (see Table 12.4); I am against buying them for the wrong reasons.

The Myth of Government Confiscation

Dealers will often tell prospective customers that numismatic coins are exempt from government confiscation, thus implying (and sometimes stating) that nonnumismatics coins are subject to it. This argument is based on the federal government's gold seizure in 1933–1934. The stories conjure up a picture of jack-booted storm troopers pounding on doors and dragging hapless gold owners out of their houses to beat and kick them around their front yards while they ransack their houses for hidden gold.

Salesmen often state that the federal law exempts coins "having a recognized special value to collectors of rare and unusual coins."[5] According to the argument, because government exempted numismatics then, they must exempt them now. But what obligates a tyrant to be *consistent*? (And make no mistake about it, government

Table 12.4:
Suggested Investment Portfolios

Here are five portfolio suggestions, and some principles you must keep in mind. Don't let anyone *smooth talk* you into buying something you'll regret—*when it's too late to correct your mistake.*

$1,000 to $4,999 to invest	Put all in U.S. 90 percent silver coins (junk silver).
$5,000 to $24,999 to invest	Put half in U.S. 90 percent silver coin, half in gold quarter- or tenth-ounce American Eagles.
$25,000 to $74,999 to invest	Buy three bags ($1,000 face value) of U.S. 90 percent silver, $10,000 worth of quarter- or tenth-ounce American Eagles, and the balance in one-ounce Krugerrands or American Eagles.
More than $75,000 to invest	Buy eight bags of U.S. 90 percent silver, $10,000 worth of quarter- or tenth-ounce American Eagles, $5,000 worth of platinum coins (American Eagles, Nobles, Maple Leaves), and the balance in Krugerrands, American Eagles, or 100 Coronas. If you have a good deal more than $75,000 to invest, simply do multiples of this portfolio.
More than $1,000,000 to invest	Buy silver and gold, as in the previous portfolio, but also consider investing in other hard assets (e.g., collectibles—including numismatic coins—gems, art, etc.).

confiscation of private property *is* a tyrannical act.) No, if they played by the rules (i.e., the Constitution) they wouldn't be stealing your gold. If the government chose to seize gold and silver again, nothing would obligate them to follow the 1933–1934 precedent.

Numismatic dealers may tell you that "the law defines a numismatic coin as one with a premium of 15 percent or more over its gold value." That's also *not true*. No such law or regulation exists. A regulation was *proposed* in the *Federal Register*,[6] but, as far as I can tell, it was never adopted.

By statute, the only coins defined as "numismatic" are American Eagle gold and silver coins minted since 1985 and other currently minted *commemorative* coins. No statute or regulation defines U.S. $20 gold pieces (or any other U.S. gold or silver coin) minted before 1934 as "numismatic."

But there's a more important reason why government confiscation is highly unlikely: *because the monetary system today is not based on the gold standard.*

In 1933 gold formed the basis of the monetary system. It was the primary monetary reserve and probably accounted for about 35 percent of all American bank reserves. When the banks were threatened by the loss of gold (people withdrawing their gold from banks in the Depression-induced panic), the government moved to protect the banks. They seized the monetary base—gold—in order to reliquefy the banks. But the law that authorized the 1933 seizure has been *repealed*.

Today, what forms the basis of our monetary system? Debt, primarily *government debt*. Therefore, a threat to the banks, or a systemic threat to the monetary system or the financial system, will not have anything to do with *gold* disappearing from the banking system, but rather a disappearance of the present basis of the monetary system—debt.

What could cause the debt to evaporate? Markets would refuse to buy government debt, and its value would sink. Bank credit, another part of the monetary system, is backed by private debt. If enough companies default on their private debt—particularly as a result of Y2K—then bank assets will shrink, and the money supply will shrink with them.

If the government wanted to keep the banks liquid in a financial or banking crisis today, seizing gold would have zero effect. Rather, they would need to shore up debt, especially the debt of the federal government and of banks. Possible steps would include a moratorium on payment of federal government debt—for example, no payment of bond premium and or interest, and a moratorium on withdrawals from banks. (You could withdraw only, say, $500 a week. That happened in 1984 in Ohio and Maryland when the savings and loan crisis erupted.) To protect the debt underlying the bank credit portion of the monetary system, a moratorium on bankruptcies and scaling down of interest and principal payments might be decreed.

Finally, there is one other large untapped pool of assets the government might use to shore up the banking system—*your pension funds*. Pension funds could be "frozen" or, in effect, *seized*. They wouldn't call it a seizure, of course, but they would still slow down payouts and forbid complete withdrawals, even with penalties.

Therefore, the idea that the government will again seize gold *for the same reasons that it seized gold in 1933* is highly unlikely. It would undoubtedly boomerang on us because it would make the problem of cash withdrawals *worse*. A seizure would only confirm public suspicions about the banks' soundness and create a black market in gold, thus raising its price.

The Myth of Reporting Requirements

Dealers may tell you that "U.S. $20 gold pieces are exempt from reporting when you buy or sell them," but this means nothing. *Everything* is exempt from reporting when you *buy* it, unless you pay more than $10,000 in cash. Even then it's not your gold or silver *purchase* that must be reported, only the *cash transaction*.

Contrary to the scare stories, *few things are reportable* when you sell. Under 26 CFR 1.6045-1 and *Rev. Proc. 92–103*, dealers need only report customer sales of twenty-five or more (*but not fewer*) Krugerrands, Maple Leaves, or Mexican Onzas, five bag lots ($5,000 face value) of U.S. 90 percent silver coin, kilo gold bars, 100 ounce gold bars, 1,000 ounce silver bars, or 50 ounces or 100 ounces of platinum. If you buy in lots smaller than these, the dealer reports nothing.

The Myth of the Better Investment

There's no question that, over the past decade and a half, numismatics have paid to investors a vastly higher rate of return than simple gold or silver bullion. In some cases, they have outperformed the stock market. Conversely, at this writing, gold and silver bullion are trading at near twenty-year lows. Wouldn't it make sense then, if you are going to invest in silver and gold, to invest in the form that promises the highest rate of return?

In most cases, the answer is "no" and the rationale is simple: Your goal in a crisis is to *protect* your assets rather than to *grow* them. It is my contention that, in a crisis, the value of numismatics will not only cease to grow, they could actually collapse to the lowest common denominator: their melt-down value (see Commandment #3, above).

Although your primary goal should be asset protection, I do think it is possible that silver and gold may rise dramatically over the next several months. Why? Because of the return of monetary demand.

The reason why the price of both silver and gold are so low (as of this writing) is *because of the withdrawal of monetary demand*. For the past 136 years,[7] the entire money supply has been increasingly diluted by *money substitutes* in the form of government, bank, and even private credit. Gold and silver have been marginalized, pushed aside, and reduced in importance as components of the money supply.

But a monetary crisis—a financial panic in Asia or Russia or a Y2K-anticipating bank run—effectively destroys the substitutes, bringing gold and silver back to center stage in the monetary system. To the extent this happens, the value of silver and gold go up.

What can make this happen? A private remonetization of gold and silver. What we saw in silver and gold in the late 1970s was precisely that. People weren't buying ten or twenty Krugerrands to hang around their necks. They weren't buying silver bags because they were collectors. It was *pure monetary demand*. They were afraid that the monetary system might collapse. Precisely that sort of monetary demand for gold and silver is reappearing today in the face of the Year 2000 Computer Problem.

Beyond Business as Usual

Why do I recommend such a big position in gold and silver? Because, once again, they are money—*cash*. I believe that a panic is coming, and you want to have your assets converted to cash *before* the panic begins.

Maybe gold and silver leave you uncomfortable. What alternatives do you have? Not very good ones: paper currency, bank deposits (*not* certificates of deposit), Treasury bills, or Treasury bonds. Money market funds are mutual funds, and when the stock market drops, so will mutual funds.[8]

Military history teaches us the danger of stagnating in conventional thinking. The world is littered with rotting Maginot Lines, monuments to minds that could imagine only the *last* war, and not the next. If the lives of great military leaders teach us anything, it is that half-hearted measures are worse than no measures at all. The commander who timidly commits a few of his troops at a time, always *re*-acting rather than acting, merely consigns them to a bloody, useless, and certain death. Better to wait and fight another day.

The commander who thinks for himself, develops a bold but sound plan, prepares for all foreseeable outcomes, concentrates his forces, and, then, at the right time, strikes with all his might where the enemy is weakest—that commander ends up in the history books.

The monetary and financial crises facing us today are not "business as usual." Y2K is a threat unlike any that we have seen in our lifetimes. Conventional thinking and half-hearted measures won't help—and they may get you killed financially.

But time is running out. Because the rush into physical gold and silver has been so strong in recent months, because their physical markets are so very thin, and because we can't know what sort of turmoil falling markets and Y2K fears will cause, I recommend that you move into gold and silver *now*, while you still can.

A Final Thought: What Do I Do with My Debt?

In the words of my friend, Dave Ramsey, author of *Financial Peace*, "debt is dumb," especially consumer debt. I know that. You know that. Anyone who has ever been in debt knows how expensive it is both financially and, perhaps more importantly, emotionally. Unfortunately, most of us have been in debt for so long that we no longer know what it feels like to be free of any obligation to anyone.

Getting out of debt should, therefore, be one of our top priorities. As the Bible says, our goal should be to "owe no one anything, except to love one another" (Romans 13:8).

But you must understand the hierarchy of your obligations. As important as getting out of debt is, *your commitment to provide for your family supersedes your obligation to your creditors.*

So then, should you get out of debt before Y2K? It depends. You certainly should not do it before you have made sure your family will have food, water, shelter, and protection. I am not suggesting that you should default on a payment schedule. I am recommending that you not pay more than the schedule requires until you have made your basic Y2K preparations.

For example, let's say that Bill gets a $500 bonus. He has $3,000 worth of Visa debt and is paying off $78 per month. He could apply the full $500 to the debt, or he could invest the amount in Y2K preparations—to buy a good used wood-burning stove, or $500 worth of canned and/or dry food, or some fifty-five–gallon drums for storing water.

For me, the choice would be simple. As much as I hate being in debt, I would hate even more seeing my family go cold or hungry.

Unfortunately, there are a number of financial advisers out there who are telling people to get out of debt at all costs. The truth is that this is not realistic for many people, and it is absolutely dangerous advice for some. Remember: Your commitment to your family supersedes your obligation to your creditors. It doesn't eliminate it, but it does take priority over it. My advice: Make your preparations first and then pay down debt. If you reverse these priorities, you are putting your loved ones at enormous risk.

Y2K PREP TIP #12
The Mechanics of Purchasing Silver and Gold

1. Check the spot prices of silver and/or gold as a point of reference. You can do this at <http://www.kitco.com/gold.live.html>. For example, let's say that today I want to buy a bag of silver ($1,000 face value). In checking the spot price, I see that it is selling at $5.17 an ounce.

2. Determine the melt-down value of the metal. A bag of silver contains 715 troy ounces of silver. So, multiply $5.17 by 715 to get $3,696.55. This is the melt-down value of the silver in the bag. It does not, however, include costs related to minting, distribution, and commissions. It also does not reflect the market demand of silver in coin form. The difference between the melt-down value and the price you pay is the *premium.* You want to pay the lowest premium possible.

3. Get at least two quotes, preferably three. Prices vary depending on a given dealer's current inventory and access to outside inventory. Let's say I call two dealers for quotes. I ask, "What is a bag of junk silver selling for today?" One dealer tells me $5,750; another says $5,920. Obviously, the first dealer has the lowest premium. If the price difference is modest, go with the dealer you like doing business with.

4. Lock in the price and then send a bank wire or money order. Most dealers will allow you to lock in the price with a fax, but you must send a money order or bank wire immediately. (Call your bank for information on how to do this.) When they get the money in hand, they will ship the coins to you.

5. Have the coins delivered to a mail drop—not your home. In the interest of privacy you don't want the coins delivered to your home. The best way to do this is to use a mail drop (for instance, "Mailboxes, Etc.").

6. Make sure the dealer does not put the name of his company on the return address. This will be a dead giveaway of what's in the box to anyone who cares to notice. Most dealers will do this as a matter of course. But the first dealer I ordered from didn't do it, so it's a good idea to ask.

Y2K PREPAREDNESS CHECKLIST					
Level	Action Step	Qty	Unit Price	Total Qty	Total Price
4	Discuss this chapter with your spouse. You don't want to do anything that would cause a rift in your marriage. You need to be in agreement.	N/A	N/A		
4	Determine what it's going to cost you if you "cash out."	N/A	N/A		
4	Do a "gut check." Are you willing to sacrifice this amount in order to make the balance of your funds more secure?	N/A	N/A		
4	Make sure you have taken care of "first things first" (i.e., invest in basic preparedness, items you can share, an emergency cash reserve, and barter items *before* investing in silver and gold).	N/A	N/A		
4	Set up an acquisition plan and begin converting your cash to silver and gold coins on a systematic basis.	N/A	N/A		

Part Five

Protection

Chapter Thirteen

Determine How You Will Dispose of Waste

A sound man is good at salvage—at seeing nothing lost.

—Lao-tzu, 500 BC

There was once a poor farmer who awoke early every morning to tend to his fields, care for his chickens, and milk his cows. One thing constantly worried him—the rising cost of maintaining his farm. Every year, the cost of fertilizer and pesticides continued to rise, and this year there was barely enough to make his work profitable.

He noticed that his neighboring farmer performed the same regimen that he did—arising early in the morning, milking the cows, tending to the chickens, working hard all day in the fields. He seemed to tend the same crops and sell them at market for the same price. Yet, in spite of all this, his family had lavish things, and he never seemed to suffer the hardships that the poor farmer did. The poor farmer was puzzled.

One day, the poor farmer asked, "How do you fare so well, my friend? As the costs of fertilizer and pest control continue to rise, you continue to live better and better."

"Things are not always what they seem. You are wasteful," responded the lavish farmer.

"Help me understand," replied the poor farmer.

"Waste not your waste," he said. "Why do you choose to purchase man's fertilizer and throw nature's away?" asked the lavish farmer. "Nature has provided you with the means to complete the cycle. By not taking advantage of that opportunity, you have broken nature's cycle. Use what is given to you."

With that, the lavish farmer revealed his secret to keeping his crops high and his home bright. When the crops were high, his stomach was full. When his stomach was full, his fertilizer was rich. When his fertilizer was rich, his crops were high. He had completed the cycle.

□ □ □

Although it is not the most pleasant subject, you need to address and plan ahead for how you will dispose of your waste during the Y2K crisis if outages last longer than a few days. Remember that your local water treatment plant and water pumping station rely on the same electricity that you rely on to run your home. Few of these stations have contingency plans for long-term power outages, which means that not long after your power goes out, the faucets will stop running and your toilet will no longer flush.

In our modern society, the concept of human waste has been given a negative connotation. In reality, human waste is a very useful substance—as natural fertilizer. Just as cow manure is commonly used as a fertilizer and is even found bagged at your local retail store, so can human excrement be used as an additive to soil for productive crops as a replacement for chemical fertilizers. Most Americans may be repulsed by this idea, probably due to the odor that is associated with human feces. But, did you know that, once dry, human excrement has little or no smell at all? Did you know that there are additives that are commercially available, as well as naturally occurring ones, that you can add to reduce or eliminate the smell? There are probably many options for human waste disposal that you are not aware of.

Where am I heading here? Well, if Y2K decommissions the porcelain toilets that are the standard for waste disposal, millions of American will suddenly be faced with a real problem. What will I do with my waste? By planning ahead for this problem, you can help not only to make your family less dependent on the American waste disposal system, but you can also help return what nature has given to you rather than throw it away.

The Dangers of Improper Sanitation

Few things can spread disease faster, attracting flies, cockroaches, rats, and other vermin than the improper storage of human waste. It has been widely speculated that deadly diseases of the Middle Ages in Europe, such as the bubonic plague, were spread mainly by the inadequate sewage systems of the time. You can imagine the effects that such an improper waste disposal system would cause now, with populations a thousand times what they were in the Middle Ages. Therefore, it is important to think now about what you will do as a contingency to the porcelain commode.

If you have ever attended a large public event, such as a fair or a concert, you have more than likely encountered one of the most awful inventions of the twenty-first century—the portable toilet. These hideous contraptions more often than not have a terrible odor and are breeding grounds for flies and other annoying and disease-carrying insects. Imagine what would happen if an entire population was forced to rely on these types of devices to dispose of their wastes for longer than the time span of a concert. What if we had to use them for a whole year?

Without proper maintenance, it isn't hard to imagine how quickly flies and other insects and rodents would breed and spread disease-causing bacteria from the fecal matter. Although it may be a horrifying image, it isn't hard to imagine that some plague might be brought about by such an infestation.

What will happen to our world if the toilets stop flushing? Our highly evolved network of sewage tunnels would be completely worthless. The impending crisis that would ensue might be larger than the sharpest stock market crash, the most intense earthquake, and the most powerful thunderstorm combined. Disease is a powerful force that we currently have the technology to keep at bay. If any of the technologies that we use to minimize the spread of disease in the so-called "civilized world," including the sewage system, were to fail, we may be witness to a plague the likes of which we have never seen.

Why Do They Call It Waste?

Did you know that some Far Eastern countries do not have a word for what we know as waste? Think about it for a moment. In nature, excrement is part of the natural cycle of things. When animals defecate, the matter reaches the ground, decomposes, and becomes part of the soil. The soil then gives food for healthy, nutritious plant life, which the animals eat to sustain their lives. The animals use what they need and pass the rest out as excrement. Thus the cycle begins again.

But humans have broken the cycle. We still take food from the ground and use it for nutrition, but our excrement, considered waste, is piped from our homes through a highly networked, very expensive, and very technology-driven sewer system that leads inevitably to a nearby waterway, where it is dumped according to strict disposal laws.

Down river, they take that water from the river and pass it through a water treatment plant to remove the bacteria and waste materials from it. This process is also very technology-driven and very expensive to maintain. Chemical additives are added to the water to sanitize it, and the water is superheated to kill any living disease-causing microbes that may be in it. As an alternative, the water is saturated with high levels of ozone to kill any anaerobic bacteria that may cause disease. In any case, the water must go through several levels of decontamination before it is considered "drinkable."

Have you ever been to New Orleans, Louisiana? This beautiful city lies at the end of the longest river in America, the Mississippi River. When you were there, did you drink the water? I hope not. The water in New Orleans has the most chemical taste of any that I have tasted in the United States. The reason for the chemical taste is because the water from the Mississippi is so highly contaminated, having passed through hundreds of city sewer systems and treatment plants that it must undergo harsh chemical treatment to make it safe to drink. As a result, many residents of New Orleans choose to drink bottled spring water or use an alternative source of water for their drinking and cooking. All of this inconvenience because billions of pounds of "waste" are pumped into America's waterways every day.

This situation is the same across the country, and it has been with us for many years. Read the following excerpt from the 1978 book *The Toilet Papers* by Sim Van der Ryn, a leading authority on ecologically sustaining architecture. In this excerpt, he responds to a 1974 article from *Scientific American* that describes the Hyperion Sewage Treatment Plant in Los Angeles, California. At that time, the plant was discharging 335 million gallons of urine and feces into the Pacific Ocean every day.

> The nutrients in all that [waste], much of it from flush toilets, if converted to fertilizer would be the equivalent of 200 tons of 7-14-12 fertilizer (7 percent nitrogen, 14 percent phosphorus, and 12 percent potassium). Each ton of fertilizer, when applied to soil, would provide the nutrients to grow 25 tons of vegetables. Thus, each day, L.A.'s waste provides the nutrients to grow 5,000 tons of vegetables, enough to provide everyone in Los Angeles with a pound or two of fresh produce daily.[1]

Sounds like our waste is being wasted, huh? What is going to happen to all that waste if the Year 2000 Problem brings those highly efficient sewage plants to a screeching halt? Talk about being backed up!

When it comes down to it, you have two choices about dealing with your waste. First, you can expect that your commodes will be "out of order" for as long as a year, and you can develop a long-term plan to use alternative toilet devices, such as chemical toilets or temporary outdoor toilets, until your commodes are working again. Or, you can make a resolution to change the wasteful cycle of the chemical treatment plants and sewage dumping facilities that our society has come to accept as "normal" and create an extensive permanent composting system in your home and rid yourself of the dreadful pipes altogether.

Finding a Temporary Solution

I guess I'm stretching the definition of "temporary" here. In order to prepare for the worst possible disruptions in our nation's water systems, you should be ready to provide yourself and your family with an alternative waste disposal system for at least three months. Without properly functioning sewer systems, you will be forced to deal with waste disposal quickly, day or night, rain or shine.

The options for temporary solutions to waste disposal range from the simple to the expert and from the inexpensive to the expensive. Your choice depends on your commitment, your price range, and your opinions on human waste.

Gate valve. Before you do anything, if you are living in a single-family dwelling or a duplex, and are part of the city sewer system (as opposed to a septic system), have a plumber install a "gate valve" in the line between your home and the main sewer line that services your property. If you don't, and there's a problem with the water system because of Y2K, the sewers could back up into your home. If that happens, all your other preparation will be for naught—you'll have to move out. By turning the gate valve, this risk is eliminated; however, from that point forward you will have to resort to a compost toilet or alternative. I have been told that a "check valve" is cheaper, but if the pressure is high it can blow it out. My advice is to go with the gate valve and be safe.

Shovel method. This is perhaps the most simple design for an indoor waste disposal system. It has only four ingredients: A bag, a toilet, a bucket, and a shovel. The system: Make sure there is no water in the toilet bowl. Put a heavy-duty trash bag inside the toilet as a liner. Use a bucket for urine and save the toilet for excrement. When they are full, pour out the urine in a location far from your water source and then rinse out the bucket. (Use secondary water, not your drinking water.) Use the shovel to dig a hole and bury the excrement. If you want to get fancy with this method, you can put up a privacy curtain to close off the "bathroom" and add a toilet seat to the bucket to make it more comfortable for the women in your home. Also, you can sprinkle a little lime on the excrement after each use to reduce the odor. Cost: about $5 each for the buckets, $30 for a good supply of the liners, and about $20 for a really good shovel.

Portable toilets. Portable toilets are available in the camping section of your local retail store and are pretty much miniature versions of porta-potties. They hold a reservoir of water that flushes the waste into a storage container. When the storage container is full, you can disconnect it from the toilet and empty or bury it. I believe that the most popular brand of this kind of portable toilet is made by Coleman. Check around. You may find a generic brand of the same model for less. Cost: $55.

Chemical toilets. Recently, I have become aware of a new product on the market that uses a bag-and-bucket system with a chemical polymer which turns human urine and feces into a deodorized, sanitary gel that can be safely buried or even disposed of in trash cans. These products go by the name Brief Relief and are available from American Innotek, Inc. You can learn more about Brief Relief at <http://www.briefrelief.com>. Cost: about $42 per week (plus shipping and handling) for two people.

Septic tanks. If you happen to be on a septic system, you can continue to use your toilets as long as you have water. If you don't have running water, you will have to fill up the toilet tank manually. But do not use your best water to do so! Try to use water that has already been used for other things, like washing dishes, clothes, anything. Alternatively, you can use water that has not been purified or treated.

Finding a Permanent Solution

You may choose to move beyond a temporary solution and change the way your family deals with its waste disposal in a more permanent fashion. Even though public opinion is generally against this type of thinking, the benefits of such a program are numerous. First, you are providing yourself with a rich, nutrient-filled compost to add to your garden. Second, you are saving valuable water and keeping water from being contaminated by your waste. And third, you can continue to dispose of your waste without running water, functional sewage treatment plants, or electricity.

Composting toilets. One option for convenient, indoor waste disposal is to purchase a composting toilet from a specialty retail outlet or over the Internet. In a composting toilet, urine and fecal matter are collected in a composting storage unit. An organic dry mix is then added to the top, introducing decomposing bacteria to the compost. By rotating the drum manually, you add air to the mixture, promoting the growth of aerobic bacteria that speed the decomposition of the waste matter into organic compost and stunt the growth of odor-causing anaerobic bacteria. This process can be quickened even further by adding a heat source to the composting compartment, such as a heating unit or a light bulb. But if a heat source is not available, decomposition will still occur as long as the temperature remains above fifty degrees Fahrenheit. The design of these units creates a partial vacuum, discharging little or no offensive odor.

The cost for all of these permanent solutions are high, but remember, they are permanent—you should never have to deal with septic or sewer systems again. The cost for a BioLet Composting Toilet from Y2K Prep: $990 plus shipping.* You will also need to purchase the humus-starter and add it to the toilet once a week. You can order from:

Y2K Prep
251 Second Avenue South
Franklin, TN 37064
Toll-free: (888) 925-2844
Fax: (615) 794-8860
Internet: <http://www.y2kprep.com/biolet>

Incinerator toilets. Even though these units do not allow for the use of the organic material for compost, they do effectively dispose of human waste conveniently. It works along the same principle as a self-cleaning oven, superheating the material to extreme temperatures and rendering it into a tiny pile of ashes and soot. The incinerator toilet that I have looked at by Storburn can handle about sixty uses between incinerations. The power for these units can be provided by propane or natural gas. Cost: about $2,500 from Jade Mountain, plus gas and incineration stimulant. You can get more information from:

Jade Mountain, Inc.
717 Poplar Avenue
Boulder, CO 80304
Toll-free: (800) 442-1972
Fax: (303) 449-8266
Internet: <http://www.jademountain.com/ecologyProducts/
          incinerator.htm>

Home composting systems. For the heavy-duty composter, there are available systems that can transform your existing network of sewage pipes into a high-capacity, streamlined, compost-collecting system for multiple toilets within your home. The Multrum 1 unit from Clivus, a compost toilet manufacturer since 1939, allows for a basement or crawlspace secured compost collection unit. These units, remarkably, require little or no maintenance, and require only the human intervention of stirring the compost once in a while to aerate the soil and remove odor-causing anaerobic bacteria. They require no chemicals, heat, or water, and have no

---

*As noted earlier, I do have a financial interest in this company, because I found that it offers the best value at the best price and has one of the shortest delivery times available.

polluting discharge. These systems are not inexpensive. A small residence system costs about $2,550. They, too, are available from Jade Mountain (see above). You can read more about this option on the Internet at <http://www.jademountain.com/comp.html>.

Outhouse. This old fashioned-method of waste disposal is a functional and low-cost method, provided you live in a rural area. In order to install a proper outhouse, or privy, you should first contact your local county health department for specific guidelines regarding outbuildings and their proximity to groundwater, wells, springs, streams, and property lines. Remember, you want to keep everything perfectly up to code. You don't want to have to start over.

I don't have the space here to go into detail about how to build an outhouse. If you are interested, read Sim Van der Rym's *The Toilet Papers* (see Chapter 2 for a brief description), or contact your local health department. Cost: depending on accessories and amenities, $250 to $500, plus labor.

What to Do with Your Trash

What if you took your trash can out to the corner and no one picked it up? If fuel supply lines run short, there will be no gasoline to run the garbage trucks. How long would it take for your trash can to become a trash heap?

Even if you have taken care of your sewage waste problem, you will still need to deal with your garbage disposal. Your choice will depend partly on your location—obviously, your options would be different if you live in an apartment complex compared to a ten-acre farm. Regardless of where you live, you've basically got three options: bury it, burn it, or recycle it.

Bury it. This method is probably the least effective and most strenuous method of disposing of your garbage. All you need to do is dig a large hole and throw it in. Make sure that you cover every single bag with at least six inches to twelve inches of dirt so that wild animals won't dig it back up and spread it around. And make sure that the site you choose for your "dump" is downstream from your groundwater source if you are using a well or a spring for your fresh water.

If you choose this method, it is probably better if you leave the garbage unbagged. The organic materials will decompose faster. Unfortunately, plastic products and some paper products will not decompose at all if not exposed to the sun. If the crisis lasts for a long time, this method might become problematic because of the huge amount of space, not to mention labor, that would be involved. After a few weeks of digging, you may choose to abandon this method for another one.

Burn it. Burning your trash is the easiest and least time-consuming method for disposing of your trash. Check out your property and determine which area would be best for your trash incinerator. If you have a large property, a dry, level area that is far from your house (you don't want the smoke blowing in) and away from your water source is the best. If you are planning on incinerating your garbage around your suburban home, consider picking up a fifty-five–gallon metal drum. These are good for confining the flames and can be reused many times over. In addition, you can use the ash from the fire to add to your compost pile or composting toilet to aid in decomposition and to absorb moisture.

Recycle it. If you took a moment to actually look at your garbage, you would be surprised at how much of it could be used again. First, separate all of the organic waste (food, paper, and liquids) from the inorganic (plastics, metals, styrofoam, etc.). Put all of the organics into a composting pile—these will make excellent fertilizer for your spring garden. Look closely at the rest. You may be able to reuse some of the plastic containers for storing food or water. By reusing your garbage, you will be able to decrease your waste by as much as 90 percent or more. What you don't reuse, burn or bury.

Waste Not, Want Not

So, we find that our waste is really not so bad after all. In truth, much of what we see as waste is used again in other countries and is actually beneficial to our way of life if used properly. We should take the advice of the lavish farmer to use what is given to us.

No matter what method you choose for your waste disposal, it is important that you make some decision quickly. The portable toilets are high-demand retail items and may not be available if you wait too long. For the more permanent systems, installation is a long process and will probably take more time than you think. Delivery is another matter entirely. Catalog retailers such as Jade Mountain are already experiencing extended delivery times due to customers who are concerned about Y2K. Plan ahead and order now while you still can!

Y2K PREP TIP #13
Create a Waste Disposal Center

By taking the time and resources that are available right now, you will be able to plan, build, and implement a waste disposal center on your property now for use during the year 2000. Remember, not everyone is planning as far ahead as you might be. You may be able to take advantage of the time that you might have to plan ahead for the future of your community.

Few things promote the spread of disease (not to mention foul odor) like improperly disposed garbage. Take the time now to minimize the spread of disease during Y2K by building a Community Waste Disposal Unit. The concept is simple. Get together with a local church or municipal office (the Sanitation Department or Public Works Department would be best) and plan a location for a centralized waste disposal site that would include two separate sections: a composting pile and an incineration chamber.

You can build a simple incineration chamber by digging a shallow hole (size depends on community size) and building a covered brick structure over the top to keep moisture out. Leave a doorway on one side to insert the trash, an opening on the top to allow smoke to escape, and an opening along the bottom to clean out the ash from time to time. By stocking up on matches and lighter fuel, you should be able to handle quite a bit of garbage. Depending on how you build it, you may be able to use this same chamber for firing pottery or even for baking!

You should also establish a community compost pile. The rules are simple: Bring your compost in, and you can have a portion of the compost in the springtime. Make sure to throw in the ashes from the incineration chamber, too. The compost should be kept in a warm, covered, dark spot that can be easily stirred to promote aeration.

No matter how you choose to construct your Y2K Waste Disposal Center, make sure to consult your local Fire Department and Public Works Department and obtain proper permits for operating such a structure. Express your concerns about Y2K and the need for proper contingency planning in the event of serious problems. You'll want to make sure that everything is perfectly legal so your center won't get shut down when you need it most.

	Y2K PREPAREDNESS CHECKLIST				
Level	Action Step	Qty	Unit Price	Total Qty	Total Price
1	Determine if you want to find a temporary solution or a permanent one for disposing of waste.	N/A	N/A		
1	Determine how you will dispose of your trash.	N/A	N/A		
3	Implement your temporary solution.	N/A	$50 to $600		
3	Create a Community Waste Disposal Center (see Y2K Prep Tip #13).	N/A	N/A		
4	Implement your permanent solution.	N/A	$250 to $2,550		

Chapter Fourteen

Be Prepared for Medical Emergencies

Be prepared.

—Boy Scout motto

A few years back, Joanne, a close friend of mine, was having a hard time dealing with the death of her mother. Her father, too, was having difficulties. So, in an effort to spend some quality time with one another in a peaceful setting, the two of them decided to go on a camping trip in the beautiful Appalachian Mountains.

While camping, the two spent hours talking, and slowly Joanne and her father began coming to grips with their loss and were able to enjoy themselves.

On one of the last days of the camping trip, the two decided to go on a four-mile hike through the woods to a scenic overlook. Apparently, the overlook could be accessed more easily by road, so few people took the scenic route hiking through the woods. The two decided it would be perfect "quiet time" they could spend together, away from the other campers.

As the two walked along the rugged trail, the path suddenly became treacherous. Joanne's father slipped on a moss-covered rock step and fell to the wooded landing below. She distinctly heard the snapping of his leg, followed by a howl of pain. Joanne looked around and, not seeing another soul, suddenly felt terribly, terribly alone and helpless.

▫ ▫ ▫

In our modern technological society, medical help is only a phone call away. Three simple numbers—911—can bring an army of trained medical technicians to your doorstep in a matter of minutes to deal with any number of medical emergencies and, ultimately, save a great number of lives in doing so.

What we don't think about is how fragile that ability is. Without the proper method of communicating our predicament, the 911 service would be useless. In the same way, the Year 2000 Problem has the ability to eradicate existing telecommunications systems, rendering the 911 Emergency Response System completely and totally useless and inaccessible.

In addition to 911 system failures, failures in the general medical services industry may grind hospitals, doctor's offices, and medical clinics to a halt. According to reports from the president's Office of Management and Budget (OMB), the Department of Health and Human Services is one of the federal agencies that is least prepared for transition into the year 2000 and beyond. Health and Human Services monitors the Health Care Financing Administration, which processes hundreds of millions of medical claims every year through Medicare and Medicaid. The ontime payments of medical claims through this office is the primary source of income for most health care facilities in the United States. Without that process in place, most hospitals and doctor's offices will most likely be forced to close because they do not have the funds to pay for their supplies or pay their employees.

Without assistance from medical personnel, would you be able to deal with medical emergencies on your own? Could you:

- Set a broken leg?

- Perform CPR?

- Distinguish between a poisonous bite and a harmless one?

- Aid someone who was having a seizure?

- Help deliver a baby?

Unless you are a practicing nurse or physician, your answer to these questions is probably no. Don't feel alone. Most Americans would respond in the same manner. Why should we be prepared? Our society has created a fantastic telecommunications network that can bring professionals to our doorstep in minutes. Well, folks, Y2K may very well bring that system crashing down, and we may be suddenly in the dark and forced to deal with these types of situations ourselves. By taking some steps now, while there is still time to prepare, you can learn the skills that you need in order to deal with any emergency situation that arises, whether it involves another person or yourself.

Preventative Measures

Because the Y2K problem will force us into lifestyle changes beyond our control, it is important for you to look at ways in which you can change your bad habits, dependencies, and knowledge base now, while you still have time to prepare. By following these few basic suggestions, you can train both your mind and body to prepare for unexpected changes in lifestyle, eating habits, and responsibilities.

1. Drop the vices. In essence, if you regularly partake in any of the common vices—smoking cigarettes, chewing tobacco, using illegal drugs, or drinking alcohol—stop immediately. These vices are not only damaging to your body, but your body also develops a dependency on them that you may be unable to satisfy come the year 2000. And they use up valuable money that you could be using to fund your preparations for the coming crisis. In addition, these vice items may become barter items after January 1, 2000, if they become scarce. You wouldn't want to feel tempted to trade your best flashlight for a pack of cigarettes or a week's food for a case of beer, so cut out the temptations while you still can.

If you need help with dropping your vices, you may be able to find support in your community or use over-the-counter medications to help you quit. Call your local hospital or ask your doctor or pharmacist what your options are.

2. Change your diet habits. I'm not saying that you have to give up McDonald's completely. My kids would probably organize a rebellion if I tried to do that. But what you can do is cut back on fast food and microwave dinners, and add more grains and beans to your family's regular diet to prepare them for a change in eating styles, depending on what types of foods you are planning on storing for food. Make more fresh soups and entrees.

3. Get regular exercise. Depending on your size, this will be different for every person. Joining a gymnasium may help to get you in the habit of regular exercise. Or, try to find time during the day to walk, jog, or run in your area. I personally run two miles every morning (weather permitting). This time is invaluable to me—I consider it my "thinking time," when I can think through ideas without being distracted by ringing phones or mounds of paperwork. It also allows me to think more clearly during the day and begin the day relaxed and refreshed. And it only takes about twenty-five minutes!

Exercising serves two purposes. The first is that regular exercise will help to improve your Body Fat Index (BFI), reducing your body's fat and increasing the amount of muscle tissue, making your body stronger and increasing your stamina under stressful conditions and hardships. The second benefit of regular exercise is that aerobic exercise such as running and jogging increase oxygen flow in the bloodstream, resulting in clearer thinking and fewer tired muscles.

If you can't run or jog in public in your area, or you don't have access to a local gym, consider purchasing a stationary bicycle or nonelectric treadmill for use in your own home. You can purchase these devices at sporting goods or retail stores for as little as $200. These items might be invaluable to you during the Y2K Crisis to maintain your stamina and continue your daily exercise regimen.

4. Become knowledgeable about basic medical procedures. Do you know how to perform CPR? Treat a snakebite? How about performing the Heimlich maneuver? You would be surprised how many people are unprepared to deal with simple medical emergencies. Your knowledge of a few simple medical procedures could mean the difference between life and death for someone who is choking, having a seizure, or suffering from a heart attack.

The first step in learning about basic medical procedures is to buy a manual that discusses the proper execution of these procedures and gives instructions on how to perform them and how to diagnose the proper course of action depending on the symptoms. The best book for this purpose is *The American Red Cross First Aid and Safety Handbook* by Kathleen A. Handal, M.D. (New York: Little, Brown and Company, 1992). This book can be purchased for only $17.95. Familiarizing yourself with it will enable you to handle nearly any emergency situation.

Once you are familiar with the Red Cross handbook, you may wish to enroll in a first aid training course in your area. These courses are given on a regular basis by Red Cross offices across the country and provide training in CPR, the Heimlich maneuver, and other basic medical procedures that can help save lives. The courses are taught by licensed medical professionals and can certify you to perform these procedures. Unfortunately, most courses are not free; the small fee for participation includes both a manual on the topic and professional instruction. Local Red Cross offices often teach other specialized courses, such as Infant/Child CPR, Emergency Response, and Preventing Disease Transmission. Contact your local American Red Cross office for a list of available courses.

If you have reached this point and wish to take your medical training further, consider signing up for a course to become certified as an Emergency Medical Technician (EMT). These courses are available at colleges and universities and provide more thorough training than you can get with a basic first aid course. With certification as an EMT, you will be able to handle almost any emergency situation that arises, from cuts and scrapes to gunshot wounds. Costs and lengths of these types of courses vary from college to college. For more information, contact either your local college or hospital and ask where the courses are available and how much they cost.

5. Secure copies of your medical records. It is imperative that patients obtain hard copy documentation of their medical records; furthermore, this information must be in a format easily understood by anyone administering care in an emergency. Without this information, a patient could suffer severe injury and possible fatality due to misdiagnosis or improper treatment. Using the patient's medical documents, a medical professional or a nonmedically trained person can more safely aid in the patient's health care needs or emergencies. The vital medical information for a patient should be carried with him or her at all times.

Stocking Your Medicine Cabinet

Just as every person's fingerprints are unique, so should every person's medicine cabinet be. Only you know what type of medicines your family uses on a regular basis, what flavors of cough syrup your kids will take, and what types of allergies and vitamin deficiencies your family members have.

Vitamins. Because nutritious, wholesome foods and square meals from the four food groups may become scarce during the year 2000, you need to be prepared to supplement your daily food intake with vitamins. Literally hundreds of different types of vitamins and vitamin supplements are commercially available for you to do this. Here is a checklist for specific vitamins that you need to be aware of and make sure you have plenty of to keep you healthy and strong:

- *Vitamin A.* This vitamin comes naturally from vegetables that contain carotene, such as carrots, broccoli, and squash. It helps promote healthy bones and teeth, and improves and maintains vision in young children.

- *Vitamin C.* This well-known vitamin is found in fresh fruits and green vegetables. It is important to healthy teeth and bones and helps absorbs iron from vegetables into the bloodstream. Deficiencies in Vitamin C can lead to scurvy in both children and adults. However, overabundance of Vitamin C has been found to have harmful effects on health.

- *Vitamin D.* This vitamin is absolutely essential because it helps the body absorb calcium and phosphorus, which are used to maintain strong bones. Before the use of Vitamin D–fortified milk, many developing children suffered from rickets, a deformation of the bones in the legs and skull, due to the body's inability to absorb calcium properly.

- *Vitamin E.* Found in vegetable oils and wheat germ, Vitamin E is essential for the production of healthy red blood cells. A person who takes in a proper amount of Vitamin E will have stronger muscle tissue and will have greater stamina.

- *Vitamin K.* This vitamin is essential for the coagulation of blood and blood clotting. Natural sources of Vitamin K include egg yolks, leafy green vegetables, and soybean oil.[1]

Other important nutrients not listed above include: *folic acid*, needed to form proteins and hemoglobin in the blood and also important for healthy development in pregnant women; *iron*, essential for maintaining healthy hemoglobin in the blood, thereby increasing the amount of oxygen in the body; and *niacin*, which has been shown to reduce levels of cholesterol in the bloodstream and helps release extra energy from stored nutrients.

As an alternative to purchasing these vitamins separately, I recommend you find a good multivitamin (a single vitamin pill that contains high doses of all types of vitamins) that meets your needs. Some multivitamins are designed to meet the special needs of children, men, women, and seniors. You should be able to buy enough vitamins for your entire family for under $50 from your local Wal-Mart or specialized vitamin dealer.

Herbal and other alternative medicines. Some vitamins are important for you to protect against infection, especially colds and flu viruses during the winter season. Zinc tablets have recently been found to promote healing and increase your body's natural defense mechanisms, leading to fewer infections and less illness. Other herbal alternatives to prescription medications include: *echinacea*, which boosts the immune system and prevents or shortens illnesses; *ginseng root*, which has proven to increase energy and endurance by aiding oxygen absorption in the bloodstream; and *St. John's wort*, which has been shown to alleviate moderate depression. *Colloidal silver* is also an effective treatment for infections.

Herbal alternatives offer many benefits for your medical needs. First, herbal medicines are almost always less expensive than their commercial counterparts. Second, herbal medications are healthier for your body because they contain all-natural materials and not the harmful by-products that exist in your commercial medications. Third, there is no limit to the number of herbal medications you can purchase. Unlike regular prescriptions, which can be refilled only a finite number of times, herbal alternatives are available without a prescription and with no refill limit, so you can stock up on as many packages as you need without conferring with a doctor or arguing with a pharmacist.

For more information on herbal alternatives to prescription medications, contact your local health food chain, vitamin retailer, or doctor to learn about current statistics on herbal alternatives.

Over-the-counter medications. Stop reading for a moment and go look in your medicine cabinet. I'll bet you found at least fifteen different kinds of over-the-counter medicines that you use on a regular basis, including pain relievers, fever reducers, antacids, antidiarrhea medicines, and antihistamines. Take an inventory of those medicines—you've just created your over-the-counter medications checklist for the year 2000! You see, that medicine cabinet is custom-designed for your family's specific needs.

By stocking up on the medications that are on your checklist, you can ensure that your family will not be slowed down or bedridden by simple, normally occurring illnesses like headaches, sinus problems, or diarrhea during the Y2K Crisis. Remember, your local pharmacy will probably not be open—you won't be able to rush out at 3 AM and get some more medicine if you run out. Make sure that you have an ample supply of these medications—at least enough to last your family for a year. Be sure to check the expiration dates on the medicines that you buy. Although most do not truly "expire," they may lose effectiveness and potency if kept too long after the recommended date.

If you can afford it, stock up on an overabundance of these medications. Because not everyone will be preparing for the Y2K Crisis, these items will be scarce and in great demand. You may be able to barter these items for goods and services that you may need. These items are plentiful and inexpensive now, but they quickly will become scarce and expensive once the Y2K Crisis hits.

One final note about over-the-counter medications—think for a moment about your extended family. Do you have young grandchildren, nieces, or nephews? If so, you should consider stocking up on children's versions of common medicines, such as pain relievers, antihistamines, and cough syrups. What about the elderly? Is it possible that your grandparents may be coming to stay with you? Prepare for their needs as well. It is important to look outside your immediate family when planning. If you so choose, you can also plan to stock up on medications for your friends and neighbors.

Prescription medications. If you've ever been to a pharmacy to get your prescription filled, you know that the prescription medications industry is tightly monitored for abuses and illegal activity. Therefore, I do not, under any circumstances, recommend that you try to obtain extra quantities of your prescription medications illegally. (I have a close friend who works as a pharmacist—believe me, they are fully aware of what is going on!)

Instead, I recommend approaching your doctor in a simple, straightforward manner and explain to him your concerns about the Year 2000 Computer Problem. The conversation might go something like this:

> You: "So, doc, have you guys had any problems with the Year 2000 Problem here in your office yet?"
>
> Doctor: "No, nothing yet. But I heard an associate of mine at the hospital say that they're spending a lot of money over there trying to fix it."
>
> You: "Yeah, I'm pretty worried about it. They say that if a lot of systems fail, some of the manufacturing plants might have to shut down for a while to repair it."
>
> Doctor: "Really? I guess they would have to, to bring their computers back up and fix them."
>
> You: "Yeah. I guess that means the pharmaceutical companies might have problems, too. Supplies of medicines might run pretty slim."
>
> Doctor: "I guess they probably would."
>
> You: "What would I do if I couldn't get my heart medicine?"
>
> Doctor: "That would be a problem for you. You might get pretty sick or have a heart attack."
>
> You: "Do you think you could write me a larger prescription so I can stock up? You know, just in case?"
>
> Doctor: "Well, I'm not supposed to. But I'd hate for you to have those kinds of problems. I'll write you a larger prescription. You know, just in case."
>
> You: "Thanks, doc. Let's both hope that this thing doesn't really happen and it's all just a bad dream, okay?"
>
> Doctor: "Okay."

While you have your doctor's attention, this would be a good time to ask him about antibiotics. Antibiotics attack serious bacterial infections within the human body. Since no over-the-counter antibiotics are available, you may have reasonable success in getting your doctor to write you a prescription for a longer supply of antibiotic pills in case Y2K troubles are widespread. He may accept, but only on the condition that you pass a training session on antibiotic usage.

If you choose to use birth control, don't forget to ask your doctor about an extended supply—or about longer-lasting options for birth control. Some modern methods (moving beyond the pill) involve placing a device under the skin that provides effective birth control for up to five years.

Make sure your doctor understands the risks involved here. Should your doctor say no even after you voice your concerns about Y2K, you may want to consider consulting another physician. Your life may depend on these medications.

One doctor that I know who *is* Y2K-savvy is Dr. Raghavan K. Chari, M.D., F.A.C.E.P., an emergency medicine critical care physician. He has thoroughly researched the effects of a large-scale Y2K Crisis in the health care field and has written and lectured extensively on the subject of "Medical Preparedness during Y2K." He is one of the founders of Conquest Associates, a health care organization promoting freedom, preparedness, and privacy in health care. Dr. Chari and his associates specialize in health care crisis readiness. Amazingly, they offer a free cassette tape on the subject of Y2K and medical preparedness. For a limited time, you can obtain this tape by calling toll-free (800) 580-9666. Or if you prefer, you can e-mail Dr. Chari at <conquest@us.net> or visit his website at <http://www. conquesthealth.com>. And there is a link on my website, which you can reach at <http://www.michaelhyatt.com>.

Other needs. Of course, every individual has special medical needs, and only you are fully aware of them. These other needs are the ones we pay the least attention to. I personally don't think much about my dental care until I run out of toothpaste. It's just something that I do every day. I'd be willing to bet that you don't think about a lot of things like this until they smack you in the face.

For example, if you require glasses or hard contact lenses to help you see properly, you should purchase a spare pair in case your current pair gets broken or misplaced. Many mainstream optical centers offer "Buy One Get One Free" or "Buy One Pair, Get the Second One Half Off" promotions. Use these opportunities to update your prescription and stock up for Y2K. If you wear soft disposable contact lenses, buy ten or twelve extra boxes from the least expensive retailer to help you make it through until they are available again.

Don't forget extra toothbrushes and toothpaste. You should probably store one new toothbrush for every three months for every member of your family. While you're at it, get a dozen tubes of toothpaste and a dozen packages of dental floss. They can be used as barter items, too.

Ladies, don't forget to stock up on those personal needs that you have to control your monthly menstrual cycle. Menstrual pads and tampons are inexpensive and never expire. Stock up on enough to last you for a year or more. These, too, can be used as effective barter items in an emergency situation.

I'm probably leaving out a lot of things—things that we do every day but just don't think too much about. It might help to go through a day or two with a pad and pencil, writing down all the things that you do and the instruments that you use to do them. Then, you may have a better checklist of things you need to stock up on.

Putting Together a First Aid Kit

Let me say first that a first aid kit is completely different from a medicine cabinet. A first aid kit should include many of the items that you find in your medicine cabinet, only in smaller quantities and in a small, easily portable package. I want to emphasize that neither one should be used as a substitute for the other. Do not say, "Well, I'm stocking up my medicine cabinet so full that I won't need a first aid kit." Being prepared for emergencies is simply not possible without a first aid kit.

Several "turn-key" first aid kits are available on the retail market, ranging in price from $9.99 to $100 or more, depending on the contents. These kits are better than having no kit at all, but it is by far better to put your first aid kit together yourself because only you know what your special needs are. To do so, find a small luggage tote or compartmentalized box that can be easily carried, then add the following key ingredients to make your own first aid kit.

The first key ingredient to any first aid kit is you. Well, not really your body, but your knowledge of basic medical procedures. You will be of little help in an emergency if you don't know how to use the materials in your first aid kit to help the victim. Buy a second copy of *The American Red Cross First Aid and Safety Handbook* by Kathleen A. Handal to include in your first aid kit (your other copy should be kept in your Emergency Preparedness Library). Its information is invaluable in an emergency. Make sure that you have read it and are familiar with its contents so that you can flip to the proper section quickly. Remember, seconds count in an emergency. According to the Red Cross, these items are essential for a proper first aid kit:

- Adhesive bandage strips

- Butterfly bandages

- Elastic bandage (three inches wide)

- Hypoallergenic adhesive tape (to secure dressings in place)

- Roller bandages (a roll of stretchable gauze to hold dressings in place)

- Sterile cotton balls

- Sterile eye patches

- Sterile gauze pads, four inches × four inches (individually wrapped)

- Sterile nonstick pads

- Triangular bandage (for slings or as a covering or dressing)

- Blunt-tipped scissors (for cutting bandages or clothing)

- Tweezers (to remove splinters and other foreign objects)

- Bulb syringe (to rinse eyes or wounds)

- Cotton swabs

- Small plastic cup

- Instant-acting chemical cold packs (for sprains, bruises, etc.)

- Paper cups

- Space blanket

- Thermometer (one that is easy to use)

- Activated charcoal (for poisoning emergency)

- Antiseptic wipes or antiseptic solution

- Antibiotic ointment

- Antiseptic/anesthetic spray

- Calamine/antihistamine lotion

- Sterile eye wash

- Syrup of ipecac (to use during poisoning emergency)

- Candle and matches

- Flashlight (with proper batteries)

- Pad and pencil for notes

- Packet of tissues

- Isopropyl alcohol

- Hydrogen peroxide

- Soap (for cleansing wounds)

- Safety pin (for use with triangular bandage)

- Disposable latex gloves (two pairs)[2]

Also, make sure to include a good pain reliever, as well as any special needs for you or for a member of your family. If you have children, include children's medications and comfort toys. And if you suffer from a debilitating sudden disease, such as epilepsy, make sure you write step-by-step introductions on how to administer to you in case you cannot communicate vocally.

The first aid kit should be placed in a highly visible place. You don't want to be running around frantically, screaming, "Where did I put that thing?" Under ideal circumstances, you could have two or three first aid kits in important locations where accidents might occur, such as in the kitchen, the garage, or the basement. If you are still using your vehicle, make sure to place one there, too.

Be Prepared

Joanne knew that her father was in tremendous pain. As she lay next to him on the ground along the lonely trail, she was startled by the sound of rustling leaves. A lone, stray hiker was coming up the trail.

"Help!" Joanne cried.

"What's the matter?" the hiker asked.

"He's broken his leg," Joanne replied. "Can you help him?"

Immediately, the hiker began searching the wooded area for an adequate splint. He took a small first aid kit from his backpack and gave Joanne's father some medication to relieve the pain as he wrapped the leg and the splint with bandages from the kit. He pulled out his cellular phone and handed it to Joanne. "Call the ranger. I put the number on speed dial."

Within a few minutes, a ranger and paramedic had arrived on the scene. With the added help, they were easily able to carry Joanne's father out of the area and eventually to a nearby hospital, where his broken leg was set properly. Luckily for Joanne, her father survived that ordeal without too many problems. If it had not been for the preparedness of the hiker, the outcome of that situation might have been drastically different.

Medical emergencies can happen at any time and any place. There is no doubt that there will be medical emergencies during the Y2K Crisis. But after Y2K, we may not be as fortunate as Joanne and her father—there may be no emergency services to come to your rescue. You could be left to deal with the situation by yourself, without the aid of a 911 operator or an EMT.

Being knowledgeable about simple medical procedures and having the ability to spot key symptoms of a medical condition could mean the difference between life and death if you are caught in the middle of an emergency. By following preventive measures to keep yourself healthy, you can minimize the chances of becoming ill or hurting yourself. By studying information about basic medial procedures, you can be ready to help others. And, by maintaining a properly stocked medicine cabinet and first aid kit, you can be prepared for any type of medical condition or emergency that you find yourself in.

Y2K PREP TIP #14
Get Your Family "First Aid Ready"

In the event of an emergency, a personal home first aid kit and a first aid manual are invaluable tools. Since emergency 911 services may not be available or may not be able to respond quickly, you may be the only chance that a victim has to survive or escape further harm. Being prepared for this type of situation could be second nature to you and your family if you choose to make your family "first aid ready."

Being knowledgeable about the effective implementation of basic medical procedures can mean the difference between life and death in an emergency situation. Although basic knowledge is better than no knowledge, having that information centralized in a single member of your family would not be beneficial if that member was the one who needed help. In order to be effective, every member of your family, including children, should be familiar with basic first aid procedures.

Here's how to do it. Take one of the basic first aid courses taught by the American Red Cross and make it a family affair. Bring the kids along so that they can see how to help people in an emergency. Review the procedures when you get home and on a regular basis thereafter. Once a month, bring the family together and read through the first aid manual and see who can remember how to do the procedures. You can even take it as far as trying to make a family game out of it!

Then, when you are putting together your personal family first aid kit, take your whole family shopping. Make sure that everyone understands how to use the tape, gauze, and ointments in your first aid kit. The kids might even like to pick out some special Band-Aids that they can include in the kit.

The outcome of these activities will be that both you and your family will have a better understanding of basic first aid and that you can be confident that any member of your family can deal with an emergency situation.

Y2K PREPAREDNESS CHECKLIST					
Level	*Action Step*	*Qty*	*Unit Price*	*Total Qty*	*Total Price*
1	Take up running, jogging, or walking for exercise.	N/A	N/A		
1	Take inventory of your medicine cabinet and make up a checklist of medicines to buy.	N/A	N/A		
1	Talk to your doctor about prescription medications.	N/A	N/A		
1	Order Dr. Chari's free cassette tape by calling toll-free (800) 580-9666.	N/A	N/A		
2	Stock up on 6–12 months' worth of over-the-counter medications.	Varies	Varies		
2	Stock up on vitamin supplements.	N/A	$50		
2	Take a first aid course from your local chapter of the American Red Cross.	N/A	$30		
2	Purchase an extra copy of *The American Red Cross First Aid and Safety Handbook* for your first aid kit.	N/A	$18		
2	Prepare custom first aid kits for your family needs, to be placed in different parts of your home.	N/A	$30		
3	Overstock on over-the-counter medications for barter purposes.	N/A	N/A		

Chapter Fifteen

Determine Your
Self-defense Philosophy

God grants liberty only to those who love it, and are always ready to guard and defend it.

—Daniel Webster

Suddenly, Stephen's eyes snapped open. What was that noise? No, it wasn't the children. He looked at the clock on his nightstand—2:17 AM. There it was again. Someone was downstairs!

He looked over at his wife Alice. Still asleep. He arose from the warmth of his bed and opened the closet. There, resting against the back corner, leaned his shotgun. He had fired it only once before, at his father's home, right after he bought it two years ago. In the dark he fumbled on the top shelf of the closet for the box of shells that he kept there, safely away from reach of his two children. He grabbed a handful of shells and headed for the hallway.

Once in the hallway, he stood at the top of the stairs and popped the shotgun open and inserted the two shells. "I don't know who you are," he shouted down the stairs, "but I want you out of my house, NOW!" With those final words, Stephen chambered the shells in the gun with a loud CLACK-CLACK!

He heard an utterance, but couldn't make it out. Then he heard the sound of something falling, and then a voice outside saying "Go, man, go!" Tires squealed as the intruder's car sped away outside.

Stephen stood at the top of the stairs, his hands shaking and his heart racing. He glanced at the clock at the bottom of the stairs—2:19 AM.

The right to bear arms is a right protected by the Constitution of the United States of America.[1] That right, however, has been at the center of a long-standing, heated debate between those who feel widespread gun ownership is an invitation for criminal activity and those who feel duty-bound to own a weapon to keep themselves and their families safe from harm. Though I feel strongly about the issue, it is beyond the scope of this book to try and convince you one way or another.

Rather than simply telling you to buy a gun, I want you to have as many different options as possible to provide self-defense for you and your family during the coming hard times. If 911 emergency services fail due to Y2K problems, you may not be able to pick up the telephone and call for help. That responsibility will be yours and yours alone. Our nation's devoted police forces will be very busy attending to criminal activities as best they can without proper communications and, possibly, without motor vehicles. It is not likely that they will be aware of an isolated criminal activity, such as a robbery, much less have the ability to reach your location quickly. It is important to think about how this will affect the safety of you and your family.

Your Self-defense Philosophy

Your first step in preparing to defend yourself and your family during the Y2K Crisis is to develop your own personal self-defense philosophy. This is no small decision. If you are like many Americans and have never considered what you would do in a crisis situation, many factors can affect the outcome of that decision.

Morally, you may be worried about the question, "Is it right for me to threaten another human being, much less take his life?" On the other hand, you may be asking yourself, "Don't I have an obligation to protect my own life and the lives of my family, no matter what the cost?" Your moral beliefs may keep you from using a weapon that has the potential to cause life-threatening injury. If this is so, you should consider one of the many less violent and nonlethal alternatives to owning a gun.

On a religious level, you may have objections to certain methods of self-defense. Remember "Love thy neighbor" and even "Love thine enemy"? These passages would seem to indicate that the use of lethal force is never justified. But other passages seem to justify self-defense. The Apostle Paul wrote in 1 Timothy 5:8, "If any provide not for his own, and specially for those of his own house, he hath denied the faith, and is worse than an infidel." This shows that protecting yourself and your family was important to the early Christians, as it still is today. In Exodus 22:2, we read, "If a thief be found breaking in, and be smitten that he die, there shall no blood be shed for him." In other words, if a thief in your home threatens your life and is killed in the struggle, you shall not be held accountable for his death. Jesus himself, in Luke 22:36, told His disciples, "He that hath no sword, let him sell his garment, and buy one." Study your Scriptures and consider Christ's teachings when determining your self-defense philosophy.

Your own personal self-confidence is also a major factor in determining your self-defense plan. Would you feel confident enough to hold and fire a weapon in a crisis situation? If not, you are probably not a good candidate for a firearm, which can be dangerous in unconfident hands. Perhaps a less lethal choice would be better for you.

Your personal situation is also a factor in your decision. Do you live alone? Are you currently living in a potentially dangerous neighborhood? Does your house look inviting to thieves? If you answered yes to any of these, then you should carefully consider how that affects your self-defense philosophy. You will probably be more in need of an effective self-defense plan than others.

Gun Ownership

Like it or not, the option of buying a firearm for your protection during the Y2K Crisis is a legal and effective self-defense philosophy. However, it is important here to note the inherent danger of a deadly firearm in the hands of an untrained, unconfident user.

If you choose to purchase a gun, and you have never owned, held, or fired a gun before, do not rush into this purchase as casually as you would any other. This is a serious purchase that deserves serious thought and planning.

Do not—I repeat—*do not* purchase a gun if you do not plan on following through with the proper training and safety techniques that go along with responsible gun ownership. If you do plan on taking on the responsibility of gun ownership, your choices are varied and are dependent on your lifestyle, your stamina, and your price range.

One of the best places to begin your training is to purchase *SafetyOn*, "a comprehensive interactive guide to firearm safety and responsible handgun ownership." It comes on CD-ROM (for either Macintosh or Windows) and contains twenty to forty hours of multimedia instruction on such topics as firearm basics, self-defense, and care and maintenance. It has been carefully reviewed by the National Rifle Association Training Division Staff and is fully compatible with their training and safety standards. It sells for $39.99 plus shipping. You can order it from:

SafetyOn
P.O. Box 113
New Albany, OH 43054
Voice: (614) 855-2854
Fax: (614) 855-2869
Internet: <http://www.gunsoft.com>

Handguns

For portable self-defense, a handgun is the optimal choice. Its small size makes it easy to carry in a purse or in a hip or shoulder holster under your clothes and out of sight. Your first choice when buying a handgun is the type of handgun you prefer— a revolver or a semiautomatic.[2] A revolver is a variation on the old Western "six-shooter" you've seen in the movies in which bullets are loaded into a revolving chamber and fired by pulling the trigger. This action brings the next bullet into place. A semiautomatic holds a clip of bullets in the gun handle and is the type of gun used by most police officers and government officials.

Revolvers are more cumbersome than semiautomatics, but they are generally less prone to malfunction and less expensive than semiautomatics. Semiautomatics are lighter and easier to conceal, but often take longer to master. Both revolvers and semiautomatics have advantages over the other, so you will have to do some shopping and determine your personal preference.

Let's look at a few popular choices for novice handgun owners, all of which should be available at specialty gun shops:

The .38 Special. This popular revolver is good for the novice user, due to its smaller size and minimal recoil. Novices can easily master control and accuracy of a .38 Special, and accuracy can be increased by purchasing one with a longer barrel. Holds five to six rounds. Cost: prices start at about $250.

The .357 Magnum. This revolver is more powerful than the .38 Special, and has a louder sound and stronger recoil. It will take .38 Special ammunition (which will reduce the recoil and is less expensive), and you can upgrade the ammunition to the larger caliber once you become used to firing it. Holds five to six rounds. Cost: prices start at about $250.

The 9mm pistol. This small semiautomatic is easy to carry, lightweight, and accurate if you take the time to practice with it. It is one of the more common military field pistols in use today. Holds eight to ten rounds. Cost: prices start at about $250.

The .40 pistol. This semiautomatic is my personal favorite (I have a Beretta). It has more power and will do more damage than a 9mm, but without the recoil of the .45 (see below). Holds eight to ten rounds. Cost: prices start at about $250.

The Colt .45 1911A1. This semiautomatic is also small and compares functionally with the 9mm pistol. The 1911A1 is considered by many shooters as the best handgun ever designed. Most government agents and much of our nation's police force carry this model every day to protect their own lives. Holds six to eight rounds. Cost: prices start at about $475.

Be aware that many states require a separate permit to carry a concealed weapon on your body at any time. This permit usually costs between $40 and $100 and varies by state. To obtain a license, contact your local police department or department of public safety.

Shotguns

If you do not plan to conceal your weapon on your body at all times and you only wish to have a personal security weapon for your home, a shotgun is your best bet. Shotguns have several advantages over traditional handguns, including greater range and less need for accuracy, as well as being less expensive than most handguns. However, they are bulkier and much more cumbersome to carry than a handgun.

Shotguns are available in a number of different sizes. For home defense purposes, look for a 20-gauge (smaller) or 12-gauge (larger) pump-action shotgun with an 18- to 22-inch barrel for home security. You should be able to find a good quality shotgun that fits this description for about $250 at a local retail store, such as Wal-Mart, or at a specialty gun shop. I personally recommend either of two guns. The Mossberg 50577 Model 500 is a pump action, 12-gauge shotgun with a 20-inch barrel. It has an eight-shot capacity, making it perfect for home defense. It sells for about $189 at major retailers. My other favorite is Remington 870 Express, also a 12-gauge pump action gun, and perhaps the most popular shotgun ever manufactured. It sells for about $220 at most retailers.

Another option, if you don't mind spending a little more money, is a 12-gauge semiautomatic. These shotguns hold four to five shells and do not require pumping to "chamber" the next round. This is generally easier for petite women and older children to operate. But for some the semiautomatic feature is actually a disadvantage, since semiautomatics do not make the CLACK-CLACK sound that can be a powerful deterrent to anyone who hears it.

In terms of shotgun ammunition, I recommend high brass (high powered) number 6 shot. The advantages are:

- A wider-than-normal pattern for the shooter who needs all the help he can get;

- The ability to stop a perpetrator—or at least ruin his day (along with that of the surgeon who must deal with the removal of hundreds of shot, rather than the nine found in 00 buckshot); and most importantly

- Reducing the likelihood that any walls would be penetrated, thus striking a family member.

Rifles

For practical purposes, rifles are impractical for home defense. The smaller-bore .22 caliber rifles that are commercially available are not effective against humans, although they still make an impressive show of force. The larger caliber rifles are too large for indoor use, as stray bullets may have the potential to penetrate interior walls and injure innocent bystanders. Unless you plan on using your weapon to maintain security on a large piece of property or hunt, skip past the rifles and go for the shotgun. The show of force is much greater.

Responsibility

No matter what type of firearm you purchase, the responsibility of owning it and being prepared to use it is tremendous. Nothing is more frightening to me than the thought of a gun in the hands of someone who is not trained in its use and not confident about using it.

Most states provide courses in proper handling, firing, cleaning, and storage of firearms as part of the application for carrying a concealed weapon or other gun permits. When these courses are not offered free of charge, they are available for a nominal fee. But, no matter what the cost, a training course should not be an option, nor should regular, consistent practice. If your spouse is not trained in the use of your firearm, make sure that he or she takes the course and practices with you.

Never pull a gun and point it unless you fully intend to use it for its purpose. Hesitation can lead to a dangerous situation in a single second. At the very least, it can make your opponent more aggressive.

And you should purchase a gun safe or secure place in which to place your guns and ammunition. The last thing you want is for a child to gain access to your weapon and injure or kill himself or someone else. There are many different models available that offer both convenience and security. You can generally purchase these at any sporting goods store or gun shop.

One last word: Make sure you buy *plenty* of ammunition. Since we don't know how long a Y2K-related disruption may last, and since it may be difficult to buy ammunition during the crisis, it is better to have more rather than less. Personally, my goal is to have at least one thousand rounds of ammunition per gun.

Alternatives to Gun Ownership

If your moral or spiritual beliefs lead you away from gun ownership, or you lack the confidence to handle a firearm, there are many, many alternatives. In my opinion, none of these is as safe (for you) or as effective as a gun, but for those who are not comfortable with using lethal force in a self-defense situation (and who is), here are some alternatives.

Self-defense Courses

Various courses are available on the local level that teach basic hand-to-hand self-defense. These courses are sometimes sponsored by police departments or are available (for a fee) from martial arts studios and universities. They teach how to identify potentially dangerous situations and how to avoid and/or escape them, how to break an assailant's grasp, the key attack areas on the assailant's body, and basic hand-to-hand martial arts movements. Depending on the length and location of the course, paid self-defense classes can cost anywhere from $25 to $100.

Stun Guns

Stun guns are becoming a popular choice for self-defense as an alternative to firearms. A stun gun is a device that can be held in the palm of your hand and uses two electrodes that deliver a low amperage, high-voltage shock of anywhere from 65,000 to 300,000 volts of electricity when placed against the body of an assailant for three to five seconds. The electricity disrupts muscle control, leaving the victim without muscle control for as long as ten minutes.

Unfortunately, these devices are sometimes ineffective against large body-frame assailants, as the electric charge may not affect the attacker properly. One officer told me that they were a poor choice in *any* situation. However, against small to mid-size assailants or against vicious animals, the stun gun *may* be an effective deterrent.

Pricing on stun guns vary depending on how many volts of electricity they discharge. The largest and most effective stun guns discharge 300,000 volts and run about $50. Smaller models can be purchased for as little as $25. You probably won't find these products at your local Wal-Mart. You'll probably need to venture to a specialty gun and knife shop to get a quality stun gun.

Tazers

An air tazer (or taser) gun is another hand-held device that uses compressed air to shoot two small electrodes at an assailant. The tazer has the benefit of distance over the stun gun. You do not have to be close to your assailant to use the air-powered tazer, unlike the stun gun. In fact, you can be as far away as fifteen feet and still effectively halt your assailant. Once the electrodes attach to the attacker's clothing, the device sends powerful "T-waves" through his body, disrupting nerve endings and rendering the victim paralyzed for a few minutes, allowing you enough time to escape.

Like the stun gun, the air tazer is powered by regular batteries, and if you choose to carry a tazer for self-defense, you should always check to see if the batteries are fresh—stock extra batteries!

Because of the technical nature of the tazer gun, these devices also carry a steeper price tag. Most models retail at about $200 and can be found in specialty gun and knife shops.

Pepper Spray

A simple, inexpensive alternative to electrical gadgets is pepper spray. This small, unobtrusive aerosol canister contains a solution of about 10 percent pepper and causes severe irritation to an attacker when sprayed in the face or on the skin. This defense is also effective against animals. Canisters of pepper spray are available in a variety of sizes, including containers that you can attach to your key chain or spray bottles that will fit nicely in your pocket.

Pepper spray is simple to use and very inexpensive, usually under $10 for the highest quality product. It is easily found at retail stores and at specialty gun shops. As a simple, easy-to-use self-defense item, pepper spray is a perfect option if you choose to avoid the hassle and expense of the other high-tech options.

You can order stun guns, tazers, and pepper pray on the Internet from suppliers such as D&D Security Products at <http://www.ddsp.com/stun.htm> or Family Defense Products at <http://www.familydefense.com>. These are just a few of the many on-line vendors who specialize in these types of product.

Man's Best Friend

A commonly overlooked option for self-defense is one that may already be sitting at your feet. Dogs have been used for thousands of years to offer protection from intruders and as early warning systems for visitors due to their heightened senses of hearing and smell. Depending on the breed of dog that you own or are planning to purchase, its presence may serve as a show of force, deterring would-be intruders before they even enter your home. One officer told me that he had personally investigated almost one thousand burglaries in his long career. In only three cases did the homeowners own a dog. In his words, "burglars seem to be allergic to homeowners with dogs."

Depending on the type of family that you have, different breeds of dog may fit better than others into your home. In order to pick out the right breed, call your local American Kennel Club chapter or veterinarian and spend a few minutes explaining your situation. Ask him what breed of dog would do best with your family. If you want a dog for protection beginning in January 2000, it is obviously too late to get a puppy. You'll need a full-grown dog.

Unfortunately, although having a dog may be the most pleasant option for self-defense, it can be expensive. Top-notch guard dogs are often high-quality breeding dogs and run a high price tag, sometimes as much as $300 or more. Add into that the cost of feeding the dog until and throughout the year 2000, and you can easily surpass the price of even the most expensive handguns.

An Ounce of Prevention

Perhaps the best method of all for defending yourself is not to become a victim in the first place. There are several, nonviolent ways to avoid a confrontation. The following ideas come from the November/December 1998 issue of *New Man Magazine*, in an article entitled "Guns at Home."

1. Organize a neighborhood watch program. By knowing your neighbors, you can decrease your chances of becoming a victim by agreeing to watch out for one another. You should probably contact your local police department on this idea—they can help you organize your program and offer training courses in crime prevention for your neighborhood. If you qualify, your neighborhood will be able to post highly visible signs that indicate that your neighborhood is definitely not safe for criminals.

2. Make your home unattractive to thieves. Thieves look for several factors when staking out a home to enter. By keeping your shrubbery cut low so that all windows can easily be seen from the road, you can prevent burglars from easily entering your home under the cover of bushes. If you choose, you can purchase iron bars or gratings to cover your windows, making them nearly impossible to penetrate with common tools. If you are really serious, you can replace your glass window panes with plexiglass or polycarbonate, which are much more difficult to break. And remember to lock your interior door to the garage or basement, so that thieves cannot gain access to the inside of your home under the cover of these dark areas.

3. Make lots of noise. "The best way to stop an intruder," says Bob Vernon, former assistant chief of the Los Angeles Police Department, "is to yell and scream, clank pots and pans, set off an alarm. He's not going to hang around that racket long!" Here's another situation in which a loud barking sentry dog may be the perfect solution to your home defense needs.

4. Establish a "safe" room. By renovating one room in your home into a safe room, equipped with a solid wood or metal door with a secure deadbolt lock, you can create a safe haven in your own home in case an intruder is not intimidated and will not leave. Make sure that your family has an established plan on meeting in the "safe room" in the event of a break-in. It might be a good idea to store some extra food, flashlights, and a first aid kit in the room, as well as a means of communicating with the outside world.

Your Decision

As Stephen descended the stairs into the darkened living room, he saw that the intruder had climbed into the living room through a window. On the floor by the window lay a neat stack of electronic equipment, including his stereo system and television set. The VCR had been dropped in the intruder's haste to escape quickly. A single flashlight lay close by on the floor, still turned on, the only hard evidence that an intruder had been standing there just minutes ago, only a few yards away from his sleeping wife and children.

"Stephen?"

He turned around to see his wife at the bottom of the stairs, obviously awoken by the noise from the situation. "What's going on?" she asked.

"Don't worry, dear," he said. "We're safe now."

Stephen comforted his wife and returned her to bed. As he lay in bed, unable to sleep, he thought about what might have happened if he hadn't had the option of his weapon to defend himself and his family. The thought of being helpless in that night's situation troubled him, and he found himself extremely thankful that he had had the strength and courage to stand up for his family.

No matter what your decision on self-defense, it is important to take action to provide your family with reliable security for the year 2000. Failure to do so means putting not only your own life, but also the lives of your family, in danger from intruders and assailants who will pounce if law enforcement is disabled by Y2K.

No matter if you choose a firearm, a stun gun, a tazer, or a guard dog, safety should be the number one factor when developing your self-defense plan. Make sure that you are completely familiar with the device you do choose and that you have been properly trained in its use. There is nothing more dangerous as a lethal weapon in untrained hands. Make sure that you store the device safely away from children, preferably in a gun cabinet or in a locked safe.

The second factor that should affect your decision is local laws regarding possession of self-defense devices. Contact your local police department to learn more about the law in your area. They might even be able to offer you self-defense and firearms training courses free of charge.

Finally, if you are still having difficulty determining your self-defense philosophy, visit with friends or family members who use these types of devices or weapons and spend some time talking with them about how they made their decisions. You may find that they battled with some of the same conflicts that you are dealing with, and you may be able to work through your decision more easily and more confidently than if you had to make it alone.

Y2K PREP TIP #15
Make Your Home an Uninviting Target

One way to prevent unwanted visitors or intruders in your home is to make the facade of your house seem uninviting or perhaps dangerous to approach.

FBI researchers have learned that burglars who were caught and arrested revealed that they frequently avoided houses where they saw evidence of a dog. Here's the key—you don't have to actually own a dog to make your premises look as if you do!

Put the largest dog dish you can find in an obvious place near the front door. If you want, you can go even further and purchase a dog bed and some extra-large rawhide chew bones and place them nearby as well. Do everything you can to make it seem as if Cujo sleeps on your front porch.

The FBI report added that some burglars fear a silent dog more than a loud, barking one. The reason for this is that they are unsure of the dog's location and attack discipline. So, even if the intruder doesn't see or hear a dog, he will still be wary of entering your home. For these reasons, you can expect less trouble from uninvited visitors if you follow these easy steps.

	Y2K PREPAREDNESS CHECKLIST				
Level	Action Step	Qty Per Person	Unit Price	Total Qty	Total Price
1	Determine your self-defense philosophy.	N/A	N/A	N/A	N/A
2	Purchase a stun gun and/or...	1	$50		
2	Purchase a tazer and/or...	1	$200		
2	Purchase a container of pepper spray.	1	$10		
2	Establish a "safe room" in your home.	N/A	$100		
2	Organize a neighborhood watch program.	N/A	N/A		
2	Make your home uninviting for intruders.	N/A	Varies		
3	Purchase a handgun.	1	$250+		
3	Obtain a concealed carry permit for a handgun.	1	$75+		
3	Purchase a shotgun.	1	$250+		
3	Complete a training course on gun safety.	N/A	$50+		

Epilogue

Moving Beyond Fear

There are two serious mistakes you can make regarding Y2K: (1) failing to prepare and (2) relying on your preparations.

—Chuck Missler

It was a frigid day in January. Gail and I had traveled to the Midwest, where I had agreed to speak at a "Y2K Community Briefing" for a local church. The temperature was hovering near zero, but with the wind chill, it felt like minus-22. Although the streets were relatively clear, the snow stood like concrete walls on each side of the road, precisely where the snow shovels had left it. Living in the south, we had never witnessed this much snow or temperatures this extreme. We wondered out loud how in the world people would get along next year if, God forbid, there was an extended power outage related to Y2K. Evidently, we weren't the only ones thinking about this possibility.

No sooner had I arrived at the church, when a young woman in her late twenties accosted me and demanded to know how Y2K was going to impact her family. I was taken back by her aggressiveness.

"I'll be dealing with that in my first session this morning," I replied.

This didn't satisfy her, and she continued to press me, "But how will I keep my children warm if the power goes off?" Her eyes communicated a deep concern.

I tried to reassure her. "Well, there are several possibilities, depending on your circumstances and resources. I'll share some ideas in my second session this afternoon. Will you be able to stay for both sessions?" I asked, trying to subtly communicate that I would answer all her questions in due course, but I wasn't going to get into it here in the church narthex.

"But you don't understand. I'm a single mom with three kids. I don't have any-one to help me, and I don't have any money. I'm really scared."

I put my arms around her as she began to cry. "It's going to be okay," I told her. "We're all going to get through this by working together. Just come to the presen-tation, and I promise you'll feel a lot better by the time it's over."

💻 💻 💻

As I've tried to make clear throughout this book, I don't know if Y2K will result in a speed bump or a train wreck. My guess is that it will probably be somewhere in between. So it is important to take your preparations seriously. Nevertheless, I do know that physical preparations *alone* are not enough.

To make it through the days ahead you must also be prepared psychologically and, more importantly, *spiritually*. History is full of stories of those who have met the worst with little preparation and yet somehow, by the grace of God, managed to get through it. On the other hand, other stories tell of people who were well prepared and didn't survive, simply because they didn't have the inner resources to meet the challenge. Both kinds of preparation are important, and you can't afford to neglect either.

In this brief chapter I want to turn from the physical obstacles we face in prepar-ing for the Millennium Bug to what I believe is the greatest inner obstacle: fear. I think that all of us, if we are honest, will admit that we have had bouts with this emo-tion as we have considered Y2K. Perhaps it has manifested itself as simple *denial* or *procrastination*. I talk with hundreds of these people every week. Others *worry* about how much there is to do and how little time there is to do it. I know I've had a few restless nights, feeling overwhelmed with what must be done. A few even experience a kind of *panic*, feeling that their lives are in imminent danger. All of these emotions can be debilitating and unproductive.

We all have to handle fear in our own way. Unfortunately, I can't offer a simple list of products to buy or steps to take, as I have for other aspects of Y2K preparation. All I can do is tell you how I *personally* deal with fear, whenever it rears its ugly head. Whenever I feel fearful or anxious about the future, I remind myself of four things:

First, not all fear is bad. Fear can be a God-given, built-in mechanism for ensuring that we get out of harm's way. The kind of fear that motivates a person to take action—locking the doors at night, looking both ways before crossing traffic, or fleeing from a would-be attacker—is healthy. Conversely, any emotion that leads to denial, feelings of helplessness, or procrastination is not productive. Seeing fear as a friend rather than a foe can help disarm it.

Second, taking action dispels fear. The Apostle Paul says that "God has not given us a spirit of fear" (2 Timothy 1:7). In the Greek, the word for "fear" means *timid-*

ity. The timid person is the one who is afraid to act. In any crisis—a war, a natural disaster, an economic downturn, or any other calamity—the timid people suffer most. On the other hand, those who act—the bold—are the ones who remain calm, rising above their circumstances and getting safely from one side of the crisis to the other. In other words, preparation is the antidote to panic. In all my travels, I have never met a person who was both panicking and preparing. You do one or the other.

Third, you can do only so much. To quote insurance magnate and motivational speaker A.L. Williams, "When all you can do is all you can do then all you can do is enough." When the Disciples were faced with feeding five thousand hungry people, they initially dismissed the task as impossible. But Jesus didn't let them off the hook so easily. He asked them to take inventory of their resources. They found that they had only five loaves of bread and two fish—hardly enough to meet the needs of the assembled crowd. But Jesus took the Disciples' meager resources, blessed them, and gave them back to distribute to the people. Amazingly, they all ate and were filled. When they had finished, there were twelve baskets left over! (See Luke 9:12–17.)

I think God often puts us—as he did the Disciples—in a position where we are unable to meet all of our own needs, so that we may learn to trust in Him. The lesson from the Disciples is that if we will take whatever resources we have, whether small or great, and offer them up to the Lord, asking for His blessing, we will discover that we have *more than enough* to meet our needs. It really comes down to a matter of faith and stewardship. If you faithfully do what you can with what you have, it is sufficient. Your focus needs to be on what you can do, not what you can't.

Fourth, I am not facing the future alone. Unfortunately, there is much that we don't know about the future. I wish I could tell you with some level of certainty exactly what is going to happen in the year 2000. But I can't. I often feel that the more I learn about Y2K, the less certain I am about what we are facing. But, in the final analysis, it doesn't really matter. As a Christian, the one thing I know for absolute certain is that "God is with us" (Isaiah 8:10) and that "He will never leave us nor forsake us" (Hebrews 13:5). I may not know what the future holds, but I know *Who* holds the future. More than that, I know that He loves me and is working all things together for good—even Y2K—to those who love Him and are called according to His purpose (Romans 8:28).

Perhaps you are not a Christian. You might not believe in God at all. My intention is not to preach to you or offend you. But I know that my faith provides me the spiritual strength to endure a Y2K crisis, and that God never intended for us to go through life *alone*. If you don't have a personal relationship with Jesus Christ, I can only encourage you to begin by reading the Gospel of John in the Bible. In the end, it is our inner resources that we need as much as—or perhaps more than—physical preparations.

Y2K PREP TIP #16
How to Combat Fear

The Bible can be a tremendous resource for people who find themselves in difficult, turbulent times. There are thousands of verses you can memorize and bring to mind to fight fear and anxiety. Here are ten that I have found particularly encouraging. (All verses are from the New King James Version of the Bible, unless otherwise noted.)

Deuteronomy 31:8—And the Lord, He is the one who goes before you. He will be with you, He will not leave you nor forsake you; do not fear nor be dismayed.

Psalm 37:5—Yet I have not seen the righteous forsaken, nor his descendants begging bread.

Psalm 46:1—God is our refuge and strength, a very present help in trouble. Therefore we will not fear, even though the earth be removed, and though the mountains be carried into the midst of the sea.

Jeremiah 29:11—For I know the plans I have for you, says the Lord. They are plans for good and not for evil, to give you a future and a hope (Living Bible).

Matthew 28:20—I am with you always, even to the end of the age.

John 16:33—These things I have spoken to you, that in Me you may have peace. In the world you will have tribulation; but be of good cheer, I have overcome the world.

Romans 8:28—And we know that all things work together for good to those who love God, to those who are the called according to His purpose.

Romans 8:32—He who did not spare His own Son, but delivered Him up for us all, how shall He not with Him also freely give us all things?

Philippians 4:6–7—Be anxious for nothing, but in everything by prayer and supplication, with thanksgiving, let your requests be made known to God; and the peace of God, which surpasses all understanding, will guard your hearts and minds through Christ Jesus.

Philippians 4:19—And my God shall supply all your need according to His riches in glory by Christ Jesus.

Appendix A

An Overview of Y2K

've owned a personal computer in one form or another since 1982, the year after the IBM-PC was introduced. I was one of those naive but enthusiastic souls who paid $5,000 for an off-white box that contained an 8088 processor, 64 kilobytes of RAM, a single 160k single-sided floppy drive, and an ugly phosphorous green monitor. I did this, of course, in pursuit of the Holy Grail of modern business—increased personal productivity.

Ever since, I've updated my hardware every couple of years. I've purchased the latest software. I've become a beta tester for various software companies, and when that wasn't enough, I taught myself Pascal and three dialects of BASIC. I've done my best to stay on the leading edge of computer technology.

You would think that with all this experience I could figure out how to back up my hard disk on some sort of semiregular basis. But I have a confession to make: I rarely do it. Even though I've gone through hundreds, if not thousands, of computer crashes and even a couple of hard-disk failures, I just can't seem to discipline myself to make regular backups.

As a result, whenever I take my disabled machine to the computer repair shop, the technician (with a smug little grin) always asks, "Do you have a backup?"

And, like some pathological liar, I always answer, "Of course." Meanwhile I'm thinking, *Of course I don't have a backup; that would be way too easy. I would rather spend the next two weeks of my life piecing together all the data I've lost and reinstalling the programs that were trashed!*

As I leave the repair shop, I vow to myself that I am going to absolutely, positively start making backups on a regular basis. My resolve lasts a day or two, but then I go right back to my old habits.

It is probably safe to say that everyone who has ever owned a personal computer has, at one time or another, experienced a computer crash. Most of us, unfortunately, are not prepared for it when it happens. As a result, we often spend days—if not weeks—putting our computer system back together just so that we can pick up where we left off.

But as disrupting as a computer crash is to our personal or professional lives, none of us has ever experienced the kind of worldwide computer crash that might happen as a result of what is called the "Year 2000 Computer Problem," or "Y2K" for short.

When the clock strikes midnight on January 1, 2000, computer systems all over the world, unless they are repaired in time, may start spewing out bad data or simply stop working altogether.

Forward to the Past

The Year 2000 Computer Problem, also called the Millennium Bug, is a sort of "digital time bomb." And when that bomb goes off, it will be similar to a giant hard disk failure—but a billion times worse than the worst computer crash you've ever experienced or could possibly imagine. It will affect personal computers, mainframe computers, and even embedded computer chips in various appliances, instruments, and other devices. And when it happens, you may pine for the good old days when the worst you could expect was a personal computer malfunction.

The January 1999 issue of *Vanity Fair* painted what it called "the nightmare scenario":

> It is an instant past midnight, January 1, 2000, and suddenly nothing works. Not ATMs, which have stopped dispensing cash; not credit cards, which are being rejected; not VCRs, which now really *are* impossible to program. The power in some cities isn't working, either, and that means no heat, lights, or coffee in the morning, not to mention no televisions, stereos, or phones, which—even in places with power—aren't working, either. Bank vaults and prison gates have swung open; so have valves on sewer lines. The 911 service isn't functioning, but fire trucks are on the prowl (though the blaze had better be no higher than the second floor, since the ladders won't lift). People in elevators are trapped, and those with electronic hotel or office keys can't get anywhere, either. Hospitals have shut down because their ventilators and X-ray machines won't work—and, in any case, it's now impossible to bill the HMO.
>
> Traffic is a mess, since no streetlights are working. Trains are running, but their control switches aren't, which is bad news for supermarkets, utilities, car dealers—and international trade, which can't move by ship

either. Only the brave or the foolhardy are getting on airplanes—but with so many countries degenerating into riots and revolution, it's wiser to stay home anyway. There are no newspapers to read or movies to go to or welfare checks to cash. Meantime, retirees are opening letters saying that their pensions have been cancelled because they are –23 years old. Many banks and small businesses have gone bust, and it will be weeks—if ever—before the mess that is the broker's statement is sorted out.

On the brighter side, no one can punch a time clock; on the darker, most of the big manufacturing plants have shut down because their lathes and robots aren't working. Pharmacies aren't filling prescriptions; the DMV is not processing license renewals, and everyone's dashboard keeps flashing SERVICE ENGINE NOW. Mortgage payments sent on time have been marked late, and everyone's phone bill is messed up because of all those calls that began in 1999 and ended in 1900. On the Internet— where thousands of Web sites are suggesting how to find God and when to move to the wilderness—the acronym for what's occurring is TEOT-WAWKI: The End Of The World As We Know It.

Will it happen? "Yes," "No," and "Maybe," say the experts. And that's the most unnerving thing about the phenomenon variously known as "Y2K," "The Year 2000 Problem," or "The Millennium Bug": no one will know the extent of its consequences until *after* they occur.[1]

Unless the Millennium Bug is tracked down and exterminated, you, your family, your friends, and your business associates are at risk. And many of the things you have learned to depend on and take for granted could suddenly disappear, leaving you, for all practical purposes, in the year 1900. The difference, of course, is that at the beginning of the twentieth century, people could cope with life without the aid of computers. In our high-tech, computer-controlled society, very few could.

Perhaps you are wondering: How in the world did we end up in this mess?

Abort, Retry, Fail

In the early days of computers, data storage was limited and very expensive. As you may know, the first computers used punch cards. It took a handful of these cards to store the amount of information that we can store today in a space smaller than a speck of dust. Computer storage cost about 10,000 times—that's a million percent— as much as it does today. With the advent of magnetic tape, costs decreased slightly. Regardless, programmers embraced any method that could save storage space or memory.

One of the methods they adopted was to reduce four-digit years to two digits. For example, 1967 became "67," 1984 became "84"—much as we do today when we hand-write a personal check. The century portion of the date was shaved off, cutting the storage requirements in half.

This simple device posed no problem so long as the dates being used pertained to the current century. However, when you get to the year 2000, you have a problem—a big problem. With only two digits available, the computer stores the year 2000 as "00" but interprets it as the year 1900! Why? Because the programmers built into the software the assumption that every two-digit year was preceded by the number "19."

Based on the rate at which technology was changing, these programmers did not think that the programs they were writing then would still be in use today. But they were wrong. Many of these programs are still in use today, and have become the information processing backbone of modern society. Worse, even when programmers have written entirely new programs, they have often blindly followed this two-digit convention.

The Millennium Bug creates enormous problems in all kinds of date-based calculations. Consider, for a moment, a corporate pension program that uses a simple date-based calculation to determine eligibility for benefits. It follows this rule: Every employee who is 65 or older gets a check; everyone who is younger than 65 does not.

Consider a person born in 1933. If you subtract this year from 1999, you get 66, an age that makes the person eligible to receive a pension check. This calculation yields the same result, whether you use two digits or four. But in the year 2000, the SSA's computers, unless they are repaired, will attempt to subtract 33 from 00, and incorrectly calculate that the person is –33 years old. Thus, from the computer's perspective, this person hasn't even been born yet—and certainly isn't old enough to receive a benefit check.

On some systems, these kinds of errors simply crash the computer. Frankly, this is the better result; at least then you know something is wrong. The bigger problem is when these sorts of errors create corrupt data and pass it on from one computer to another. Before long, even compliant systems (that is, those that can correctly handle dates after January 1, 2000) can crash or miscalculate data.

But we don't have to wait until January 1, 2000, to begin seeing problems with the Y2K issue. Already, it is affecting us. According to Cap Gemini, an international computer consulting and research firm, 55 percent of all corporations have already experienced at least one Y2K-related computer failure.[2] These include:

Electric utilities at risk. In the summer of 1998 a midwestern electrical utility ran a test for Y2K compliance. According to *U.S. News & World Report,* "When the test clock turned over to 2000, a safety system mistakenly detected dangerous operating conditions, and the power generators completely shut down. Programmers worked on the problem for three days, then re-ran the test. A different sector of the system failed, shutting down the system again. Technicians have yet to fix the problem. This underscored one of the most unsettling aspects of the Y2K bug: Fixing the program that runs one piece of equipment can have disruptive effects on other parts of the system."[3]

Y2K upgrade causes chaos in U.S. Senate offices. A new Y2K-compliant financial management computer system was installed in the Office of the Secretary of the U.S. Senate in October 1998. For months individual Senate offices faced fiscal chaos. The Disbursement Office was unable to process payments for Senate expenses. Overdue bills piled up for state office rents, credit cards, staffers' travel expenses, cell phones, and pagers. Some Senate staffers faced eviction from their state offices because of grossly past-due rent payments.[4]

Problems on the factory floor. According to Ralph Szygenda, chief information officer for General Motors, "At each one of our factories there are catastrophic problems. Amazingly enough, machines on the factory floor are far more sensitive to incorrect dates than we ever anticipated. When we tested robotic devices for transition into the year 2000, for example, they just froze and stopped operating."[5]

Interest miscalculation in the banking industry. The consumer loan system at a Fortune 500 financial services company in the Midwest sent two hundred customers a bill for ninety-six years' worth of interest when it encountered a "00" date in a program that looks four years ahead. It reportedly took the company one month to fix the problem by expanding two-digit–year fields to four. However, the fix blew up interrelated systems the next month when they couldn't handle the four-digit years.[6]

Dumping of dangerous chemicals into the water supply. According to Senator Bob Bennett (R-Utah), when a water purification plant in Utah set its clock ahead to test for Y2K compliance, the plant malfunctioned, dumping dangerous quantities of chlorine and other chemicals into the water.[7]

Credit cards still being declined. With less than a year to go, Visa is still saying that it receives 100 to 150 reports a month that credit cards have been declined by point-of-sale systems because a card's expiration date is in the year 2000.[8]

Like an Iceberg

When most of us think of computers, we think of the monster that sits on our desk at home or at work, the personal computer. There are approximately 300 million of these machines worldwide.[9] They can be affected by the Millennium Bug at four different levels: hardware, operating system, application software, and data. All must be checked to make sure that they are Y2K ready.

But as much as you may use your personal computer on a day-to-day basis—or even if you don't use one—it is the least of your worries. It's like the tip of the iceberg, and like most icebergs the part that is below the surface, the part you can't see, threatens to do the most damage. This includes mainframe computers and embedded chip systems that exist just below the level of our conscious awareness.

Wherever you have large volumes of transactions—whether in health care, or banking and finance, or telecommunications, or simply billing systems for large corporations—you're going to find mainframe computer systems. The rumors of their death have been greatly exaggerated; those mainframe systems have not gone away. They haven't been replaced by client-server systems or microcomputers.

If anything, mainframes have proliferated over the last decade. In fact, according to one source, they have increased 20 percent per year for each of the past several years and, moreover, 55 percent of all the large-scale mainframe systems running today are less than two years old.[10] Today, there are approximately 700 billion software functions running on mainframe computers.[11] Much of it is custom software and can't be easily upgraded. And all of it is vulnerable to the Millennium Bug.

But the dirty little secret of Y2K—the reason why we're not going to get 100 percent of these systems fixed before January 1, 2000—is what is called the embedded chip system problem. An embedded chip is a computer chip that has the software code actually burned onto it. In other words, the code is wedded to the chip.

Embedded chips are everywhere. They're in satellites. They're at the bottom of the North Sea regulating the flow of petroleum. They're in traffic lights and weapon systems, fax machines and cell phones. They have permeated our culture and become, as *ComputerWeekly* magazine called them, "the unseen guardians of our lives."[12]

The standard estimate for the number of embedded chips is 25 billion worldwide. In his testimony before Congress, David Hall, a recognized expert on embedded systems, estimated that there were likely 40 billion.[13] *Datamation* magazine, a leading trade publication for computer professionals, put the number at 70 billion.[14] The good news is not many of them are date sensitive. Exactly how many? That's anyone's guess. For example:

- Peter de Jager, one of the first to sound the alarm on Y2K, suggests that the number is less than 0.1 percent.[15]

- *Datamation* estimates that on average about 7 percent are date sensitive.[16]

- David Hall states that "in tests accomplished so far, anywhere from 1 percent to 10 percent of an enterprise's systems and equipment items exhibit Year 2000 impacts… these impacts range from minor to catastrophic."[17]

- Action 2000, the British government's official Y2K awareness agency, states, "According to research conducted over the past year, around 5 percent of simple embedded systems failed Millennium Bug tests. For more sophisticated embedded systems, failure rates of between 50 and 80 percent have been reported. In manufacturing environments, the overall failure rate is around 15 percent."[18]

The bad news is that, whether it's one-tenth of 1 percent or 10 percent, *we don't know where they are without checking 100 percent of them.* One television commentator said that that was the equivalent of tracking down and replacing every bolt in every bridge on earth in the time we have left between now and January 1, 2000—an unbelievable, impossible task. And unfortunately, the vast majority of enterprises haven't even started. By late 1998 only 11 percent of businesses and government agencies had begun to assess their embedded system risks.[19]

The Typical Y2K Project

To understand where a particular organization is in its Y2K repairs, you need to understand what is involved in the typical Y2K project. It generally consists of three phases:[20]

1. Inventory and assessment. The first thing a company must do is identify all of its automated systems and determine the likelihood of Y2K problems. This is generally 7 percent of the project's total work.

2. Review and repair. In this step, the company begins the tedious process of reprogramming the computers. In the case of embedded chip systems, it is to identify those systems, contact the manufacturers (assuming they are still in business), and ask whether the chips are Y2K-compliant (assuming they still support that particular chip). This step is about 35 percent of the total job.

3. Regression testing. The most arduous, most tedious, and most time-consuming part of any Y2K project is the testing phase, which accounts for 58 percent of the total workload. As an industry average, computer programmers introduce about one error (or "bug") for every ten lines of code they write. The only way to ferret out those bugs is to test the code over and over again, in an attempt to make the computers run as reliably as possible.

With these phases in mind, let's examine some of the systems that we depend on most.

Our Core Infrastructure

What makes the Millennium Bug so menacing is that it threatens our core infrastructure. By *infrastructure* I mean that vast array of computers that operate silently in the background of our existence, providing us the kinds of services and products that we depend on for our modern way of life.

To understand the concept of infrastructure, consider a four-legged stool. One leg of the stool represents electricity. Another represents telecommunications, another transportation, and another water. The seat on top of the legs represents banking and finance. Government, business, and individual citizens sit perched on top of this stool. Most of the time we never think about the infrastructure. We sit happily above it and conduct our lives and business, unaware of the systems that make it possible. But we are dependent on this infrastructure in ways that we cannot begin to comprehend. And, in fact, the various infrastructure components themselves are mutually dependent on one another. According to Joel Willemssen of the General Accounting Office (GAO) in his January 1999 testimony before Congress:

> America's infrastructures are a complex array of public and private enterprises with many interdependencies at all levels. These many interdependencies among governments and within key economic sectors could *cause a single failure to have adverse repercussions in other sectors* [emphasis added].[21]

Leg 1: Electricity. If there is one thing that we are more dependent on than even computers in this society, it's electricity. It animates virtually everything within our field of experience. Without electricity we can't even keep the computers up after January 1, 2000, to continue working on them.

The more than 7,800 electric utilities in the United States are completely computer-dependent.[22] Computers are used in billing systems, power generation, and power distribution. To complicate matters, the nation's electric companies are tied together into four regional power grids. The North American Electric Reliability Council (NERC) notes, "Each of the four Interconnections is a highly connected network. A major disturbance within one part of an interconnection will rapidly have an impact through the interconnection and has the potential to cascade the effect to the entire interconnection."[23] In other words, the grid is vulnerable to what is sometimes called "the domino effect."[24]

So far, not one U.S. electric utility has announced that it is Y2K-compliant.

In June 1998 the Senate Special Committee on the Year 2000 Technology Problem surveyed the ten largest electrical power utilities in the country, serving some fifty million Americans.[25] You would assume that these would be "the best and the brightest" of all utility companies, certainly the ones with the most available resources to address the problem. Here's what it found:

- Only two of the ten utilities—20 percent—had completed phase one

- None was confident that its suppliers would be compliant

- None had a contingency plan

- One didn't have any idea how much computer code it had

- One of the ten reported 300,000 embedded-chip systems

In response to this survey, Senator Christopher Dodd (D-Connecticut), vice-chairman of the committee, said,

> Quite honestly, I think we're no longer at the point of asking whether or not there will be any power disruptions, but we are now forced to ask how severe the disruptions are going to be.[26]

Senator Bennett, chairman of the committee, echoed his concerns: "I think there is a virtual certainty that we'll have brownouts and some regional blackouts."[27] He went on to say:

> We still have 18 months [from June 1998], and nobody really knows. So there is a very slim possibility that everything will work just fine. I think the chances of regional blackouts and heavy brownout activity throughout the grid are about 80 percent.[28]

Of course, that was the summer of 1998. Where are we now? At the time of this writing, in early 1999:

- Not one publicly-held electric utility is Y2K-compliant (this is according to their own 10-Q filings with the SEC).[29]

- By the end of 1998, these same publicly-held utilities had spent only 30 to 35 percent of their Y2K budgets.[30] If we assume that there is a correlation between money spent and work completed, this does not bode well for finishing on time. And lest you think the work is actually being accomplished more efficiently and that companies are spending less than they had budgeted, in late January 1999 Senator Bennett remarked, "At the corporate level, the price of fixing Y2K problems keeps outstripping original estimates."[31] Thus, these figures may signal that *less work* has been completed, since in most cases Y2K budgets are being revised upward.[32]

- Seventeen percent of the utilities reporting to NERC had completed repairs and testing on less than 10 percent of their systems. Sixty-six percent (two-thirds) of the utilities had completed less than 50 percent of their systems.[33]

- Energy companies like Chevron, Exxon, and Mobil are also behind schedule.[34] These are the companies that provide the fuel for many power plants.

In early 1999 Senator Bennett suggested this analogy:

> The recent blackout in San Francisco affected nearly a million residents. It was a microcosmic look at what we may face as the calendar ticks over to 2000. Although the blackout was not caused by Y2K problems, it shows how a simple technological malfunction—in this case, one caused by human error—can have major cascading effects. Multiply this problem by a thousand, or a hundred, or even ten and we begin to see the possible consequences that we face.[35]

All of these reports are, to say the least, disturbing. If we lose electricity, everything else falls in succession: telecommunications, banking and finance, food distribution, water treatment and delivery, and shipping and transportation. Without electricity our modern way of life grinds to a halt.

Leg 2: Telecommunications. The telecommunications infrastructure is almost as important as electricity. In fact, modern banking and finance cannot survive without telecommunications. Even the electrical utility industry uses telecommunications to synchronize transmissions across the grid.

Telecommunication companies are also computer-dependent. And, because of deregulation, fixing these computers is even more complicated. Today we have long-distance carriers, regional Bell operating companies, Internet service providers, competitive local exchange carriers, equipment manufacturers, and much more.

The biggest long distance carriers are spending enormous sums of money getting their computers ready for the next century. For example, AT&T, the largest long-distance carrier, has more than 500 million lines of computer code and now plans to spend $700 million on the problem[36] (up from its estimate of $520 million in May 1998). MCI has 350 million lines of code and is spending approximately $400 million.[37] And Sprint has more than 100 million lines of code and is planning to spend more than $250 million.[38] Altogether, the seven major telcos are spending $2 billion on Y2K.[39]

What kind of progress are they making? According to Federal Communications Commission (FCC) Commissioner Michael Powell, "The ways in which the year-2000 problem could affect telecommunications companies seem to be almost unlimited."[40] As of early 1999, AT&T, generally considered to be the furthest along, had spent less than half of its $700 million budget.[41] And according to a report from the GAO, the telecommunications industry's largest telecommunications providers will not be ready until June 30, 1999—leaving only six months for testing.[42] This is particularly disconcerting when you realize that industries that are dependent on the telecommunications infrastructure (such as banking and electricity) can't do end-to-end testing until sometime after this deadline. While the larger telecommunications providers will likely meet the deadline, according to FCC Commissioner Powell, "At this point in time, we can say with assurance there are people who aren't going to make it."[43]

Leg 3: Transportation. The transportation industry is the link that furnishes the supplies the other infrastructure providers need to deliver their services.

On September 10, 1998, the Senate Special Committee heard testimony on the transportation industry's progress on Y2K.[44] Prior to the hearings, the Senate surveyed the nation's leading transportation providers, including airlines, airports, railroads, maritime shippers, trucking companies, and city transit agencies. What were the results? According to the Senate survey:

- Only a third of the respondents had completed a preliminary assessment of what systems would be affected (phase one)

- None had completed contingency plans; only half had begun to create them

- Surprisingly, half expected to be involved in litigation over the problem

Based on the survey, Senator Bennett said, "I am concerned that the transportation sector as a whole may not be able to transition through the millennium without major disruptions."[45] And well he should be. According to information available in early 1999:

- The FAA pushed back its Y2K-compliance date to September 30, 1999[46]—this after it had previously announced publicly that it would be 99 percent compliant by September 30, *1998*, a full year earlier.[47] In a study released by Proma Creative Solutions in December 1998, the forty major airlines on average had spent only 36 percent of their Y2K budgets. According to Proma's CEO, "Companies have been working on the problem for at least two years, and the fact that only 36 percent of the airlines' projected remedial budget has been spent is definite proof that the airlines will have much work to do before we can safely board their planes on January 1, 2000."[48]

- The usually optimistic John Koskinen, the president's Y2K czar, admitted to *USA Today*, "'We are deeply concerned about the railroads. We have no indication that they are going to make it."[49] When you consider, for example, that coal is shipped by rail to coal-firing power plants, you can see the potential for disruptions *even if* the power generating utilities are compliant.

- On December 7, 1998, the U.S. Coast Guard's chief information officer, Rear Admiral George Naccara, said the embedded-chip problems in some ships could come close to halting them dead in the water. "Some [vessels] may have problems crossing the ocean," which could also crimp the nation's oil supply.[50] A few days later, Koskinen told a group of journalists that 95 percent of all imported goods enter the United States via maritime shipping.[51]

- In late January 1999 the State Department warned U.S. citizens that those "with more limited resources or expertise, or who are not paying appropriate attention to the [Y2K] problem, may experience significant difficulties.... All U.S. citizens planning to be abroad in late 1999 or early 2000 should be aware of the potential for problems and stay informed about Y2K preparedness in the location where they will be traveling."[52]

Leg 4: Water. Obviously, we are also highly dependent on clean water. People can survive for only about three days without water. And we also depend on water for sanitation and personal hygiene. Like all of our other core infrastructure, water treatment and delivery are also computer dependent.

Many water utilities are aware of the Y2K problem and are working on it. Some are not. Based on my own research, this industry segment is the furthest behind.

In the course of my research, I called my local water utility in mid-September 1997 and asked to be connected to the person in charge of Information Technology. (I live in a small municipality outside of Nashville, Tennessee, with a population of about 22,000.) When I was transferred to the appropriate person, I asked him what his utility was doing to address the Year 2000 Computer Problem. There was a long pause, so I asked him if he was even familiar with the Year 2000 Problem. There was another pause, and then he said, "Well, I've heard of it, but I'm not sure exactly what it is." I was shocked, to say the least, so I double-checked to make sure I was speaking to the head of the computer department. "Yep, I'm the right guy," he assured me.

I explained the Year 2000 Problem and asked if his systems were Year 2000-compliant. "Well, I don't know, but it sounds like this is something we ought to check into." Indeed.

We have approximately seventy thousand such water utilities in the United States. According to a recent American Waterworks Association survey (November 1998):[53]

- 61 percent have a formal Y2K plan

- 51 percent have completed the inventory and assessment phase

- 26 percent have inquired about the status of vendors and suppliers

- 12 percent have contingency plans

In short, there is a serious question as to whether some of these utilities will be able to provide safe, clean water to their customers at the dawn of the new millennium.

The Seat: Banking. The banking and financial infrastructure of our society is at great risk. It's the means by which we all complete our daily transactions. Whether it is by check or by credit card, we depend on digital money moving around at the speed of light from one institution to the another in order to make our payments, pay our bills, receive paychecks, and all the rest. And the same is true for businesses and agencies. They depend on that same infrastructure in order to pay their employees and suppliers, generate a cash flow, and do everything else necessary to have a viable enterprise.

One of my questions as I was doing the research for *The Millennium Bug* was how much of the money in our economy is actual cash. In other words, of all the deposits on record in U.S. banks—my money and yours—how much of it is paper currency you could put your hands on if you wanted to and how much of it is digital. As noted, what I found was very disturbing. Only about 1.13 percent of the money supply is cash.[54] The rest of it—98.87 percent—is nothing more than a digital entry on a computer.

Think about what this means. If we had a bank run and people wanted to withdraw all of their money (and assuming that everyone had exactly the same amount of money on deposit) only the first eleven people out of a thousand would get their money back; the rest would be turned away. Or, to think of it another way, every depositor would get $1.13 for every $100.00 on deposit.

With so much money being digital, there is a great deal at risk if the computers go down. If the Millennium Bug causes the bank's computers to fail or generate corrupted data, then suddenly we will find we are in an "Alzheimer economy"—a situation in which computers may not be able to remember how much money is in your bank account or even whether you have an account with that particular institution.

So how is the banking and financial services industry progressing? Compared to other industry segments, it is leading the pack. According to a recent FDIC survey, 94 percent of its six thousand member banks are making "satisfactory progress."[55] However, this means that 6 percent are not making adequate progress. Furthermore:

- This information is self-reported. It has not been independently verified. (This, by the way, is the problem with almost all of the data we have.)

- It does not refer to banks that are Y2K-ready (none is yet compliant); it refers only to banks making satisfactory progress. You need to keep in mind that 73 percent of all corporate software projects are late.[56]

- It does not include banks outside the United States.

- It does not take into account other dependencies like electricity and telecommunications, two things modern banking cannot function without.

- The FDIC itself is not yet compliant.[57]

Tweedledee and Tweedledum

You would think that with this much at stake, with our critical infrastructure at risk, Y2K would be the federal government's top priority. Unfortunately, the federal government is even further behind.

The House Subcommittee on Government Management Information and Technology, chaired by Congressman Steve Horn (R-California), issues a quarterly report card on the progress of twenty-four key federal government agencies relative to their Y2K progress. In the subcommittee's report card, issued at the end of 1998, the federal government was given a "D."[58] Why? Because, based on current rates of progress, nine of those twenty-four agencies will not get even their most mission-critical systems repaired until well after January 1, 2000. Please note: This does not refer to all of their computers; it refers only to a fraction of the systems, the ones they have classified as "mission critical." Worse, more than half the agencies do not have contingency plans to ensure that service will continue in the event their mission-critical systems fail.

Seven agencies earned a grade of "D" or "F." These include the following, along with their expected dates of completion.[59] (All dates are based on current rates of progress.)

At this writing, only two agencies can claim 100 percent compliance of its mission critical systems: the Social Security Administration (SSA)[60] and the Small Business Administration (SBA).[61]

In summarizing a previous report (September 9, 1998), Congressman Horn said: "This is not a grade you take home to your parents, and it is definitely not a grade to take home to the voters and taxpayers."[62] He continued:

Table A.1:
Seven Federal Agencies Making the Worst Y2K Progress

Agency	Grade	Expected Completion
Department of Transportation	D	2000
Department of Defense	D–	2000
Department of Justice	F	2001
Department of Energy	F	2001
Health and Human Services (including Medicare)	F	2001
Agency for International Development	F	2023
State Department	F	2034

When was the last time you heard of the government putting a new computer in place on schedule?... There is no room for the usual slippage. There is no margin for error.[63]

In the summary report, issued a month later (October 8, 1998), Congressman Horn stated that the government of the United States of America is "on the edge of failure."[64]

Speaking of the Clinton administration in the most recent report, Congressman Horn said:

The Year 2000 computer problem is not receiving the attention it deserves from the President. It is essential that the President begin to address the Year 2000 issue much more frequently. President Clinton and Vice President Gore cannot continue to act as if this problem is going to solve itself.[65]

Four Reasons Y2K Won't Get Fixed in Time

All the experts agree that there is not enough time to get all the computers repaired before January 1, 2000. There are at least four reasons this is so and why we must stop pretending and begin making contingency plans now.

Reason #1: We got started too late. Consider the SSA. In many ways, this agency has been the "Y2K poster child" in the most positive sense. It started early—way back in 1989. The SSA needed two full years to do its inventory and assessment. At the end of that phase, it believed it had 30 million lines of computer code that had to be reviewed and repaired. In 1991 it assigned 2,800 employees, including 700 full-time programmers, to the task and began the arduous job of actually rewriting the code.[66]

On December 28, 1998, President Clinton announced that the SSA had achieved 100 percent compliance.[67] Forget for a moment that it discovered additional code along the way, including another 33 million lines of code in its state offices. And forget that it doesn't actually write the checks itself; they are written by the Financial Management Service (FMS), which is not scheduled to be compliant until March 1999.[68] Still, the SSA has done an outstanding job.

But what about other government agencies that have more work and have gotten started much later?

Take the IRS, for example. It didn't get started until late 1996 and has 100 million lines of code—more than three times that of the SSA.[69] This is the same agency that a few years ago wrote off a $4 billion computer modernization project because it could not successfully bring the work to completion.

Or consider the Department of Defense. At last count it had more than a *billion* lines of computer code, and this doesn't even include its embedded systems problem.[70] In the spring of 1998 it reported to Congress that it was only 9 percent of the way complete,[71] although it is now miraculously claiming to be 52 percent complete.[72]

Reason #2: We have too many computer languages. In 1996 the software productivity research catalog of programming languages identified almost five hundred different languages in current use.[73] COBOL is by far the most prevalent, accounting for almost 70 percent of all current software running on mainframe computers today. It also has, by far, the most plentiful supply of Year 2000 automated tools and services available. In fact, it may have more support than all the other languages combined.

But guess what? COBOL is no longer taught in most universities. And this still leaves approximately 499 languages without adequate support, even though they impact only 30 percent of the programs in use. These include languages such as BASIC, FORTRAN, ADA, Pascal, Modula, and a host of others.

But beyond these, some of the languages are *proprietary*. This is especially true in the Department of Defense, where languages were developed to keep hackers out or to accommodate specialized functions. In these situations, the language developers are often retired—or even dead.

The problems are further compounded by the fact that many applications are written in multiple languages. Some have estimated that this may involve almost 30 percent of all programs.

Reason #3: We have too few programmers. It is estimated that the shortfall of programmers to get the job done by the year 2000 is 30 percent worldwide for COBOL alone.[74] At present, we have only about 500,000 mainframe programmers in the United States.[75] But many them are retired. In an article in the *Washington Post*, Dr. Howard Ruben, professor of Computer Science at Hunter College in New York City, estimated that the United States will need an additional 500,000 to 700,000 experienced COBOL programmers between now and the year 2000.[76]

Reason #4: Much of the computer source code is missing. The computer language that humans read and write is called source code. Consider the following example:

```
    If CurrentYear – BirthYear => 65 Then
        PrintCheck
    Else
        DisplayMessage ("Does not qualify!")
    End If
```

This brief source code program tells the computer to evaluate how old a person is by subtracting the year in which he was born from the current year. Translation: If this number is greater than 65, then run the check printing routine; otherwise notify the operator that the candidate does not qualify.

When the programmer finishes writing the source code, he runs it through a compiler, which reduces it to machine language. This is the language the computer reads and writes, and it consists basically of binary information—zeros and ones. It looks something like this:

```
011100100101001000011110001000110001
100100101001000011110001000110001011
001001010010000111100011101100010110
```

Here's the kicker: Without the source code, the computer programmers have no easy way to repair the software. Unfortunately, the source code is sometimes misplaced, accidentally discarded, or intentionally bypassed. When that happens, the software generally has to be completely rewritten from the ground up.

Through a Glass Darkly

Thus far, I've tried to stick to the facts and substantiate my statements with links to the original sources. As a result, I hope that you are on your way to being convinced that the computer code is broken and will malfunction if it is not repaired. This is beyond dispute. In addition, hardly anyone challenges the fact that it is too late to get all of our critical systems fixed in time. According to Senator Bennett in a January 27, 1999, article:

> Our government is not going to get all of its critical systems fixed in time for the century change. The evidence for this is overwhelming.... The General Accounting Office (GAO) cites countless other vulnerabilities. State and local systems that process Federal benefit checks are not likely to be fully remediated. County-operated "911" systems may have failures. At the corporate level, the price of fixing Y2K problems keeps outstripping original estimates. Many companies, like Chevron and General

Motors, are now conceding that they cannot guarantee their service as of January 1, 2000.

Even John Koskinen, chairman of the President's Council on Year 2000 Conversion, has publicly acknowledged that the time to begin Y2K remediation has passed, and the time has come for crisis management and contingency planning.[77]

The bottom line is that *disruptions are now inevitable*. The only debate is in regard to the nature and severity of the crisis that awaits us.

But now I want to turn a corner and speculate about the future. This is always dangerous. The truth is that no one really knows what's going to happen on January 1, 2000. I certainly don't, and I don't know of anyone who does. All of us, regardless of our professional credentials, are guessing. That's why I outline and develop three different scenarios in my book *The Millennium Bug*. What will happen? You decide.

The Brownout Scenario

This scenario could last anywhere from a couple of weeks to a couple of months. It is largely a scenario of inconvenience and frustration, one in which the electricity works only intermittently. Sometimes you get a dial tone, and sometimes you don't. Some goods are scarce, and unemployment rises. But the disruptions are local—or at worst, regional—and limited. Somehow we muddle through and get to the other side.

Even in this scenario, however, we don't get through completely unscathed. We can expect a severe global recession, which, as Dr. Edward Yardeni has forecasted, will be like the recession of 1973–1974.[78]

The problem with this scenario, from my perspective, is this: *If we can't get our computers fixed in the months we have remaining between now and January 1, 2000, how do we think we can get them fixed in the few weeks after January 1, 2000, when we're operating in a chaotic and unstable environment?*

The Blackout Scenario

This scenario could last anywhere from four months to two years. The linchpin for this scenario is the electrical power grid. Without electricity, water can't be treated or pumped; people get sick drinking from alternative sources; disease begins to spread from untreated sewage. Planes are grounded, the majority of other vehicles stop running as petroleum products are used up. Basic food items cannot be delivered; supermarkets are empty; people are hungry. There are no phones, and the Internet is down. Many banks are closed—perhaps all of them—and some will never reopen. Perhaps the president invokes the Emergency Powers Act, and martial law could be declared.

Whereas the brownout scenario is one of inconvenience and frustration, this is a scenario of fear and panic. It may also involve widespread rioting and looting, and even a global economic depression. (Unfortunately, Y2K is not our only worry. We are now experiencing a global deflation that threatens to undo our economy even before January 1, 2000, arrives.)

The Meltdown Scenario

This is the scenario that I pray doesn't come to pass. But I think we have to consider it and realize it is a possibility. Technologically, it's not any different from the Blackout scenario. The electricity goes off, and everything else falls like dominos after that. But sociologically, it's vastly different.

One of the things we have to recognize is that the social context today is vastly different from what it was, say, in the Great Depression. Since that time we have had decades of moral relativism. We have produced an extremely self-centered culture in which people have less regard for their neighbors than they once had.

My fear is that people today would not do what they did years ago, when everyone believed he was his brother's keeper and extended a helping hand to those in need. We don't live in that kind of world anymore, and our situation could quickly degenerate into the sort of situation we have to expect when there is a blackout, when there is a race riot, or, in Third World countries, when people are starving. In those situations, social stability deteriorates very quickly.

So what's it going to be: brownout, blackout, or meltdown? Again, I want to reiterate that *I don't know* and neither does anyone else. Senator Bob Bennett says:

> With less than a year remaining until the year 2000, our nation is at a critical crossroads in its approach to the looming Y2K crisis. The press tends to characterize Y2K as one of two extremes: "end of the world" on the one hand, or "no big deal" on the other. They either focus on the most dire Y2K predictions—the "Chicken Little" approach—or they summarily dismiss Y2K as a non-issue.
>
> Both approaches are wrong. The first road leads to public alarm, or even panic, the consequences of which could be even worse than those caused by the Y2K technological problem itself. The second road is equally dangerous. Deceptively smooth and far easier to traverse in the short term, it leads to a precipice that will not be seen until there is no time left to change direction. And there are no brakes on the vehicle in which we are traveling. Each day brings us closer to the brink.

I do know, however, that the time is long past for responsible figures in government, industry, and the media to be telling the American people that Y2K will have simple, easily managed consequences.[79]

It seems, therefore, that the safest course is to stubbornly steer a middle course of hoping for the best but preparing for the worst.

Conclusion

If you are like most people, when you think of everything that needs to be done between now and January 1, 2000, you probably feel overwhelmed. The problem is, if that emotion is left unchecked, it can turn into procrastination, and procrastination can quickly turn into paralysis. And *that's* your number one enemy. Time is not on your side; you've got to get started now. Preparing for the Year 2000 Computer Crisis is like tackling any other large project. You must take it one step at a time and do a little bit every day, preparing incrementally. If you do that you will be prepared and won't be caught by surprise when the Millennium Bug bites.

Here are a few final principles to consider as you prepare.

Act, or be acted upon. You don't have to be a victim; you've been forewarned, and you've been given some resources to begin preparations. Like the Nike advertisement says, "Just Do It."

Don't let the best be the enemy of the good. I know this is the reverse of what you normally hear, but perfectionism will only result in procrastination. Perhaps you can't do everything, but you can do something, and some preparation is better than none, so get started.

The sooner you start, the less you will spend. As more and more people realize that a crisis of some proportion is inevitable, the more they will scramble to prepare. And because more and more dollars will be chasing fewer and fewer supplies, prices will begin rising—you can be sure of that. The longer you wait to prepare, the more expensive it is going to be. So start now.

Appendix B

Y2K Preparedness Checklist

The checklists here are drawn from each of the chapters in the main body of the book. The only difference is that here the items have been grouped together by *level*. This way you can work on the lower levels first and then progress to the higher ones. In the first column (marked with a "✔"), check off the items as you complete them. If you decide that it doesn't apply to you, or you simply don't want to do it, write an "X."

	LEVEL 1: THE 72-HOUR CHECKLIST				
✔	*Action Step*	*Qty*	*Unit Price*	*Total Qty*	*Total Price*
	Take inventory of important records. Determine which ones you already have.	N/A	N/A		
	Determine how you will file/store these records for safekeeping.	N/A	N/A		
	Create a "follow up" chart for your important records.	N/A	N/A		
	Assign task of monitoring "follow up" chart to a family member.	N/A	N/A		

(Continued)

	LEVEL 1: THE 72-HOUR CHECKLIST *(Continued)*				
✔	*Action Step*	*Qty*	*Unit Price*	*Total Qty*	*Total Price*
	Faithfully request, and re-request, the documents until you have them all. Do not let more than 2 weeks pass without working on this chore.	N/A	N/A		
	Visit recommended Y2K Internet sites—print out useful articles, lists, product descriptions, etc. File with preparedness books.	N/A	No cost		
	Purchase the Bible if you don't already have a copy.	1	$20		
	Purchase *The American Red Cross First Aid and Safety Handbook.*	1	$18		
	Purchase *Spiritual Survival During the Y2K Crisis.*	1	$13		
	Purchase *The Complete Book of Survival.*	1	$25		
	Assign research jobs to family members.	N/A	N/A		
	Buy an AM/FM radio, preferably one with shortwave capabilities.	1	$100		
	Purchase canned foods.	Varies	Varies		
	Purchase Styrofoam cups.	Varies	Varies		
	Purchase paper plates and utensils.	Varies	Varies		

✔	*Action Step*	*Qty*	*Unit Price*	*Total Qty*	*Total Price*
	LEVEL 1: THE 72-HOUR CHECKLIST *(Continued)*				
	Purchase napkins and paper towels.	Varies	Varies		
	Purchase baby foods (if necessary).	Varies	Varies		
	Purchase matches (for candles, cooking, etc.).	Varies	Varies		
	Purchase cooking timer (wind-up).	1 per family	Varies		
	Purchase crayons, pencils, pens, paper.	Varies	Varies		
	Purchase needles, thread, safety pins.	Varies	Varies		
	Purchase work gloves.	2 pairs/ person	Varies		
	Collect empty 2-liter bottles.	50	$0		
	Buy bottles of unscented Clorox and an eye-dropper.	N/A	$5		
	Fill 2-liter bottles (plus 4 drops unscented bleach); store in cool, dark place.	N/A	$0		
	Make a checklist of what tools you need for your Y2K Tool Kit.	N/A	N/A		

(Continued)

	Action Step	Qty	Unit Price	Total Qty	Total Price
	LEVEL 1: THE 72-HOUR CHECKLIST *(Continued)*				
✔	Do mental exercise: Imagine your neighborhood without electricity, water, and police protection. Honestly assess how your family would fare.	N/A	N/A		
	Have long talk with spouse and/or family about the issue of location.	N/A	N/A		
	Determine if you can keep your present job if you move (work-at-home arrangement or commute).	N/A	N/A		
	Purchase extra underwear for every member of your family.	N/A	N/A		
	Purchase long underwear, if appropriate for your climate.	N/A	N/A		
	Purchase extra socks for every member of your family.	N/A	N/A		
	Make sure you have a sufficient number of jackets, hats, gloves, and boots for every member of your family.	N/A	N/A		
	Purchase a down comforter or extra blankets for every bed in your home.	N/A	N/A		
	Purchase a sleeping bag for every member of your family (optional).	1	$50 to $300		
	Purchase fire extinguisher(s).	1	Varies		

LEVEL 1: THE 72-HOUR CHECKLIST *(Continued)*					
✔	*Action Step*	*Qty*	*Unit Price*	*Total Qty*	*Total Price*
	Purchase battery-operated carbon monoxide monitor.	1	$40		
	Purchase waterproof matches.	1	Varies		
	Purchase a Coleman cook stove.	1	$50 to $100		
	Purchase some Sterno as a back-up.	1	Varies		
	Decide whether or not you have the resources to pursue alternative energy and how much you have to spend.	N/A	N/A		
	At the very least, come up with an alternative source of light.	N/A	N/A		
	Start with at least a 72-hour emergency cash reserve fund.	N/A	N/A		
	Determine if you want to find a temporary solution or a permanent one for disposing of waste.	N/A	N/A		
	Determine how you will dispose of your trash.	N/A	N/A		
	Take up running, jogging, or walking for exercise.	N/A	N/A		
	Take inventory of your medicine cabinet and make up a checklist of medicines to buy.	N/A	N/A		

(Continued)

	LEVEL 1: THE 72-HOUR CHECKLIST *(Continued)*				
✔	*Action Step*	*Qty*	*Unit Price*	*Total Qty*	*Total Price*
	Talk to your doctor about prescription medications.	N/A	N/A		
	Order Dr. Chari's free cassette tape by calling toll-free (800) 580-9666.	N/A	N/A		
	Determine your self-defense philosophy.	N/A	N/A		

	LEVEL 2: THE 1-WEEK CHECKLIST				
✔	*Action Step*	*Qty*	*Unit Price*	*Total Qty*	*Total Price*
	Purchase safe, fire-box, and/or file cabinet to store your important documents. Recommend choice: Sentry Fire-Safe Model 1175 Security File.	1	$84.96		
	Purchase *The Home Water Supply*.	1	$19		
	Purchase *The Toilet Papers*.	1	$11		
	Consider two-way communication. Discuss options with your family, friends, and neighbors.	N/A	N/A		
	Buy one or more two-way radios, either CB or FRS.	Varies	Varies		
	Purchase dried foods (pasta, macaroni, beans, etc.).	Varies	Varies		

✔	Action Step	Qty	Unit Price	Total Qty	Total Price
	LEVEL 2: THE 1-WEEK CHECKLIST *(Continued)*				
	Purchase salt, sugar, honey, cooking oil, spices.	Varies	Varies		
	Purchase thermometers.	2 per family	Varies		
	Purchase special treats (candies, puddings, cookie mix).	Varies	Varies		
	Purchase dishwashing liquid.	Varies	Varies		
	Purchase can opener (heavy-duty, hand operated).	2 per family	Varies		
	Purchase manual kitchen utensils.	Varies	Varies		
	Purchase aluminum foil, plastic wrap.	Varies	Varies		
	Purchase knife and utensil sharpeners.	Varies	Varies		
	Purchase board games and cards.	Varies	Varies		
	Purchase rubber gloves.	4 pairs	Varies		
	Purchase clothesline and clothespins.	Varies	Varies		
	Purchase laundry detergent.	Varies	Varies		
	Purchase 55-gallon food-grade drums.	N/A	$43		
	Investigate job/real estate markets in more rural location.	N/A	N/A		

(Continued)

	LEVEL 2: THE 1-WEEK CHECKLIST *(Continued)*				
✔	*Action Step*	*Qty*	*Unit Price*	*Total Qty*	*Total Price*
	Meet with real estate agent—assess value of your present home.	N/A/	N/A		
	Consider purchasing a fireplace insert.	1	$1,200 to $2,000		
	Consider purchasing a wood stove.	1	$200 to $1,500		
	Consider purchasing a kerosene space heater.	1	$180 to $300		
	Purchase firewood (price per cord).	1	$120		
	Purchase kerosene (price per 55-gallon drum, including the drum).	1	$80		
	Acquire a one-week supply of cash.	N/A	N/A		
	Determine where you will stash your cash.	N/A	N/A		
	Make list of "smart" barter items. Be sure to diversify.	N/A	N/A	N/A	N/A
	Immediately begin buying some of these items *each* week. Do not skip a week.	N/A	N/A		
	Go to flea markets, swap meets, etc., and sharpen your barter skills.	N/A	N/A	N/A	N/A
	Stock up on 6–12 months' worth of over-the-counter medications.	Varies	Varies		

✔	Action Step	Qty	Unit Price	Total Qty	Total Price
	LEVEL 2: THE 1-WEEK CHECKLIST *(Continued)*				
	Stock up on vitamin supplements.	N/A	$50		
	Take a first aid course from your local chapter of the American Red Cross.	N/A	$30		
	Purchase an extra copy of *The American Red Cross First Aid and Safety Handbook* for your first aid kit.	N/A	$18		
	Prepare custom first aid kits for your family needs to be placed in different parts of your home.	N/A	$30		
	Consider purchasing a stun gun.	1	$50		
	Consider purchasing a tazer.	1	$200		
	Purchase a container of pepper spray.	1	$10		
	Establish a "safe room" in your home.	N/A	$100		
	Organize a neighborhood watch program.	N/A	N/A		
	Make your home uninviting for intruders.	N/A	Varies		

	LEVEL 3: THE 30-DAY CHECKLIST				
✔	*Action Step*	*Qty*	*Unit Price*	*Total Qty*	*Total Price*
	Purchase *Emergency Survival Communications.*	1	$20		
	Purchase *How to Live Without Electricity.*	1	$14		
	Consider getting an amateur radio license.	1	$10		
	Consider buying a ham radio for long-range, two-way communication.	1	Varies		
	Purchase long-term food-storage program (per person price).	1 year	$850		
	Purchase long-term food-storage program (per four-person price).	1 year	$3,350		
	Purchase food-grade storage buckets (amount assumes no packaged long-term foods).	12/year	$6		
	Purchase desiccants—One Unit Clay, Unit Pak.	1	$10		
	Purchase oxygen absorbers—FT-750.	1	$5		
	Purchase cast iron skillets.	2 per family	Varies		
	Purchase cast iron Dutch oven.	1 per family	Varies		
	Purchase colander.	1 per family	Varies		

✔	Action Step	Qty	Unit Price	Total Qty	Total Price
	LEVEL 3: THE 30-DAY CHECKLIST *(Continued)*				
	Purchase food scale.	1 per family	Varies		
	Purchase shoelaces.	Varies	Varies		
	Purchase Katadyn ceramic water filter (long term), or...	1	$269		
	Purchase Katadyn filter (short term).	1	$87		
	Set up cisterns near house downspouts.	N/A	N/A		
	Purchase all the tools you lack for your needs.	Varies	Varies		
	Study how to use all of your tools.	N/A	N/A		
	Purchase a repair manual for your Y2K Emergency Preparedness Library.	1	Varies		
	Make the decision to move or stay.	N/A	N/A		
	If you stay, make self-defense plans with neighbors.	N/A	N/A		
	If you stay, arrange "half-way relocation" plan... just in case.	N/A	N/A		
	If you move, get to know new neighbors and become part of new community.	N/A	N/A		

(Continued)

LEVEL 3: THE 30-DAY CHECKLIST *(Continued)*					
✔	*Action Step*	*Qty*	*Unit Price*	*Total Qty*	*Total Price*
	If you are going to pursue alternative energy, determine how you can "lighten your load."	N/A	N/A		
	Fill out a chart similar to Table 9.1 in order to determine your electric demand.	N/A	N/A		
	Identify your alternative energy resources.	N/A	N/A		
	Order Stan Pierchoski's *Power House* video tape.	1	$154		
	Acquire a one-month supply of cash.	N/A	N/A		
	Determine whether you have a valuable skill or service. If so, obtain needed supplies/tools and practice your skill.	N/A	N/A		
	Implement your temporary waste disposal solution.	N/A	$50 to $600		
	Create a Community Waste Disposal Center.	N/A	N/A		
	Overstock on over-the-counter medications for barter purposes.	N/A	N/A		
	Consider purchasing a handgun.	1	$250+		
	Obtain a concealed carry permit for a handgun.	1	$75+		

✔	Action Step	Qty	Unit Price	Total Qty	Total Price
	LEVEL 3: THE 30-DAY CHECKLIST *(Continued)*				
	Consider purchasing a shotgun.	1	$250+		
	Complete a training course on gun safety.	N/A	$50+		

✔	Action Step	Qty	Unit Price	Total Qty	Total Price
	LEVEL 4: THE 3-MONTH CHECKLIST				
	Purchase *Making the Best of Basics.*	1	$20		
	Purchase *Portable Wealth.*	1	$12		
	Purchase basic grains, beans, corn (popcorn), rice, etc. (amount assumes no long-term foods).	40 lbs/ month	Varies		
	Purchase a grain mill (Whisper Mill, Family Mill, or Country Living Mill).	1	$229 to $366		
	Locate self-sufficient water source (well, spring, stream, etc.).	N/A	N/A		
	Decide how much more you want to stockpile and begin making incremental withdrawals.	N/A	N/A		
	Revisit where you are hiding your money. Make sure it is as secure as you can make it.	N/A	N/A		

(Continued)

	Action Step	Qty	Unit Price	Total Qty	Total Price
✔					
	If you are going to withdraw more than $10,000 send a letter to your banker (see Table 10.5).	N/A	N/A		
	Determine whether you can manufacture barter items during a crisis. If so, obtain needed supplies/tools.	N/A	N/A	N/A	N/A
	Discuss Chapter 12 with your spouse. You don't want to do anything that would cause a rift in your marriage. You need to be in agreement.	N/A	N/A		
	Determine what it's going to cost you if you "cash out" of your convention investments.	N/A	N/A		
	Do a "gut check." Are you willing to pay the price of getting out of conventional investments in order to make the balance of your funds more secure?	N/A	N/A		
	Make sure you have taken care of "first things first" (i.e., invest in basic preparedness, items you can share, an emergency cash reserve, and barter items *before* investing in silver and gold).	N/A	N/A		
	Set up a precious metals acquisition plan and begin converting your cash to silver and gold coins on a systematic basis.	N/A	N/A		

LEVEL 4: THE 3-MONTH CHECKLIST *(Continued)*

LEVEL 4: THE 3-MONTH CHECKLIST *(Continued)*					
✔	*Action Step*	*Qty*	*Unit Price*	*Total Qty*	*Total Price*
	Implement your permanent waste disposal solution.	N/A	$250 to $2,550		

LEVEL 5: THE 1-YEAR CHECKLIST					
✔	*Action Step*	*Qty*	*Unit Price*	*Total Qty*	*Total Price*
	Purchase *The Encyclopedia of Country Living.*	1	$28		
	Purchase *Square Foot Gardening.*	1	$17		
	Purchase nonhybrid seeds.	1 pkg/ family	$129 to $159		

Appendix C

Making Sure Your
Personal Computer Is Y2K-OK

As I often remind people when I speak on Y2K, your personal computer is the least of your worries. Nevertheless, if you use a personal computer, you will definitely want to make sure it is Y2K-compliant. There's no sense adding more misery to your life by failing to get your own computer ready for the new millennium.

You need to understand that a personal computer can be affected at three levels: the hardware level, the operating system level, and the application software level. You must check each of these in turn.

Checking Your PC's Hardware

The good news is that if you are using a Macintosh computer it is already Year 2000–compliant, at least at the hardware level and operating system level. You can read Apple's Y2K compliance statement on the Internet at <http://www.apple.com/about/year2000>. A simple Y2K test for Macintosh systems can be found at <http://www.macnologist.com/y2k/test.html>.

If you are using an IBM or IBM-compatible, you will have to check the system, using one of the many utilities now available. One such utility is Ontrack Y2K Advisor. You can download a noncommercial version free from <http://www.ontrack.com>. I do *not* recommend setting the clock forward to 12/31/99 at 11:55 PM and letting it roll forward. Most users won't experience any problems, but some systems have had unexpected results.

A more comprehensive utility is Tic Toc Pro. It sells for $129.00. It has the approval of the federal government's General Services Agency. You can read more about it at <http://tic-tocpro.com>. A minimal free test is available on the website.

Don't assume that just because you have bought a new computer it is ready for the next century. Believe it or not, many manufacturers are still shipping computers infected with the Millennium Bug. If you are in the market for a new machine, make sure that you get the manufacturer to guarantee *in writing* that the computer is Year 2000–compliant. If they won't do so, find another manufacturer.

Generally speaking, the process of making your hardware compliant is as simple as downloading a software patch from the manufacturer's website or ordering the patch on disk over the phone. Here is a list of the more popular hardware manufacturers with links to the Year 2000 sections of their websites.[1]

Table C.1:
Year 2000 Information for Popular PC Hardware

Manufacturer	Website
Compaq	<http://www.compaq.com/year2000>
Dell	<http://www.dell.com/year2000>
Gateway	<http://www.gateway.com/year2000>
Hewlett-Packard	<http://www.hp.com/year2000>
IBM	<http://www.ibm.com/year2000>
Packard-Bell	<http://support.packardbell.com/year2000/default.asp>
Sony	<http://sawebp1.sel.sony.com>
Toshiba	<http://www.toshiba.com/Y2K>
Winbook	<http://www.winbookcorp.com/_technote/y2k.html>

Checking Your PC's Operating System

Once your hardware is Year 2000–compliant, you need to check your operating system. DOS and most versions of Windows are not Year 2000–compliant. (So much for the hope that Bill Gates is smart enough to solve this problem!) Windows 98 is not even Y2K-ready out of the box—it has some minor Y2K issues that you can resolve by visiting Microsoft's website. In addition, with Windows 98, you must manually set the date format to accommodate four-digit years. Here's how:

1. Select **Start** | **Settings** | **Control Panel.**

2. Double-click on the **Regional Settings** icon.

3. Click on the **Date** tab.

4. Note that you can change the "pivot date" if you want in the **Calendar** section. Ninety-nine percent of the time, the default settings are fine.

5. In the **S̲hort date style** field, select one of the four-digit year options.

6. Click on **OK**.

If you are not using Windows 98, you may want to upgrade. This may not be possible, however, depending on your hardware resources. In the case of other operating systems, you may be able to download and install a software patch from Microsoft's website. You can check your particular operating system at <http://www.microsoft.com/technet/year2k/product/product.htm>. (Please note: Microsoft has changed the web addresses of this page three times in a period of ninety days, so I can't guarantee the link will still work when you are reading this. Currently, its main Y2K site is <http://www.microsoft.com/technet/year2k>.)

Checking Your PC's Applications Software

If you are in the habit of purchasing regular upgrades to the software you use most often, you will probably be fine. If you have any doubt, check with the software publisher. Some of the more popular ones are listed below with links to their Year 2000 pages (only the most recent versions are listed). For those products marked with an asterisk you must select the exact product from a drop-down list box. Whatever you do, make sure your custom applications are Year 2000–compliant. If there is any question, check with the software developer.

Table C.2:
Year 2000 Information for Popular PC Application Software

Publisher	Website
Act!*	<http://www.symantec.com/y2K/y2k.html>
CorelDRAW*	<http://livewire.corel.com/cfscripts/y2k/index2.cfm>
Corel Paradox*	<http://livewire.corel.com/cfscripts/y2k/index2.cfm>
Corel Ventura*	<http://livewire.corel.com/cfscripts/y2k/index2.cfm>
Corel WordPerfect*	<http://livewire.corel.com/cfscripts/y2k/index2.cfm>
GoldMine	<http://www.goldminesw.com/html/year_2000.htm>

(Continued)

Table C.2:
Year 2000 Information for Popular PC Application Software *(Continued)*

Publisher	Website
Lotus 1-2-3	<http://www.lotus.com/home.nsf/tabs/Y2K>
Lotus Approach	<http://www.lotus.com/home.nsf/tabs/Y2K>
Lotus Freelance*	<http://www.lotus.com/home.nsf/tabs/Y2K>
Lotus Notes*	<http://www.lotus.com/home.nsf/tabs/Y2K>
Lotus Organizer*	<http://www.lotus.com/home.nsf/tabs/Y2K>
Lotus Word Pro*	<http://www.lotus.com/home.nsf/tabs/Y2K>
Microsoft Access	<http://www.microsoft.com/technet/year2k/product/ product.htm>
Microsoft Excel	<http://www.microsoft.com/technet/year2k/product/ product.htm>
Microsoft Explorer	<http://www.microsoft.com/technet/year2k/product/ product.htm>
Microsoft FoxPro	<http://www.microsoft.com/technet/year2k/product/ product.htm>
Microsoft FrontPage	<http://www.microsoft.com/technet/year2k/product/ product.htm>
Microsoft Money	<http://www.microsoft.com/technet/year2k/product/ product.htm>
Microsoft Outlook	<http://www.microsoft.com/technet/year2k/product/ product.htm>
Microsoft Powerpoint	<http://www.microsoft.com/technet/year2k/product/ product.htm>
Microsoft Project	<http://www.microsoft.com/technet/year2k/product/ product.htm>
Microsoft Publisher	<http://www.microsoft.com/technet/year2k/product/ product.htm>
Microsoft Word	<http://www.microsoft.com/technet/year2k/product/ product.htm>
Norton Anti-Virus*	<http://www.symantec.com/y2k/y2k.html>
Norton Utilities*	<http://www.symantec.com/y2k/y2k.html>
pcANYWHERE*	<http://www.symantec.com/y2k/y2k.html>
Peachtree Accounting	<http://www.peachtree.com/year2000>
QuickBooks	<http://www.intuit.com/support/year2000.html>
Quicken	<http://www.intuit.com/support/year2000.html>
TurboTax	<http://www.intuit.com/support/year2000.html>
WinFax Pro*	<http://www.symantec.com/y2k/y2k.html>

Appendix D

Getting Your Local Community Ready

Individual preparedness is for those who can; community preparedness is for those who can't.

—Paloma O'Riley,
The Cassandra Project

When I think about preparing an entire community, I am reminded of a letter that I received from a Y2K community organizer in the northeastern United States. In it, he wrote of the unusual circumstances that brought about his community's preparedness group.

He had first learned about Y2K Problem on the Internet, and had been studying the problem for months, reading all the books and websites. He was firmly convinced that this was going to be a serious problem, but he was afraid to talk about Y2K because he believed his friends and neighbors would think he was crazy. Instead, he began quietly preparing his family for the crisis on his meager paycheck.

One night, at a locally organized family fun night at his church, the subject was brought up by a close friend of his. After a few minutes of discussing the concept, he discovered that a lot of people were aware of Y2K in his neighborhood, and they had all been afraid to talk about it from fear of ridicule! The group met again and formed an official group to talk about their preparation plans on a regular basis.

Inspired by the success in his neighborhood, he called to make an appointment to speak to his minister about Y2K. The minister, too, had read about Y2K, but he had not brought it up because he worried that such a "radical" topic might split the church down the middle. The two talked for a long while and decided to address the issue together in front of the congregation. Surprisingly, many of the members had quietly been worrying about the problem at home, afraid to discuss the problem in public.

In the end, the church agreed to be a central repository for Y2K supplies, and the surrounding neighborhood voted to pool its supplies to create a Y2K food pantry. The townspeople began collecting money to purchase food and supplies in bulk at wholesale prices and have now succeeded in stocking their pantry so full that they can feed not only themselves and their families, but also those who did not have the foresight or resources to prepare for themselves.

What Is Community Preparedness?

A community can be whatever you define it to be. Depending on where you live, your community may include an urban city of thousands of people, an apartment building with hundreds of people, or your street with only a dozen people. No matter how you define your community, you need to begin preparing now how to alert your community to the Year 2000 Problem and urge people to begin storing food, water, and supplies to support the group during the coming crisis.

There is no single definitive plan for community preparedness. Your options are as varied as the types of communities in which they are implemented. You, yourself, must evaluate the resources that are available and decide the best method for implementing a community action plan in your area.

Remember the old adage, "There is strength in numbers"? This is absolutely true in Y2K preparedness. Even though we should all strive to be completely independent and prepare ourselves and our families, we need to remember that the power of a group is much greater than the power of an individual. More people will listen to a group of voices than a single one. You will find that your efforts will snowball as more people join in the preparations.

Do not think that community preparedness is an alternative to individual preparations. Obviously, you want your community to be able to provide for those who have not prepared themselves, but you also don't want your needs to be a drain on the community's reserves. So, some combination of personal individual preparedness and community preparedness is best in most situations.

Benefits of Community Preparation

In my opinion, we will never reach 100 percent awareness of the Y2K Problem in the United States. There will be those who deny the possibilities of such a crash all the way up to the last minute—when it all comes crashing down. What should be done with these individuals when they come knocking on the door of the Ark? They cannot be left in the cold with no food to eat or water to drink. Just like the biblical hero Joseph, we should store enough for everyone, so that when the time comes, we can look beyond family relations and church affiliations and fulfill the needs of our entire communities.

With Y2K, we have been given the opportunity to reach out to our communities and help those who cannot help themselves. Let us not take that responsibility lightly.

The benefits of promoting community preparation are apparent in many ways. Here are just a few:

Reducing the potential for violence. When the food and water supply lines run short, people will begin searching seriously for these vital resources. In fact, depending on your community, they may resort to threats and violence if they are not successful.

By stocking a Y2K pantry full enough to serve the needs of the entire community, and then publicizing your preparations, people will know where they can go to find the food and water that they need and they will not be tempted to invade your home or your property to get it. You may want to post a sign on your door that reads, "There is no food or water here for you, but you are welcome to come to the First Harvest Y2K Pantry at Southern Hills Community Center if you are in need."

Bringing the community together. Depending on what type and size neighborhood you live in, you may not know your neighbors too well. If not, Y2K provides a tremendous opportunity to get to know them. By getting to know your neighbors, you may discover the strengths your community already possesses. For example, if a member of your neighborhood is an Emergency Medical Technician (EMT), you can use him to head a medical emergency Y2K task force. One member of your community might work for the city public works department and might be able to get a good deal on a generator for the community center. You never know what treasures lie beneath your own nose until you go looking for them.

Providing an opportunity for evangelism. According to Bill Mindel, pastor for the Harbor Light Community Chapel in Harbor Springs, Michigan, Y2K may be the greatest opportunity for Christian evangelism in our lifetimes, possibly in the history of the world. He hopes that his community food reserves draw in the meek of his community, so that he can spread the Gospel to them. "The exciting thing about this is that when people come to get the wheat, or to get the beans, or to get the honey, or whatever we have that would be here for them, this gives us the opportunity to share the most important news with them—Christ—who is the one who has promised to sustain them and to supply them for all their needs."

What People Are Already Doing

Communities across the United States and in other parts of the world have already begun to organize themselves to deal with the problems that will surely result from Y2K. By taking a look at what others have already done, you can develop your own plan for community preparedness and avoid the time-consuming process of "reinventing the wheel."

Harbor Light Community Chapel (Harbor Springs, Michigan). A community food pantry storehouse since 1992, the Harbor Light Community Chapel officially became a community Y2K food pantry in 1998, when Pastor Bill Mindel was introduced to the Y2K Problem by one of the church's members. Since then, the church has used its home mission funds to build a Y2K food storehouse and stock the pantry with foods with adequate shelf lives. The church has reached out to the community to tell it about the events that might ensue during the year 2000.

In addition to stocking the pantry, the church holds meetings twice every week to teach how to survive in a nontechnological world. These classes include canning, leather tanning, water storage, and cooking with dried foodstuffs. The church members are also hard at work attempting to set up a complex communications system, which includes its own FCC license and several relay stations.

According to Mindel, "Y2K is just something we have to get through. If the crisis is extended, then we'll be ready. If the disruptions are minor, we're already talking about how to distribute the excess supplies to other areas of the country and around the world."

Rogue Valley Y2K Task Force (Medford, Oregon). The Rogue Valley Y2K Task Force was established in May 1998 and has become one of the leading communities advocating Y2K preparedness in the United States. The RV-Y2K Task Force has developed six carefully coordinated action teams to work out the Y2K preparations of the community. These teams include:

- an education action team for educating the public

- a faith communities and service organizations action team for alerting other organizations with different spheres of influence about Y2K

- a food and water action team for instructing proper methods for storing these items

- a health care action team to ensure the proper emergency medical care during the crisis

- a utility and infrastructure action team to alert local utilities and to instruct individuals on methods to deal with service disruptions

- a web design action team to provide information on preparedness to the Internet and to allow RV-Y2K members to communicate with one another; you can visit the website at <http://www.rv-y2k.org> or write to the organization at P.O. Box 4247, Medford, Oregon 97501

Community Awareness in Atlanta, Georgia. On September 12, 1998, a highly publicized community-wide Y2K awareness seminar was held in Atlanta, Georgia. The event was coordinated by the Atlanta-based Joseph Project 2000, founded by Shaunti Feldhahn, author and former Federal Reserve Bank analyst turned Y2K community preparedness advocate. According to Feldhahn, "This was our kickoff event and will be used as a model for more events like this in the future." Since that time, similar events have been held across the United States.

The Atlanta event was anchored by keynote speaker Jim Lord, a widely read Y2K columnist and author of the book *Surviving the Y2K Crisis.* He discussed the basic underlying cause of the Y2K problem and the extent to which it will affect the public's day-to-day activities and our modern infrastructure. Following Lord, Michael Hale, the State of Georgia chief information officer and Y2K czar, spoke about the state's progress and plans for contingencies in the event of a large-scale failure. Larry Burkett, founder and president of Christian Financial Concepts, followed Hale and spoke about methods to reduce current debt and acquiring important documents before the crisis.

This event drew more than three thousand attendees from the Atlanta area and marked one of the first Y2K gatherings for a major metropolitan area.

Who Can Help You?

Thankfully, many organizations have spearheaded campaigns to promote Y2K awareness and provide resources for community briefings. By contacting these organizations, you can get more information on updates, speakers, and funding to promote Y2K awareness and preparation in your community. As always, continue to check my website at <http://www.y2kprep.com>. There are many resources there that you can use for community preparedness. In addition, you will want to contact the following organizations:

The Cassandra Project. In Greek mythology, it was Cassandra's curse to always speak the truth and never be believed. You may feel this way when speaking about Y2K to your friends and neighbors. The Cassandra Project is a grass-roots community preparedness organization based in Boulder County, Colorado, and spear-headed by Paloma O'Riley. The Cassandra Project offers a wide variety of pre-paredness materials, including plans for community meetings, questionnaires, community press releases, and study courses for community preparations. All of this information is available absolutely free of charge from the Cassandra Project web-site at <http://www.cassandraproject.org>. You can also contact the Cassandra Pro-ject by mail at P.O. Box 8, Louisville, CO 80027.

The Joseph Project 2000. According the Bible, God told Joseph that a terrible famine would be coming during a time of plenty and that he needed to prepare. True to God's word, the famine came and people were hungry. Joseph had obeyed God's word and stored enough food to feed not only himself, but also all of the people in Egypt. Due to Joseph's forethought and trust in the word of God, he was able to save the lives of his country's people. The Joseph Project 2000, founded by Shaunti Feld-hahn, author of *Y2K: A Balanced Christian Response*, is a nonprofit Christian organi-zation that encourages community preparations and instructs church groups on how to plan a Year 2000 Project. For more information, visit the organization's website at <http://www.josephproject2000.org> or write to: 6409 Bells Ferry Road, Wood-stock, GA 30189-2324.

Y2K News Magazine. *Y2K News Magazine* is a biweekly magazine that is published in Crossville, Tennessee, by publisher and speaker Tim Wilson. They have also pro-duced a special issue entitled Y2KCPR (Critical Preparation Resource) which they offer at tremendous bulk discounts for church and nonprofit fundraising programs. You can order large quantities of these magazines and use them as donation incen-tives, fundraiser items, door-to-door sales, or whatever you choose to earn extra money to fund your preparedness project or stock your Y2K pantry. By effectively using this product, your community can tackle the single most challenging problem for most small organizations—money. For ordering information, contact *Y2K News Magazine* on the Internet at <http://www.y2knews.com> or by calling (931) 484-8819. Or, if you prefer, request information by writing to 20 Our Way Drive, Crossville, TN 38555.

Where Can I Start?

At this point, you might be feeling a bit overwhelmed about what exactly you need to do to begin preparing your community for the year 2000. This is completely natural. The important first step is to make a list of what you want to do and begin acting on that list as soon as possible. Here are a few places you can look to in your community to your preparations. Start at the top and begin calling and writing letters.

Churches. An October 1998 survey by the Christian Broadcasting Network and the Barna Research Group shows that 75 percent of all church pastors are aware of the Year 2000 Problem, but only 13 percent have actually mentioned it to their congregations. Consider writing to or calling the leaders of every church in your local area. Make sure to explain the need for community preparations for Y2K and the opportunity for Christian evangelism. If possible, try to arrange a time to meet with the pastor or even the elders of the church and show them a video or read selections from this book. Giving them a copy of Appendix A is also a good first step for people who need to be brought up to speed quickly.

Municipal leaders. Contrary to what is often joked about, municipal leaders are interested in hearing what their constituents are concerned about. By sending a message to your municipal leaders, including your city's mayor, city council, and other local offices, you can alert them to the growing concern in your community about preparing for Y2K.

Nonprofit organizations. Most midsize and large cities will have local offices for the Federal Emergency Management Agency and the American Red Cross. Get the addresses from your phone book and write or call them to ask where they are in their preparations. Find out if they are planning on having extra staff on hand to deal with potential emergencies in the year 2000. Ask if they will be offering special preparedness classes for Y2K. Inform them that you are preparing, and that you might be able to help coordinate if they are planning on doing nothing. Don't forget to contact the fire department, too. In Baton Rouge, Louisiana, the ladder systems on the city's fire trucks failed in a test to function after the year 2000. Ask if your local department has performed similar tests.

Government offices. Where is your city's police department, water department, and electric department in their Y2K preparations? Call or write and ask them. Tell them that they have a responsibility to inform the public about the status of public health and safety systems. Above all, plead for full disclosure. People can handle the truth. What they can't handle is a sudden admission in December 1999 that these officials had been overly optimistic and the deadline won't be met.

Local industry. A few localized industries often employ the bulk of a given community. If a large plant goes down in your area, many citizens may suddenly be out of a job. With sudden high unemployment, the local economy can plummet quickly, creating even more layoffs. You can see the domino effect that would ensue. So consider writing to the director of operations and the Information Systems director for the plant in order to ask them about their status on Y2K and inform them of the repercussions of failing to meet the deadline.

Here is a template for a letter for a local city government or business.[1] Obviously, you can adjust the letter in any way you see fit:

Table D.1:
Sample Y2K Inquiry Letter

[Date]

[Contact Name]
[Title]
[Organization]
[Address]
[City, State Zip]

Dear [Contact Name]:

I am greatly concerned about the Year 2000 Problem, and its possible impact on the reliability and continuity of the services you provide. Specifically I have the following questions:

1. Do you have a Year 2000 (Y2K) remediation project?
2. What is the status of your Y2K activities?
3. How many mission critical systems do you have?
4. Have you developed contingency plans to ensure continuity of services to residents in your jurisdiction in the event Y2K failures occur?
5. Have you developed contingency plans to ensure continued operation should third-party (suppliers, vendors) failures occur?
6. What steps are being taken to ensure the public's health and safety should critical infrastructure (e.g., power, water, traffic systems, etc.) fail?
7. Will you publicly inform residents of your Y2K efforts and their progress? If so, when, and by what means?

I would appreciate a written response to my concerns, as well as assurance that your services will continue after December 31, 1999.

I look forward to receiving your reply soon. Thank you for your time and attention.

Sincerely,

[Your Name]
[Address]
[City, State Zip]
[Phone]

The important thing is not to take yes for an answer. You don't want to settle for some glib assurance that all is well. Keep pressing until you get specific, detailed information.

Strength in Numbers

Your next step is to find other people who are concerned about the year 2000. You will probably find them by contacting churches or civic organizations, as explained above. Once you have a group of people who are knowledgeable about Y2K and are ready to begin preparing, you will have effectively begun your community preparedness project. Of course, you will need to adapt your project to the specific needs of your community. Here are a few more tips on successfully preparing your community:

Use your talents. Every person has talents that others do not. Interview every member of your Y2K preparedness group to determine their talents and how you can harness those existing abilities to your advantage. For example, you may already have an EMT in your midst, and can use him to teach a class in first aid and basic medical procedures. Put him in charge of your emergency medical plan and have him put together your community first-aid cabinet. Additionally, you may have an individual who is a ham radio enthusiast. Put him in charge of your alternative communications systems. You get the idea.

Take good notes. Designate one of your members as a secretary. It will be his or her job to record the day-to-day journal of how your organization prepared for Y2K, including the mistakes as well as the successes. If you are successful—and I hope you are—you will undoubtedly have other communities coming to you for information on how to prepare effectively. And, as the time until Y2K grows shorter, the margin for mistakes grows shorter as well. Your notes will be a God-send for other communities who are trying to piece together a preparedness plan.

Use the media. The media are an extremely powerful tool if used properly, but they can also be damaging if used improperly. The best possible situation is for you to have a member of the media, whether newspaper, radio, or TV, among your members. If you do not, you might choose to invite the media to one of your meetings, where you could present a good Y2K video and loan out some Y2K preparedness books for them to look at. The media usually like to cover community events, such as carnivals, craft fairs, or celebrations. Perhaps you could plan a fundraising event that the media could cover in a positive way to promote your message. In addition, it would probably be good to appoint one of your members as a media relations specialist to deal with the media on the phone and speak in front of the cameras.

Final Thoughts

I hope that this information helps you prepare your community for Y2K. Of course, as I have stated, there is no one definitive plan for creating your preparedness group. My suggestion to you is to begin simply, gathering momentum slowly and learning from groups that are already established. Contact the groups that I have listed for more information and gather as many resources as possible. Use the talents that your members already have and develop a concrete plan about how you will deal with problems as they occur and how you will distribute food, water, and supplies during the Y2K Crisis. And, make sure to take good notes along the way in case you are asked by the media or other organizations how you have done all that you have done.

Y2K PREP TIP #17
Host a "Y2K Community Briefing"

Last year, I spoke at a "Y2K Community Briefing" for the people in our subdivision. Amazingly, sixty-five people showed up. (Earlier in the day, I had told one of my daughters that I didn't think we should expect more than twenty.)

During the first hour, I gave an overview of the Y2K Problem following the standard outline I use in my "America Offline" speech (essentially the same material provided in Appendix A). Following this, I opened up the floor for questions. Surprisingly, there were no naysayers. Everyone seemed concerned, but they were also excited about the prospect of working together. One of the unexpected benefits of having a meeting like this is the opportunity to get to know one another.

There are at least three reasons why you need to consider doing something similar in your neighborhood:

First, you need the motivation that comes from doing things in a group. Preparing for Y2K is difficult. It's easy to begin doubting the whole thing and fall back into denial or procrastination. But if you are preparing in a group, you can encourage one another and keep going when you're ready to quit. You can help solve one another's problems and jointly shoulder the burden. Perhaps most important, it gives you the validation that you really aren't crazy (or if you are, you're not the only one!).

Second, you probably don't have enough resources to prepare on your own. Preparing for Y2K can get expensive, particularly if you believe that the disruptions may be long-term. But there are many costs that can be shared and are better done in the context of a community. For example, not everyone needs to build his own emergency preparedness library, stockpile medical emergency supplies, or come up with an alternative way to dispose of waste. These issues can better be solved in a group. But even beyond the cost, you probably don't have the time to become an expert on everything. This is where you can let the division of labor work for you. One person in your group can research and become an expert on food storage and preparation, another on alternative sources of water, and another on self-defense. This saves everyone time and lets you accumulate far more information and expertise than you could ever do on your own.

Third, you have a responsibility to the larger community. There are, no doubt, many in your community who cannot prepare. Some of these simply don't have the foresight to prepare for themselves. No matter what you tell them, they just don't "get it." Others are convinced, but they don't have the resources. This is especially true of the poor, the elderly, and the sick. At a practical level, if you don't make provisions for these people, they will become a problem—perhaps even a threat—once the crisis begins. At a moral level, you are your brother's keeper. You currently receive the benefits of living in a community and you owe something to that community.

Beginning a group is not that difficult. We followed these steps:

1. We contacted the president of the homeowner's association, making sure we had his support before we proceeded.
2. We made arrangements with the local junior high school to use the school theater for the meeting.
3. We elected a speaker to make the formal presentation (guess who got elected?!).
4. We delivered a flyer announcing the event to everyone's home.
5. We delivered a "reminder" flyer the day before the event.
6. We invited the local press—and they came!
7. We started the meeting on time, and we ended on time.
8. At the end of the meeting, we asked for volunteers to serve on the official "Y2K Taskforce." We had several volunteers.
9. We appointed a chairperson to plan the first taskforce meeting.
   Since the initial meeting, we have had several other meetings. Each of them has been fruitful and encouraging. If you haven't started yet, what's keeping you?

Appendix E

Shelf Life and Storage Tips for Various Foods

The following tables[1] contain the storage length (shelf-life) of various foods along with specific handling tips. Please note that my estimates may be overly conservative, but I would rather be safe than sorry. The foods are organized into four tables: staples, mixed and packaged foods, canned and dried foods, and miscellaneous foods. Also, keep in mind that you may not be able to refrigerate foods if you lose electricity and do not have an alternative energy source.

Table E.1:
Staples

Item	Storage Length At 70°F (21°C)	Handling Tips
Baking powder	18 months	Keep dry and covered
Baking soda	2 years	Keep dry and covered
Bouillon cubes or granules	2 years	Keep dry and covered
Bread crumbs, dried	6 months	Keep dry and covered
Cereals		
ready-to-eat (unopened)	12–18 months	
ready-to-eat (opened)	2–3 months	Refold package liner after opening
cooked	6 months	Keep cool
Chocolate		
pre-melted	12 months	Keep cool
semi-sweet	2 years	Keep cool
unsweetened	18 months	Keep cool
Cocoa mixes	8 months	Cover tightly

(Continued)

Table E.1:
Staples *(Continued)*

Item	Storage Length At 70°F (21°C)	Handling Tips
Coffee		
cans (unopened)	2 years	N/A
cans (opened)	2 weeks	Refrigerate after opening
Instant (unopened)	1–2 years	N/A
instant (opened)	2 weeks	Use dry measuring spoon
Cornmeal	12 months	Keep lid tightly closed
Cornstarch	18 months	Keep tightly closed
Flour		
white	6–8 months	Keep in airtight container
whole wheat	6–8 months	Keep refrigerated and airtight
Gelatin (all types)	18 months	Keep in original container
Grits	12 months	Store in airtight container
Honey	Indefinitely	Cover tightly. If it crystallizes, warm jar in pan of hot water
Jellies and jams	12 months	Keep tightly closed
Molasses		
unopened	12 months	N/A
opened	6 months	Keep tightly closed
Marshmallows	2–3 months	Keep in airtight container
Mayonnaise (unopened)	2 months	Refrigerate after opening
Milk		
condensed or evaporated	12 months	Invert cans every 2 months
non-fat dry		
unopened	6 months	N/A
opened	3 months	Place in airtight container
Pasta (spaghetti, macaroni)	2 years	Once opened, store airtight
Rice		
white	2 years	N/A
flavored or herb	6 months	Keep tightly closed
Shortenings, solid		
unopened	8 months	Refrigeration not needed
opened	6 months	Refrigeration not needed
Sugar		
brown	4 months	Place in airtight container
confectioners	18 months	Place in airtight container

Table E.1:
Staples *(Continued)*

Item	Storage Length At 70°F (21°C)	Handling Tips
Sugar *(Continued)*		
granulated	2 years +	Cover tightly
artificial sweeteners	2 years +	Cover tightly
Syrups	12 months	Keep tightly closed
Tea		
bags	18 months	Place in airtight container
instant	3 years	Cover tightly
loose	2 years	Place in airtight container
Vinegar		Keep tightly closed. Slightly
unopened	2 years	cloudy appearance is OK.
opened	12 months	Distilled vinegar keeps longer than cider vinegar.
Non-dairy coffee creamers (dry)		
unopened	9 months	N/A
opened	6 months	Keep lid tightly closed.

Table E.2:
Mixed and Packaged Foods

Item	Storage Length At 70°F (21°C)	Handling Tips
Biscuit, brownie and muffin mixes	9 months	Keep cool and dry
Cake mixes	9 months	Keep cool and dry
Casseroles, complete or add meat	9–12 months	Keep cool and dry
Cookies (packaged)	2 months	Keep tightly closed
Crackers (unopened)	8 months	Keep tightly closed
Hot roll mix (unopened)	18 months	If opened, put in airtight container
Pancake mix (opened)	6-9 months	Put in airtight container
Pie crust mix (unopened)	8 months	Keep cool and dry
Potatoes, instant (unopened)	6–12 months	Keep in airtight package

(Continued)

Table E.2:
Mixed and Packaged Foods *(Continued)*

Item	Storage Length At 70°F (21°C)	Handling Tips
Pudding mixes (unopened)	12 months	Keep cool and dry
Rice, mixes (unopened)	6 months	Keep cool and dry
Sauce and gravy mixes	6–12 months	Keep cool and dry
Soup mixes (unopened)	12 months	Keep cool and dry

Table E.3:
Canned and Dried Foods

Item	Storage Length At 70°F (21°C)	Handling Tips
Canned foods (unopened)	2 years	Keep cool
Canned fruit juices	9 months	Keep cool
Canned foods (opened)		
baby foods	2–3 days	All opened canned foods:
fish and seafood	2 days	refrigerate and cover
fruit	1 week	tightly. To avoid metallic taste,
meats	2 days	transfer food to glass or plastic
pickles and olives	1–2 months	storage containers.
poultry	2 days	
sauce, tomato	5 days	
vegetables	3 days	
Fruits, dried	6–12 months	Keep cool in airtight container
Vegetables, dried	6–12 months	Keep cool in airtight container
Catsup, chili sauce		
unopened	12 months	N/A
opened	1 month	Refrigerate for longer storage
Mustard, prepared yellow		
unopened	2 years	N/A
opened	6–8 months	Stir before using

Table E.3:
Canned and Dried Foods *(Continued)*

Item	Storage Length At 70°F (21°C)	Handling Tips
Spices and herbs		Store in airtight containers in dry
whole spices	1–2 years	places away from sunlight and
ground spices	6 months	heat. At times, check aroma; if
herbs	6 months	faded, replace. Whole cloves,
herb/spice blends	6 months	nutmeg, and cinnamon sticks maintain quality beyond two-year period.
Tuna (unopened)	4–6 years	Keep cool and dry
Vanilla		
unopened	2 years	Keep tightly
opened	12 months	closed. Volatile oils escape.
Other extracts, opened	12 months	Keep tightly closed. Volatile oils escape.

Table E.4:
Miscellaneous Foods

Item	Storage Length At 70°F (21°C)	Handling Tips
Cheese, parmesan (grated)		
unopened	10 months	Refrigerate after opening
opened	2 months	Keep tightly closed
Coconut (shredded, canned)		
unopened	12 months	
opened	6 months	Refrigerate after opening
Instant breakfast	6 months	Keep in original package
Nuts		
in shell or pkg'd (unopened)	6 months	
vacuum can (unopened)	12 months	Refrigerate or freeze for longer storage
other packaging	3 months	

(Continued)

Table E.4:
Miscellaneous Foods *(Continued)*

Item	Storage Length At 70°F (21°C)	Handling Tips
Peanut butter		
unopened	6–9 months	Refrigeration not needed. Keeps
opened	3 months	longer if refrigerated.
Peas and beans, dried	12 months	Store in airtight container in a cool place
Popcorn	2 years	Store in airtight container
Whipped topping, dry	12 months	Keep cool and dry
Yeast, dry	Check expiration date	N/A

Appendix F

Where to Stash Your Cash and Other Valuables

Earlier this year, I posted the Y2K Prep Tip about "Where Not to Cash Your Stash" on my website at <http://www.michaelhyatt.com>. Immediately, one of my readers suggested that I come up with a list of where to put it.

"Okay, Mr. Smarty Pants, if you're going to tell us where *not* to put it, then at least tell us a few places where we can stash it." *Good idea*, I thought. So I invited the thirty thousand or so readers who visit my website on a weekly basis to help me with the task. I was flooded with responses. Here are the best ideas from your fellow citizens. They are arranged in no particular order. Some of the ideas are better than others. Scan through the list and see which ones make sense for you. Remember: Don't put everything in one place!

- Inside empty cassette or CD covers
- Inside empty video covers with your video collection
- An empty box of cereal in your cupboard
- Bottom of a tool box
- Behind some books in a bookcase
- Inside a spare tire in your car
- In an envelope stapled to the back of your bed's headboard
- Under the files in a packed file cabinet
- Shoe box in your closet
- A kitchen cabinet with a false back
- Scarf box under the couch
- Taped to the inside of your piano
- Inside a guitar case
- At the bottom of a dried herb jar
- Hollowed out books on the shelf with your other books

- A Ziploc bag submerged in a toilet tank
- A Ziploc bag buried in a flower or plant pot
- Behind pictures in frames
- An envelope taped to the bottom of a china cabinet or free-standing shelf
- In a box of tampons
- Inside porcelain knick-knacks or statuary
- In a coffee can buried in a garden
- In hollow plastic broom handles
- In a Ziploc bag placed inside the clean-out drawer of a chimney
- In an empty vitamin or herb bottle, placed with your real ones
- In a coffee can in the garage with nails on top of the cash
- Behind a suspended ceiling
- Inside a Thermos or Tupperware container
- Under the corner of a carpet under a piece of heavy furniture
- Behind the knee board of your piano
- Inside old sneakers or other shoes
- Inside a board game
- Inside stuffed animals or toys
- Inside the back of a wall clock
- Inside the kick plate under your bathroom cabinet
- Under the insulation in the attic
- Inside socks in your dresser
- Inside gloves in the closet
- In a box of Christmas decorations stored in the garage or attic
- Inside a buried PVC pipe with closed ends
- Wrapped in some fabric inside a box of sewing supplies
- Inside an empty paint can and stored with your other paint cans
- Inside a return air vent
- Inside a false electrical outlet
- Behind a mirror
- Inside the breast pocket of a suit or coat
- Inside some luggage stored with your other luggage
- Inside a pillow
- Inside a curtain valance, especially the puffy kind
- Inside a hollow-core door
- Inside a hot water bottle or—enema bag!
- In a sleeping bag stored with other camping equipment
- On top of a kitchen cupboard or free-standing cabinet
- Under the microwave

- In a fake milk carton or soda bottle in the refrigerator
- In a bag of charcoal
- Inside a first aid kit
- Inside a child's toy chest
- In an envelope taped under a coffee table
- Inside a photo album
- Inside a recipe box
- In a fake box of laundry detergent
- Inside an empty mayonnaise bottle that has the inside painted white
- Under a dog house
- Under a wooden step going to the basement or garage

Notes

Introduction

1. Prepared Testimony of Michael S. Hyatt, Author of *The Millennium Bug: How to Survive the Coming Chaos* (Washington, DC: Regnery, 1998), before the Subcommittee on Government, Management, Information, and Technology of the Committee on Government, Reform, and Oversight and the Subcommittee on Technology of the Committee on Science, U.S. House of Representatives, 24 September 1998, 2. Available from <http://www.michaelhyatt.com/mrgoes.htm> (16 December 1998); INTERNET.
2. Bob Brewin and Orlando De Bruce, "DOD Reports More Systems Need Y2K Fix," *Federal Computer Week* 24 August 1998. Available from < http://www.fcw.com/pubs/fcw/1998/0824/fcw-newsdody2k-8-24-98.html > (16 December 1998); INTERNET.
3. Standish Group International, "Year 2000—A Date Odyssey," 1998. Available from <http://www.standishgroup.com/ad.html> (16 December 1998); INTERNET.
4. Yes, I know that it was often management that failed to head the warnings of the programmers, but I also know that programmers continued to utilize the two-digit date convention long after memory prices plummeted and there was no practical reason for continuing the outdated practice.

Chapter 3. Develop an Alternative Communications System

1. Dave Ingram, *Guide to Emergency Survival Communications* (Columbus, OH: Universal Electronics, 1997), 23.
2. Ibid, 82.

Chapter 4: Stockpile Food and Common Household Goods

1. You can also call the Customer Service number on the can. They can give you the shelf life of that particular item, plus specific directions on how to read the expiration codes.

2. Please note: Because of volatility and market conditions, these prices can change rapidly and without notice. I anticipate rapidly escalating prices as 1999 progresses.
3. This is not to suggest that real meat products are necessarily better for you. However, they are generally more pleasing to the taste, especially for committed meat-eaters.
4. Be advised that this is *not* a good option for people with hemochromatosis, a potentially fatal blood/iron inherited disease. Those with this disease should *never* eat food prepared in cast iron cookware.

Chapter 5: Develop an Alternative Source of Water

1. This material is taken from a web site maintained by the Metropolitan Government of Nashville and Davidson County, Department of Water and Sewerage Services. Available from <http://www.nashville.org/ws/h2o_use.html> (21 December 1998); INTERNET. Note: this table does not include water used for washing dishes and clothes or gardening and lawn care.
2. James Talmage Stevens, *Making the Best of Basics* (Seattle: Gold Leaf Press, 1997), 61.
3. Ibid., 62.
4. Stu Campbell, *The Home Water Supply* (Pownal, VT: Storey Books, 1983), 133.

Chapter 6: Acquire a Basic Selection of Tools

1. The SureFire brand of NiCad laser lights is actually brighter, but it is very expensive. SureFire laser lights start at about $120 and go up from there. They are the first choice of many law enforcement agencies. You can see SureFire's full line of products at <http://www.surefire.com>.
2. James Talmage Stevens, *Making the Best of Basics* (Salt Lake City: Peton Corp, 1975), 225.
3. Ibid. 224.

Chapter 8: Secure an Alternative Source of Heat

1. Bonnie Camp, "Shining the Light on Electric Utility 10Q Y2K Disclosures," *Electric Utilities and the Year 2000*, 21 December 1998. Available from <http://www.euy2k.com/guest2.htm> (29 December 1998); INTERNET.
2. William Ulrich, "Energy Companies Seem Far Behind on Year 2000," *ComputerWorld*, 14 December 1998. Available from <http://www.computerworld.com/home/print.nsf/all/981214829E> (29 December 1998); INTERNET.
3. Ibid.
4. *Y2KWatch News*, 7 January 1999. You can subscribe to *Y2KWatch News* at <http://y2kwatch.com>.

Chapter 10: Build an Emergency Cash Reserve

1. You can obtain this book by writing to The Federal Reserve Bank of Chicago, P.O. Box 834, Chicago, IL 60690–0834 or call (312) 322-5111.
2. Ibid., 3.

3. These numbers are from the Federal Reserve Bank of St. Louis. You can check the figures for yourself on the Internet at <http://www.stls.frb.org>.

Chapter 11: Collect Items You Can Use as Barter

1. Rainer Stahlberg, *The Complete Book of Survival* (New York: Barricade Books, 1998), 73.

Chapter 12: Change Your Investment Strategy

1. Edward Robb Ellis, *A Nation in Torment: The Great American Depression, 1929–1939* (New York: Kodansha International, 1995), 45. This book is "must reading" for anyone who believes the stock market will never crash again.
2. Ibid., 24.
3. When I use the term "bond," I am actually referring to all kinds of debt-based instruments, including government, municipal, and corporate bonds. Although it is perhaps less obvious, even your checking account, money market fund, and savings accounts, are, in effect, loans that you make to the bank. This is what fractional reserve banking is all about. You deposit your money (i.e., loan it to the bank), and the bank turns around and loans it out to borrowers, paying you a modest interest rate for your nominal risk.

    Perhaps even less obvious is the fact that our currency is also a debt-based instrument. It is borrowed into circulation. This is why a dollar bill says "Federal Reserve *Note*" at the top. A *note* is a loan made by the Federal Reserve Bank to the U.S. Treasury. Here's how it works:

    Congress decides it need to make an appropriation. It passes a law and goes to the U.S. Treasury for funding. If the Treasury is out of money—which it often is—it must borrow the money from the Federal Reserve, the nation's central bank (which is not, of course, a government agency but a private banking cartel). The Fed says, "no problem," and hands over a billion or two of paper money in exchange for the U.S. government's promise to pay back the money with interest at a future date. The government then says "thank you very much" and begins to spend it into circulation, buying whatever is necessary in the original appropriation.
4. I am indebted to Franklin Sanders for much of this material. It has appeared in slightly different form on his website at <http://www.the-moneychanger.com> and in his newsletter, *The Moneychanger*. It is used with his permission.
5. Presidential Executive Order of 5 April 1933, § 2(b).
6. Vol. 49, No. 3, 5 January 1984.
7. This has been true since the Greenback Act of 1863.
8. If you insist on staying in stocks and bonds, then at the very least hedge your investments with some cheap out-of-the-money gold and silver call options. Buy the call options that expire in December 1999, or June or July 2000. At this writing, the December 1999 gold call option with a strike price of 380 sells for about $100. The December 1999 silver call option with a strike price of 7.50 costs about $450. (A gold call option controls a futures contract for 100 ounces of gold; a silver call option controls a futures contract for 5,000 ounces of silver.) If a Y2K panic into gold and silver unfolds, these options will skyrocket. How much can you lose? Only the price that you pay for the option.

Prices on these options change all the time. Right now they look undervalued. You can buy these options through any commodity broker (sorry, a stock broker can't help you) or call Sue Rutsen or Teddy McAleer at Fox Investments in Chicago, (800) 621-0265, but they have a $5,000 account minimum.

Chapter 13: Determine How You Will Dispose of Waste

1. Sim Van der Ryn, *The Toilet Papers: Recycling Waste and Conserving Water* (Sausalito, CA: Ecological Design Press, 1978), 34–35.

Chapter 14: Be Prepared for Medical Emergencies

1. "Vitamin," *Microsoft® Encarta® Encyclopedia*. Funk and Wagnalls Corporation, 1996.
2. Handal, Kathleen A., *The American Red Cross First Aid and Safety Handbook* (New York: Little, Brown, and Company, 1992), 6–7.

Chapter 15: Determine Your Self-defense Philosophy

1. Article II of the Bill of Rights states, "A well regulated militia being necessary to the security of a free State, the right of the people to keep and bear arms shall not be infringed." Being part of the common law, the Constitution supersedes and is antecedent to all statutory law. Another way of saying it, the right to bear arms is an inalienable right. It is not granted by the state and thus cannot be taken away by the state.
2. With a semiautomatic weapon, the trigger must be pulled once for each round (shot). With a fully-automatic weapon, once the trigger is pulled, the gun continues to fire until you let up on the trigger.

Appendix A: An Overview of Y2K

1. Robert Sam Anson, "The Y2K Nightmare," *Vanity Fair*, January 1999, 80. Available from <http://www.remarq.com/default/transcript.pl?group=comp.software.year-2000: 50034064:50034064&update=1770> (1 February 1999); INTERNET.
2. Cap Gemini, "Many Major Firms Have Already Experienced Year 2000-Related Computer Failures," Press Release, 29 December 1998. Available from <http://www.usa. capgemini.com/news/press/pr122998.html> (1 February 1999); INTERNET.
3. Douglas Stanglin and Shaheena Ahmad, "Year 2000 Time Bomb," *U.S. News & World Report*, 8 June 1998, electronic edition. Available from <http://www.usnews.com/usnews/ issue/980608/8y200.htm> (1 February 1999); INTERNET.
4. "Senate Isn't Paying Bills on Time," *Roll Call On-line*, 11 January 1999. Available from <http://www.rollcall.com/4GEbBL43/newsscoops/5thscoop.html> (1 February 1999); INTERNET.
5. Gene Bylinsky, "Industry Wakes Up to the Year 2000 Menace," *Fortune*, 27 April 1998. Available from <http://www.pathfinder.com/fortune/1998/980427/imt.html> (1 February 1999); INTERNET.

6. Lynda Rodosevich, "Millennium Bug Already Taking Its Toll," *InfoWorld*, 10 January 1998. Available from <http://www.infoworld.com/cgi-bin/displayStory.pl?980110. ey2k.htm> (1 February 1999); INTERNET.

7. Brent Israelsen, "Utah Water Managers Are Battling Y2K Problem in Advance," *The Salt Lake Tribune*, 18 January 1999. Available from <http://www.sltrib.com/1999/jan/ 01181999/utah/75860.htm> (1 February 1999); INTERNET.

8. Bruce Caldwell, "Millennium Bug Bites Retailers," *Information Week*, 25 January 1999. Available from <http://www.techweb.com/se/directlink.cgi?IWK19990125S0080> (1 February 1999); INTERNET.

9. John MacCleay, "Mainframe Rush Leaves PCs in Peril," *The Australian*, 6 October 1998, electronic edition. Available from <http://www.theaustralian.com.au/extras/ 007/4235583.htm> (19 December 1998); INTERNET.

10. Testimony of Bruce H. Hall, Research Director, Applications Development Methods and Management, before the Subcommittee on Technology and the Subcommittee on Government Management, Information and Technology, 20 March 1997. Available from <http://www.house.gov/science/hall_3-20.html> (19 December 1998); INTERNET.

11. Associated Press, "Y2K: A Race Against Time," *USA Today*, 18 August 1998. Available from <http://www.usatoday.com/life/cyber/tech/ctd294.htm> (20 December 1998); INTERNET.

12. Julia Vowler, "The Heart of Embedded Systems," *ComputerWeekly*, 8 May 1997. Available from <http://www.computerweekly.com/cwmain/cwmainfram.asp> (1 February 1999); INTERNET.

13. Testimony of David C. Hall, Senior Consultant, Year 2000 Infrastructure and Embedded Systems Engineering, CARA Corporation, Before the Subcommittee on Government Management, Information and Technology of the Committee on Government, Reform, and Oversight, U.S. House of Representatives, Field Hearing on Year 2000 Efforts, Chicago, Illinois, 3. September 1998. Available from <http://home.swbell.net/adheath/ dhall.htm> (1 February 1999); INTERNET.

14. Lauren Gibbons Paul, "The World's Biggest Easter Egg Hunt," *Datamation*, September 1998, electronic edition. Available from <http://www.datamation.com/PlugIn/issues/ 1998/september/09y2k.html> (19 December 1998); INTERNET.

15. Neil Winton, "Millennium Bug Expert Shouts for Action," *Reuters*, 16 October 1998. Available from <http://infoseek.go.com/Content?arn=a0589LBY752reulb-19981016 &col=NX> (1 February 1999); INTERNET.

16. Ibid.

17. David C. Hall.

18. "Embedded Systems: How Big is the Problem," Action 2000, n.d. Available from <http://business.bug2000.co.uk/search/index.shtml> (1 February 1999); INTERNET.

19. "Year 2000 Risk Assessment and Planning for Individuals," The GartnerGroup, 28 October 1998. Available from <http://gartner12.gartnerweb.com/public/static/home/ 00073955.html> (1 February 1999); INTERNET.

20. Summarized from "CA 2000 White Paper: Meeting the Year 2000 Challenge," State of California, Department of Information Technology. Available from <http://www.year2000. ca.gov/correspondence/CA2000WhitePaper.asp> (19 December 1998); INTERNET.

21. Prepared Testimony of Joel Willemssen, Director, Civil Agencies Information Systems, Accounting and Information Management Division, U.S. General Accounting Office, Before the Subcommittee on Government, Management, Information, and Technology, of the Committee of Government, Reform, and Oversight, U.S. House of Representatives, 20 January 1999. Available from <http://www.house.gov/reform/gmit/hearings/testimony/990120jw.htm> (2 February 1999); INTERNET.

22. *Directory of Electric Power Producers 1998*, 106th edition, Edison Electric Institute as quoted in "The Number of Electricity Suppliers in Today's Power Market," Edison Electric Institute, October 1998, electronic edition. Available from <http://www.eei.org/Industry/structure/3electri.htm> (19 December 1998); INTERNET.

23. North American Electric Reliability Council, "Preparing the Electric Power Systems of North America for Transition to the Year 2000," 17 September 1998, 10. Available from <ftp://ftp.nerc.com/pub/sys/all_updl/docs/y2k/y2kreport-doe.pdf> (19 December 1998); INTERNET.

24. See Michael S. Hyatt, *The Millennium Bug: How to Survive the Coming Chaos* (Washington, DC: Regnery Publishing, 1998). In Chapter 3: "One Bad Apple Spoils the Whole Bunch," I describe the domino effect in some detail.

25. Opening Comments of Senator Bob Bennett (R-Utah), Chairman, Special Committee on the Year 2000 Technology Problem, United States Senate, "Hearing to Discuss Chances the Millennium Bug Will Cause the Nation's Power Grid to Fail," 12 June 1998. Available from <http://www.senate.gov/~y2k/statements/61298bennett.html> (19 December 1998); INTERNET.

26. Opening Comments of Senator Christopher Dodd (D-Connecticut), Vice-Chairman, Special Committee on the Year 2000 Technology Problem, United States Senate, "Hearing to Discuss Chances the Millennium Bug Will Cause the Nation's Power Grid to Fail," 12 June 1998. Available from <http://www.senate.gov/~y2k/statements/61298dodd.html> (19 December 1998); INTERNET.

27. Robert A. Rankin, "'Y2K' Bug May Lead to Brownouts," *Ft. Worth Star-Telegram*, 11 June 1998, electronic edition. Available from <http://www.netarrant.net/news/doc/1047/1:COMP56/1:COMP56061198.html> (19 December 1998); INTERNET.

28. Ibid.

29. Bonnie Camp, "Shining the Light on Electric Utility 10Q Y2K Disclosures," *Electric Utilities and the Year 2000*, 21 December 1998. Available from <http://www.euy2k.com/guest2.htm> (29 December 1998); INTERNET.

30. William Ulrich, "Energy Companies Seem Far Behind on Year 2000," *ComputerWorld*, 14 December 1998. Available from <http://www.computerworld.com/home/print.nsf/all/981214829E> (29 December 1998); INTERNET.

31. Senator Bob Bennett, "Ready or Not: Y2K Is Coming," *Y2KToday*, 27 January 1999. Available from <http://www.y2ktoday.com/modules/news/newsdetail.asp?id=736> (2 February 1999); INTERNET.

32. For example, if a company says it has spent $35 million of its $100 million budget (35 percent), and then increases its budget to $120 million, that same $35 million now represents 29.16 percent of its budget. Thus the earlier assumption about the amount of progress is, compared to the new budget, overstated.

33. Bonnie Camp, "Does the NERC Data Really Paint a Bright Picture for Power? One Y2K Student's Analysis," *CBN News*, 14 January 1999. Available from <http://www.cbn.org/ y2k/insights.asp?file=990114o.htm> (1 February 1999); INTERNET.

34. William Ulrich.

35. Senator Bob Bennett, "Ready or Not: Y2K Is Coming," *Y2KToday*, 27 January 1999. Available from <http://www.y2ktoday.com/modules/news/newsdetail.asp?id=736> (2 February 1999); INTERNET.

36. "AT&T Y2K Costs Up," *ComputerWorld*, 30 November 1998, electronic edition. Available from <http://www.computerworld.com/home/print.nsf/all/9811307E32> (19 December 1998); INTERNET.

37. Kate Gerwig, "MCI Gets Serious With SNA," *TechWeb*, 6 July 1998. Available from <http://www.techweb.com/se/directlink.cgi?INW19980706S0017> (19 December 1998); INTERNET.

38. From Sprint's "Year 2000 Securities and Exchange Commission (SEC) Filing" as provided on their website. Available from <http://www.sprint.com/y2k/SEC2000filing.html> (19 December 1998); INTERNET.

39. Mary E. Thyfault and Bruce Caldwell, "Are Telcos Ready for the Year 2000," *TechWeb*, 22 June 1998. Available from <http://www.techweb.com/se/directlink.cgi?IWK 19980622S0100> (19 December 1998); INTERNET.

40. Margaret Johnston, "Year-2000 Testimony Disconcerting for Senate Committee," *InfoWorld*, 3 August 1998. Available from <http://www.idg.net/idg_frames/english/content. cgi?vc=docid_9-66973.html> (1 February 1999); INTERNET.

41. AT&T Has Spent Half of Its Projected $600 Million Budget," *Reuters*, 8 January 1998.

42. Prepared Testimony of Joel Willemssen, Director, Civil Agencies Information Systems, Accounting and Information Management Division, U.S. General Accounting Office, before the Subcommittee on Government, Management, Information, and Technology, of the Committee of Government, Reform, and Oversight, U.S. House of Representatives, 20 January 1999. Available from <http://www.house.gov/reform/gmit/hearings/testimony/ 990120jw.htm> (2 February 1999); INTERNET.

43. "FCC Commissioner Says Failures Are Certain," *International Herald Tribune*, 27 November 1998.

44. Opening Comments of Senator Bob Bennett (R-Utah), Chairman, Special Committee on the Year 2000 Technology Problem, United States Senate, "Transportation and Y2K: Can We Get There From Here?" 10 September 1998. Available from <http://www.senate.gov/ ~y2k/statements/091098bennett.html> (19 December 1998); INTERNET.

45. Ibid.

46. Margaret Allen, "D/FW Airport Expects to Fly Through Year 2000," *Dallas Business Journal*, 4 January 1999. Available from <http://www.amcity.com/dallas/stories/1999/ 01/04/story7.html?h=y2k> (2 February 1999); INTERNET.

47. Cassandra Burrell, "FAA Flying Through Its Computer Renovations," *Fox News*, 29 September 1998. Available from <http://www.foxnews.com/js_index.sml?content=/ news/wires2/0929/n_ap_0929_241.sml> (2 February 1999); INTERNET.

48. "On Average, Only 36% of the Major Airlines' 'Year 2000' Project Budget Has Been

Spent," Proma Creative Solutions, 15 December 1998. Available from <http://actor.act-com.co.il:8080/ows-wis/pr31.htm> (2 February 1999); INTERNET.

49. M. J. Zuckerman, "Y2K: Minor Glitch or Major Disaster?" *USA Today*, 7 January 1999. Available from <http://www.usatoday.com/life/cyber/tech/cte068.htm> (2 February 1999); INTERNET.

50. Bob Brewin, "Coast Guard Raises Y2K Warning Flag," *Federal Computer Week*, 7 December 1998. Available from <http://www.fcw.com/pubs/fcw/1998/1207/fcw-newscoast-12-7-98.html> (2 February 1999); INTERNET.

51. 120-Plus Countries Ponder Global Effects of Y2K," *CNN Interactive*, 12 December 1998. Available from <http://cnn.com/TECH/computing/9812/12/y2k.un> (2 February 1999); INTERNET.

52. U.S. Warns of Millennium Bug Problems for Overseas Travelers," *TechServer*, 29 January 1999. Available from <http://www.techserver.com/noframes/story/0,2294,12633-21362-156624-0,00.html> (2 February 1999); INTERNET.

53. "Voluntary Year 2000 Preparedness Survey," American Water Works Association, November 1998. Available from <http://www.awwa.org/y2ksrvey.htm> (19 December 1998); INTERNET.

54. This number is derived by dividing the *cash reserves* held by U.S. banks (approximately $43.5 billion) by the *deposit obligations* of those same banks (approximately $3.8 trillion). This amount equals 1.13 percent. See Chapter 10 of Michael Hyatt, *The Y2K Personal Survival Guide* (Washington, D.C.: Regnery Publishing, 1999).

55. "FDIC: Bank Balances Y2K Proof," *Wired News*, 28 September 1998. Available from <http://www.wired.com/news/news/politics/story/15283.html> (20 December 1998); INTERNET.

56. Standish Group International, "Year 2000—A Date Odyssey," 1998. Available from <http://www.standishgroup.com/ad.html> (16 December 1998); INTERNET.

57. Testimony of Donna Tanoue, FDIC Inspector General, Before the Committee on Banking and Financial Services, United States Senate, 17 September 1998. Available from <http://www.fdic.gov/publish/speeches/98spchs/sp17sep.html> (20 December 1998); INTERNET.

58. "Horn Releases Last Set of Y2K Grades for 1998: Executive Branch Merits an Overall 'D'," Press Release from Subcommittee on Government, Management, Information, and Technology, 23 November 1998. Available from <http://www.house.gov/reform/gmit/y2k/981123.htm> (20 December 1998); INTERNET.

59. "Year 2000 Progress Report Card, Year 2000 Progress for Federal Departments and Agencies," issued by Subcommittee on Government, Management, Information, and Technology, U.S. House of Representatives, 23 November 1998. Available from <http://www.house.gov/reform/gmit/y2k/gradecard1123.pdf> (20 December 1998); INTERNET.

60. From a press release by the White House entitled, "Remarks by the President at Social Security and Y2K Event," White House Office of the Press Secretary, 28 December 1998. Available from <http://www.whitehouse.gov/WH/New/html/19981228-13153.html> (2 February 1999); INTERNET.

61. "Year 2000 Progress Report Card."

62. "Horn Releases Y2K Grades: Executive Branch Merits an Overall 'D'," Press Release from Subcommittee on Government, Management, Information, and Technology, 9 September 1998. Available from <http://www.house.gov/reform/gmit/y2k/980909.htm> (20 December 1998); INTERNET.

63. Ibid.

64. Report by the Committee on Government, Reform, and Oversight, U.S. House of Representatives, 8 October 1998. Available from <http://www.house.gov/reform/gmit/y2k/y2k_report/IIreport.htm> (20 December 1998); INTERNET.

65. "Horn Releases Last Set of Y2K Grades for 1998: Executive Branch Merits an Overall 'D'."

66. Melanie Goldman, "Social Security Says Check's in the Mail for Y2K," *Atlanta Business Chronicle*, 14 December 1998. Available from <http://www.amcity.com/atlanta/stories/1998/12/14/focus5.html?h=y2k> (22 December 1998); INTERNET.

67. From a press release by the White House entitled, "Remarks by the President at Social Security and Y2K Event," White House Office of the Press Secretary, 28 December 1998. Available from <http://www.whitehouse.gov/WH/New/html/19981228-13153.html> (2 February 1999); INTERNET.

68. This information was directly from FMS's home page on February 9, 1999, at <http://www.fms.treas.gov/y2k/irsfact.html>.

69. Bob Violino and Bruce Caldwell, "And Now For The Bad News—Year 2000 Projects Can Drain Funding and Talent from Other Operations, Forcing IS Managers to Delay—Even Kill—Vital Initiatives," *InformationWeek*, 21 April 1997. Available from <http://www.techweb.com/se/directlink.cgi?IWK19970421S0045> (20 December 1998); INTERNET.

70. Robert Molter, Chairman of the Defense Department's Year 2000 Working Group and Member of the Interagency Year 2000 Committee. Quoted in Andrew C. Braunberg, "Defusing the Millennium Time Bomb," *Signal Magazine*, June 1996, 3 (electronic edition). Available from <http://www.us.net/signal/Archive/June96/defusing-june.html> (20 December 1998); INTERNET.

71. Stanglin and Ahmad.

72. Year 2000 Progress Report Card, Year 2000 Progress for Federal Departments and Agencies."

73. Capers Jones, "The Global Economic Impact of the Year 2000 Software Problem," Revision 5.2, 23, January 1997, 7–8. Available from <http://www.spr.com/html/year_2000_problem.htm> (20 December 1998); INTERNET.

74. Warren S. Reid and Steven Brower, "Beyond Awareness: Ten Management and Legal Pitfalls Regarding the Year 2000 Computer Problem That You May Not Have Considered, Yet!", *Year2000*, 22 June 1997. Available from <http://www.year2000.com/archive/beyond.html> (20 December 1998); INTERNET.

75. Some 200,000 are still in the workforce. There are an additional 300,000 who are retired. See Jonathan Krim, "Retired Troops Available for Year 2000 Emergency," *Chicago Tribune*, 1 December 1997, Business section, 2.

76. Rajiv Chandrasekaran, "Older Programmers May Fix Future," *Washington Post*, 2.March

1997, A01. Available from <http://www.washingtonpost.com/wp-srv/frompost/features/mar97/2000.htm> (20 December 1998); INTERNET.

77. Senator Bob Bennett, "Ready or Not: Y2K Is Coming," *Y2KToday*, 27 January 1999. Available from <http://www.y2ktoday.com/modules/news/newsdetail.asp?id=736> (2 February 1999); INTERNET.

78. Edward Yardeni, "Year 2000 Recession?", *Y2K Reporter*, Version 9.1, 2 November 1998. Available from <http://www.yardeni.com/y2kbook.html> (20 December 1998); INTERNET.

79. Senator Bob Bennett, "Ready or Not: Y2K Is Coming," *Y2Ktoday*, 27 January 1999. Available from <http://www.y2ktoday.com/modules/news/newsdetail.asp?id=736> (2 February 1999); INTERNET.

Appendix C: Making Sure Your Personal Computer Is Y2K-OK

1. Please keep in mind that website links can change or disappear without notice. If one of these links does not work, you will have to do a search on one of the more popular Internet search engines. For example, to search for Gateway's Year 2000 page, enter "Gateway + 2000" in the search box. This tells the search engine to find all pages that include both "Gateway" *and* "2000."

Appendix D: Getting Your Local Community Ready

1. This letter was adapted from one provided by the Cassandra Project.

Appendix E: Shelf Life and Storage Tips for Various Foods

1. Adapted and supplemented from: Mark L. Tamplin, Ph.D., Fact Sheet HE 8490 from the Home Economics Department, Florida Cooperative Extension Service, Institute of Food and Agricultural Sciences, University of Florida, February.

Acknowledgments

No book is ever the product of one person's vision or work. That is especially true with this book. I had a great deal of help from a number of different people. Without their support and encouragement this book would have never been written.

First of all, I would like to thank my wife, Gail, who has been exceedingly patient and supportive since the beginning of my research into Y2K. Rather than being jealous of my time, she has demonstrated a true servant's heart again and again as she has rolled up her sleeves and asked, "What can I do to help?" Her continuous joy and love are contagious, and I am grateful beyond words.

I would be remiss if I failed to mention my five daughters, Megan, Mindy, Mary, Madeline, and Marissa. They have each offered encouragement in their own way and also been patient while Dad has been in "his own world" writing or traveling from one end of the country to the other for speaking engagements. I love each of you more than words can express.

My business partner and agent, David Dunham, has been my constant and faithful adviser. He has multiplied my efforts in innumerable ways and been a steadfast friend through thick and thin. What are we going to do next year, pal?

Next, I want to thank my superiors at Thomas Nelson Publishers, including Sam Moore, Chuck Moore, and Rolf Zettersten. You men have been incredibly generous in allowing me to speak and write on the subject of Y2K while being a full-time employee of the company. I know you think I'm going to quit any day now and become a full-time author. Don't count on it. I'm having too much fun working with you guys!

I also want to acknowledge my friends and colleagues at Thomas Nelson, including Rob Birkhead, Victor Oliver, Janet Thoma, Cindy Blades, Brian Hampton, and my personal assistant, Elizabeth Shelton. Each of you has been a blessing and an encouragement. Thanks for your support and good humor.

Without the vision and commitment of the Regnery Publishing staff, *The Millennium Bug* would have "died on the vine." I'm especially grateful to Jeff Carneal, Alfred Regnery, Richard Vigilante, Harry Crocker, Jed Donahue, and Harry McCullough. A special word must be said about Sandy Callender and Sarah Jane Fremont, the world's two best publicists (full body wag). Without your determination and tenacity, the first book would not have been successful enough to warrant a second. I am grateful beyond words.

My fellow laborers at St. Ignatius Orthodox Church are deserving of special mention. If absence makes the heart grow fonder, then all of my traveling has only made me love and appreciate you more than ever. To Father Steven Rogers, Father Bob Sanford, Deacon Keith Hansen, Deacon Richard Jones, and Deacon Ed Martin, thanks for "holding the fort down" and covering for me when I've been on the road. I especially appreciate the effort you've made, Father Steven, to alert our congregation and help us prepare—physically *and* spiritually.

My fellow soldiers in the race to get people prepared for Y2K include Shaunti Feldhahn, Steve Farrar, and Tim Wilson. Thanks for your encouragement and support.

Now to the people who actually helped prepare the manuscript: Bob Allen, Bill Dunn, Randy Guidry, and Franklin Sanders. There's no way this book could have been written if it hadn't been for your thorough research and assistance. I continue to be amazed by your dedication and skills. While I must take responsibility for any faults, this book is as much yours as mine. It was definitely a team effort and your fingerprints are all over it. Thank you.

As I finished each chapter, I posted it on my website and solicited public comment. I was amazed at the response I received—more than two thousand e-mail messages! My readers corrected my facts, offered alternative suppliers, and helped me hone certain passages. What a great way to write a book! "Better to stumble before a few than fall before the masses."

In particular, I want to thank the following readers who offered wonderfully helpful suggestions or questions that stimulated my thinking: A.T. Hagan, A.W. Miller, Adam Andrews, Al Roka, Alan L. Jones, Alec Mckelvey, Alice Panethiere, Andrea Mathews, Andrew J. Heller, Angela Branch, Anthony Buck, Aron Roberts, Baaron Schulte, Barbie Johnson, Barry Van Koevering, Bettye Megason, Beverly A. Whiting, Beverly Allen, Beverly Mouse, Bill and Gail Bethke, Bill Bennett, Bill Burden, Bill Justin, Bill Moriarty, Bill Neef, Bill Raemisch, Bill Stewart, Bob Franco, Bob Jones, Bob Tyrka, Bobbie Ford, Bonnie Coles, Bonnie Rieke, Brad and Vickie Hall, Brad Thone, Brad Wyckhouse, Brandon Burbach, Brent and Michelle McFarland, Brian J. Peets, Bruce Bellamy, Bruce Broweleit, C.J. Stegner, Caleb

Foulks, Carl Wells, Carol and Jess Fellows, Carol Randall, Caroline March-Long, Charles Walker, Charles Walker, Cheryl Phillips, Chris Augeri, Chris Busby, Chris Douglass, Chris Root, Christian S. Young, Christian Young, Connie Snipes, Craig Olson, Craig Reisinger, Craig Tabler, Dale Bourke, Dale Mosher, Dan and Rhonda Auld, Dan Young, Daniel Lowe, Daniel Stitzel, Darrell Wallen, Darren Potasky, Darren.B.Smith, David A. Mayberry, David and Julie Savitt, David Delikat, David King, David Nygren, David Williams, Dawn Weissman, Dean T. Miller, Debi Kelly, Debra Johnson, Dennis Monroe, Deran Eaton, Diane Baugh, Dick Wheeler, Dinah E. Northrip, Don Burns, Don Carll, Don Kulha, Don Lennox, Donald Mundorff, Donald Mundorff, Donna Moss, Doris Rosenhaus, Dottie Feder, Doug Raymond, Dr. Steven Lawhon, Duane McClun, Ed Ankers, Ed McCullough, Ed McGuckin, Eric and Carol Sluder, Eric Steffens, Faith Harrison, Farlan Clutters, Frank Hoffman, Gail Parker, Gail Vass, Gary Brant, Gary M. Smith, Gary Upton, Gayle Cameron, Gene Peterson, Geoff Gleason, George Meicke, George Strasser, Ginger Houston-Ludlam, Glenda G. Gordon, Grant Bell, Greg and Pat Delong, Greg Roy, Gregory John, Gwenn Franco, Gwyneth Beynon, Harold Thorne, Harvey Chinn, Hedi Label, Herrick Kimball, Hilarie Hall, Irene Crowe, J. Bell, J. W. Mason, Jack Boyce, Jack M. Caron, James Drake, James E. Jolley, James Shannon, James T. Vaughn, Jamey and Michelle Nichols, Jay Mulqueen, Jay Sheldon, Jay Stehle, Jay York, Jeanne Winrich, Jeff and Shoshanna Szuch, Jeff and Sue Townsend, Jeff Hartzell, Jeff Hyatt, Jeff Sims, Jeff White, Jeremy Naylor, Jeri Callan, Jerome Thomas, Jerry and Bobbie Lange, Jerry Maguire, Jerry Reynolds, Jim Feeney, Jim Miller, Jim Saad, Joan Figueroa, Joan Stieber, Joe Ann Mcfarlin, Joe Crews, John and Alanna Pasquale, John Falero, John Fogh, John Jasper, John Kirby, John Lichtenberger, John Riordan, John Stewart, John W. Eddings, John Wilkinson, John Wolfe, Joseph B. Williams, Joy Curtis, Joy Washburn, Judge Doug Revard, Judy Lea, Judy Mellon, Judy Redmon, June Howard, Karen Cheney, Karen Spearman, Karen Tamminga, Kate Casagrande, Katheryn Pate, Kathy Bungard, Kathy Chumley, Kathy Wilson, Keith Costa, Keith Girard, Ken Flynn, Ken Lapoint, Kendall Marr, Kent Crockett, Kevin Lemke, Kurtis S. Smith, Leonard D. Nelson, Jr. M.D., Linda Hayase, Linda Mullen, Lisa Swaim, Lois Kleinsasser, Lona Ann White, Lonnie Johnson, Lori Dwornik, Lori Flanagan, Lou Wilson, Luis Amarilla, Lyndon Anderson, Mark and Colleen Ma, Mark Evans, Mark Hungerford, Mary T. Chase, Matt Bickhard, Matt Bolton, Matt Long, Michael Bailey, Michael D. Leifer, Michael F. Khanchalian, Michael K. Mcdonald, Michael L. Dunn, Michelle Kendall, Mike and Diane Whaley, Mike and Lisa Moratz, Mike Joffrion, Mike McNatt, Mike Murray, Mike Turner, Moreen Petrella, Neil Hoover, Nora Lenz, Pat Jones, Pat Mcdermott, Pat Spadaccia, Paul Angus Sullivan, Paul Lewis, Peggy Mills, Randy Grimm, Randy Guidry, Regina Martin, Reginald Wagner, Rich Harrell, Richard and Julie Noe, Richard F. Desmond, Richard P. Howiler,

Richard Paulos, Rick Buck, Rick Wygant, Robert L. Stephens, Roberta M. Savitt, Robin Sahr, Robin Tyner, Robyn Looney, Robynn Reilly, Roger Fitzsimonds, Roman Swatzyna, Ron Lane, Ron Miller, Ronald J. Hipwell, Ronald J. Renski, Russ A. Wright, Russell A. Spoto, Ryan Booth, Sally Martens, Sam Hansen, Sandra Ghost, Sara Heesaker, Sarah E. Toombs, Scott C. Tadler, M.D., Scott Crossman, Scott K. Spearman, September Lee Dordick, Shawn Labelle, Shawn Woollen, Sheree Deyo, Sherrill Fink, Stan Heeres, Steve Bury, Steve Knox, Steve Shapero, Steve Vannattan, Steven and Kathleen Herr, Steven Hunt, Steven Nickell, Steven O'Saile, Steven Pollack, Steven S. Pyle, Stewart L. MacDonald, Stuart Von Rathjen, Susan Farmer, Susan L Berger, Susan Stanley, Suzanne Line, Suzanne P. McLaughlin, , Tammy Heiston, Tammy Prailey, Teresa Ludwig, Terri Reid, Terry Vanderkolk, The Gayders, Timothy Barney, Timothy Rebman, Todd R. Lepine, M.D., Tom Lusk, Tonn, Thomas, Tony Bennett, Tony Holicki, Tony Soper, Ty Hadman, Uusitalo Olli, Van C. Evans, Viser Mail, Wade Miller, Walt Heck, Walter Beckmann, Walter Lee, Warren Dunnavent, Wayne Agostino, Wayne Greulich, Wendy Barrett, Wesley G. Zottman, Will Babilonia, William Ringland, and William Winters.

Index